Reattachment Theory

A *Camera Obscura* book

Reattachment Theory
QUEER CINEMA OF REMARRIAGE

Lee Wallace

DUKE UNIVERSITY PRESS   DURHAM AND LONDON   2020

© 2020 Duke University Press
All rights reserved
Printed in the United States of America on acid-free paper ∞
Designed by Amy Ruth Buchanan
Typeset in Whitman by Westchester Publishing Services.

Library of Congress Cataloging-in-Publication Data
Names: Wallace, Lee, [date] author.
Title: Reattachment theory : queer cinema of remarriage / Lee Wallace.
Description: Durham : Duke University Press, 2020. | Series: A camera obscura book | Includes bibliographical references and index.
Identifiers: LCCN 2019034742 (print)
LCCN 2019034743 (ebook)
ISBN 9781478006817 (hardcover)
ISBN 9781478008101 (paperback)
ISBN 9781478009139 (ebook)
Subjects: LCSH: Same-sex marriage. | Marriage. | Lesbianism in motion pictures. | Homosexuality in motion pictures.
Classification: LCC HQ1033 .W35 2020 (print) | LCC HQ1033 (ebook) | DDC 306.84/8—dc23
LC record available at https://lccn.loc.gov/2019034742
LC ebook record available at https://lccn.loc.gov/2019034743

Cover art: *A Single Man*, Tom Ford, 2009. Courtesy of Photofest.

For the Stanleys of this world

There is no marriage without remarriage.
—Stanley Cavell,
Cities of Words

CONTENTS

Acknowledgments xi

1 Queer Skepticism and Gay Marriage 1
2 From Gay Marriage to Remarriage 27
3 Dorothy Arzner's *Wife* 53
4 Tom Ford and His Kind 82
5 Lisa Cholodenko's Attachment Trilogy 111
6 Reattachment Theory 134
7 The Remarriage Crisis 162

Reacknowledgments 183

Notes 191

Bibliography 225

Index 239

ACKNOWLEDGMENTS

The world is an imperfect place.

How we meet imperfection, and what we say about it, is up to us. Imperfection, as a rule, lends itself to criticism and critique. One of the strengths of queer theory is that it tends to grasp imperfection generously. It tells many hopeful stories about damage and shame and failure, things that are elsewhere considered as stains on the way the world or people should be. Yet, despite its counterintuitive allegiance to various orders of inadequacy and deficiency, queer theory has met the imperfection of marriage with radical skepticism. Whether it regards the phenomenon of marriage, including same-sex marriage, as an institutional failure (a mechanism for reproducing social inequality) or an ethical failure (an interpersonal contract that promotes sexual standards no one keeps), queer critique renders marriage a contemptible, not a redemptive, object.

Yet for all its imperfections, the world—including the world of marriage—is also an enchanted place. But, as anyone who has ever fallen in or out of love will know, enchantment is even harder to grasp than imperfection and still harder to trade in the languages in which we have learned to speak to each other, both personally and professionally. This book is an attempt to change the story we tell ourselves about marriage and to reenchant us to its queer possibilities as they appear in what Stanley Cavell refers to as the ordinary language of film. Cavell, who died in June 2018, around the same time that I completed the manuscript of this book, is not usually counted among queer theory's fellow travelers but, as I hope *Reattachment Theory* demonstrates, his account of film's capacity to capture the extraordinary in the ordinary, including the ordinary of married life, is an extraordinary resource for anyone wanting to think queerly about imperfection.

Like Cavell, I am drawn to the popular vehicle of narrative film as a medium in which the marriage plot is sustained and transformed through the generic means of comedy, tragedy, and romance. Whereas Cavell fixates on the transformation of the marriage plot that occurs in the classical Hollywood comedies of remarriage, which were made in the wake of the contemporary popular acceptance of divorce, I see a similar transformation occurring in recent films that speak either directly or indirectly to the contemporary popular acceptance of same-sex marriage. I approach the gay remarriage plot—which also turns on the possibility of remarriage—not in sociological terms but through the lens of close reading. As practiced by Cavell, close reading is less a methodology than an orientation to the entrancement of cinema and an attempt to capture the formal intuition of a particular film sentence by sentence. Prose imperfectly captures the register of film but, as both the classical and queer comedies of remarriage happily teach, the pursuit of perfection relies on getting things wrong as a way toward getting them right.

Although any mistakes ahead are all mine, for the chance to make them I am indebted to the University of Sydney and to the Australian Research Council for the award of a Future Fellowship, which allowed time for error as well as its scholarly recovery. I thank the staff at the Center for the Promotion of Gender and Women's Studies, Freie Universität Berlin, for the Visiting Fellowship across which a series of unrelated essays found their rationale in remarriage. A small grant from the Sydney Social Science and Humanities Advanced Research Centre (SSSHARC) allowed me to invite Robyn Wiegman to the University of Sydney in early 2018 to put the draft manuscript of this book through an ultimate peer review. Robyn's input into this book was both intimidating and transformative. She challenged me to draw out the field implications of my argument and make more of my methodological refusal to concede homosexuality's relation to marriage as signified by its legal state. Similarly transformative was the role played by the three readers commissioned by Duke University Press, who, like the triplicate figures of folklore, each brought different expertise to the task of turning a fledgling manuscript into a fully formed book. Their intellectually imaginative response to the first draft of this book gave me confidence that my way of reading and writing could draw others into an open-ended conversation about film and made final revisions much easier than I had any right to expect. Ken Wissoker has been a steady guide and supporter throughout. I am also grateful to Joshua Tranen for helping me navigate the process by which a manuscript becomes a book. Final acknowledgment is due to Annalise Pippard for the deft research assistance that held the various parts of this project together from beginning to end.

An early version of chapter 3 appeared as "Dorothy Arzner's *Wife*: Heterosexual Sets, Homosexual Scenes," in *Screen* 49, no. 4 (2008): 1–19; a shorter version of chapter 4 appeared under the same title, "Tom Ford and His Kind," in *Criticism: A Quarterly for Literature and the Arts* 56, no. 1 (2014): 21–44;

chapter 5 appeared as "Three by Three: Lisa Cholodenko's Attachment Trilogy" in *Camera Obscura* 102, vol. 34, no. 3 (2019): 96–125; and chapter 6 first appeared as "Reattachment Theory: Gay Marriage and the Apartment Plot," in *The Apartment Complex: Urban Living and Global Screen Cultures*, ed. Pamela Wojcik (Durham, NC: Duke University Press, 2018), 145–67.

1 Queer Skepticism and Gay Marriage

Contrary to the widely accepted idea that the rise of the same-sex marriage is coterminous with the rise of neoliberalism, I argue that the history of homosexuality—and in particular the history of lesbianism—has always been entangled with the history of marriage and therefore integral to the reimagining of affective and erotic horizons within the couple form and the wider sociality it indexes. Although I make this case primarily through an engagement with film, in this introductory chapter I briefly review influential queer critiques of the marriage equality movement in order to unsettle them via a wider argument about homosexuality and its relation to continually evolving discourses of sexual and social intimacy. I begin with a selective overview of established and trending perspectives on same-sex marriage within social theory and legal theory before arguing for the ongoing salience of narrative as a framework for thinking differently about marriage post–marriage equality. This will ultimately allow me to replot contemporary gay marriage along the coordinates of remarriage first described by Stanley Cavell in his discussion of Hollywood comedies of the 1930s and 1940s and displace queer skepticism around marriage with a form of wry utopianism that builds on the experience of coupled love as much as its theorization. The seven films on which Cavell builds his argument about remarriage are, in the order he discusses them, *The Lady Eve* (Preston Sturges, 1941), *It Happened One Night* (Frank Capra, 1934), *Bringing Up Baby* (Howard Hawks, 1938), *The Philadelphia Story* (George Cukor, 1940), *His Girl Friday* (Howard Hawks, 1940), *Adam's Rib* (George Cukor, 1949), and *The Awful Truth* (Leo McCarey, 1937). As I will later demonstrate in relation to the films of Lisa Cholodenko and Andrew Haigh in particular, the possibility of reattachment that is central to remarriage comedy is closely tied to the question of whether one finds oneself in a tragedy, comedy, or romance. However appealing the idea, the pages ahead do not offer a theory of gay marriage as remarriage so much as insist on the importance of narrative and nonrealist reading practices in making sense of the contemporary dilemmas of long-term intimacy, for queers as for everyone.

This is to tell a different story about marriage than the one that queers have been telling for the last twenty years. Cast your mind back to 1999, a moment whose numerological cast seemed to call for apocalyptic diatribes. This was the year Michael Warner published *The Trouble with Normal: Sex, Politics, and the Ethics of Queer Life*, an energetic critique of various normativing tendencies within American neoliberalism that included a chapter-length polemic against gay marriage, which it correctly foresaw as the future of lesbian and gay mainstream activism.[1] One of the most influential aspects of Warner's argument was its insistence that the extension of the right to marry to same-sex couples is less a political achievement than a measure of the broadening reach of normativity, a benign system of social docility that readily encompasses those sexual constituencies who have traditionally been considered—and considered themselves—beyond its ken. Whereas Warner makes a strident argument for the ethical value of engaging "the perspective of those at the bottom of the scale of respectability: queers, sluts, prostitutes, trannies, club crawlers, and other lowlifes," the decades since the publication of his book have seen the global uptake and unanticipated popularization of the marriage equality movement.[2] Operating from an ever-broader social base, the respectable tenor of the marriage equality movement can be seen in the Ring Your Granny campaign that contributed to Ireland becoming the first country in the world to adopt same-sex marriage by popular referendum in 2015 and, two years later, the #RingYourRellos initiative launched in the context of the Australian Marriage Law Postal Survey, which also saw a generation of media-savvy activists reintroduced to the quaint affordances of stick-down envelopes and pillar boxes. The naffness of the mainstream embrace of the idea of gay marriage continues to bolster the outlaw appeal of Warner's argument for the value of queer counterpublics, those informal networks of friends and strangers linked together by relations of care that have no recognition in law but effectively comprise an alternative public sphere in which sexuality is valued for its social stickiness beyond the lines mandated by heterosexual kinship and family.[3]

Although she acknowledges that "the topic of gay marriage is not the same as that of gay kinship," Judith Butler has pointed out that "the two become confounded in U.S. popular opinion when we hear not only that marriage is and ought to remain a heterosexual institution and bond, but also that kinship does not work, or does not qualify as kinship, unless it assumes a recognizable family form."[4] Like Warner, Butler is interested in severing the link between reproductive heterosexuality and the kinship system over which it is presumed to exercise exclusive rights. Kinship, Butler argues, does not only radiate out from birth and child-rearing practices but includes all social practices "that emerge to address fundamental forms of human dependency" such as "relations of emotional dependency and support, generational ties, illness, dying, and death (to name a few)." She points to the long ethnographic tradition of mapping both African American and gay and lesbian kinship patterns that may or may not "approximate the family form" in order to argue that, both theoretically and in practice, "conceptions of kinship have become disjoined from the marriage assumption."[5] This conceptual separation of marriage and kinship is, as Butler notes, also furthered by those legal responses to calls for marriage equality that separate recognition of civil partnerships from the right to coparent, adopt, or access fertility services. Yet, far from weakening the heterosexual grip on kinship, this legal differentiation produces a situation in which family law is enshrined beyond marriage rights in a legally quarantined sphere that is less susceptible to the inclusion of nonnormative practice.

Variously applied in different legal jurisdictions, this apparent devaluation of marriage in association with same-sex claims to marriage-like relationships and its legal separation from other kinship practices considered integral to social reproduction is, in many senses, what queer critics of marriage have often predicted would happen when marriage by definition included same-sex relationships. Far from spreading social equity, they argued, the advent of same-sex marriage would only deepen and displace the inequities at the heart of a patriarchal institution that remains central to the governing heterosexual social order. In addition, they warned, by extending social legitimacy to those gays and lesbians who assimilate the heteronorms of marriage, same-sex marriage would further marginalize and disadvantage those who didn't. But, as Louise Richardson-Self has recently noted, these well-rehearsed "assimilative" arguments about whether to accept or reject same-sex marriage on the grounds of its reification of heteronormative privilege are most useful in clarifying that at base the same-sex marriage debate is concerned with the "*equal regard* of LGBT people" rather than marriage per se.[6]

As an objection to discrimination rather than a claim to marriage, Richardson-Self goes on to argue, the argument for marriage equality is thus based on the recognition of difference rather than the ascription of sameness. Starting from this premise, Richardson-Self argues for the need to understand marriage not as an institutional form that delivers legal privilege to some and denies it to others but as a full-scale social imaginary that facilitates structures of identity and belonging in association with certain notions of intimacy and kinship but not others. From this perspective the goal of the marriage equality movement is not winning political rights but reimagining the terrain of marriage as composed of "traditional and nontraditional" practices of affiliation and care that are "horizontally" aligned rather than ranked in a moral hierarchy. Like Butler, Richardson-Self argues for the need to bring into social circulation "a new meaning-generating story" that challenges marriage's stranglehold on notions of affective kinship. In place of current ideals of marriage, she proposes an expanded "narrative of caring-love" that "acknowledges that all persons at all stages of their life require, desire, and/or deliver care, and that care is fundamental to our flourishing as intersubjective individuals."[7] The point is not to change the institution of marriage but to change the story of marriage, an outcome that can seem wooly and imprecise in activist frameworks that agitate for legal rights and recognitions but is, I would argue, business as usual for novel and film genres that survive only to the degree that they can innovate and renew received narrative patterns for historically evolving audiences. Of course, changing the story of marriage is also business as usual for those who are married or in marriage-like relationships, including the relationships of care that Richardson-Self points to that evolve across time in relation to different expectations and abilities, not all of which are rationally geared or knowable in advance. As we will see in the chapters ahead, it is the made-to-be-broken quality of all attachment that increasingly imprints itself in stories about commitment in the era of marriage equality.

Wanting to shift the normative ideal of marriage until it becomes radically inclusive of all relations of "caring-love" leads Richardson-Self to take a stance against politically expedient arguments for the strategic adoption of current marriage norms. She points out that those countries that moved early to legalize same-sex marriage, such as the Netherlands, by and large have not seen the advent of new norms and collective behaviors that demonstrate the social acceptance of LGBT populations or their families of choice but continue to report instances of intolerance. Richardson-Self takes the persistence of homophobia in these liberal jurisdictions, like violent protest in opposition to the proposed introduction of same-sex marriage elsewhere, as evidence that marriage reform has "little real social effect" beyond the endorsement and strengthening of the narrative of traditional marriage, which men and women have always had different stakes in, and the racially and ethnically unmarked nuclear family with which it remains cognate in "the dominant shared Western social imaginary."[8] Whether gays and lesbians are allowed to marry, or not allowed to marry, its seems the story of marriage remains the story of a bleached-out familialism that knows no difference from itself. Whether exclusively heterosexual or inclusive of homosexuals, marriage is considered to be in the service of normativity or, more specifically, what Lee Edelman has called "reproductive futurism," the popularly mandated system of symbolic generationalism that defuses and redirects present-tense calls for social justice into an anodyne emotional mode that refuses to acknowledge structural injustices and their long-term racial legacies.[9] In this sense, the story of marriage is a closed book.

The drive to normalization that queer theory finds within the marriage imaginary has meant that marriage, and the affective participation in sociality it supports, has been dismissed out of hand as a research object that might warrant sustained inquiry through a range of perspectives or methodological instruments. Social scientists, who tend to be more at home with the idea of the normative and its role in generating social change, are by and large better at investigating what it is that folk achieve when they marry beyond the rights and privileges that marriage equality activists argue for and queer theorists argue against.[10] Kimberley Richman's book-length account of her quantitative and qualitative survey of same-sex-marrying couples from California and Massachusetts begins with the revelation that of the nearly fifteen hundred couples she surveyed, 70 percent were already registered domestic partners and 55 percent had already been through nonlegal commitment ceremonies. That is, the majority of lesbians and gays seeking marriage, often at great personal cost, "already had access to the *rights* associated with marriage (at least at the state level), and many had already experienced the *ceremonial* aspect of marriage."[11] In her follow-up interviews with one hundred couples, Richman draws out the diverse reasons why gays and lesbians get legally married so as to tease out "the complexity of both the meaning of marriage and the legal consciousness of those seeking it."[12] Drawing on the tripartite model of legal consciousness established by Patricia Ewick and Susan Silbey's landmark study of the role of law in everyday attitudes and actions, Richman initially confirms that the same-sex couples surveyed and interviewed identify a variety of instrumental, validating, and oppositional motivations for seeking legal marriage, often in combination with each other.[13] In addition to this expected result, however, Richman discovered that some of the couples voiced none of these motivations and that, further, many of them expressed "an unmistakable voice of romance, which did not quite fit with the tripartite model of legality, but rather expressed motives that were seemingly external to the law and legality—they were neither strategic, nor reverent, nor resistant. They were instead aimed at purely emotional, personal, or romantic drives."[14] Richman points out that while it is no surprise that marriage is considered a "mechanism for attaining these things, it is not entirely intuitive why *legal* marriage," as opposed to a wedding ceremony or equivalent ritual, "was a necessary component to satisfying these drives." As she goes on to argue, this can be accounted for only by acknowledging "the hegemonic power of law, and the way that it infuses human relations, even in barely perceptible ways."[15] Sensitive to the many motivations for marriage and orientations to law expressed across and within the couples she interviewed, Richman emphasizes the critical significance of the emotional schema engaged by her interview subjects, many of whom initially sought out marriage on completely different grounds. Not only does Richman's study reveal that "the newly emerging right to marriage for same-sex couples is one that is not confined to the instrumental, political, or even symbolic realm," but it reveals law to be "a conduit or cultivator of emotion" insofar as "the data shows us that the personal or affective impact of law is often unsought or unexpected, but nevertheless profoundly felt."[16] Arising at the point where marriage law intersects with the marriage imaginary, the bewildering experience of conjugal affect is a normative phenomenon that cannot be fully explained within either legal or sociological frameworks.

This evidence for the emotional impact of marriage law, even on those who initially bring nothing but political pragmatism to it, is extremely suggestive. It is not that people are dumb or wrong to have a feeling for marriage, or to think that they don't have any such feeling, but rather that this phenomenon, whether anticipated or unanticipated, speaks to the affective as an important and motivating reality in people's everyday public lives. Lauren Berlant has identified our collective yet highly individualized attachment to the story of emotional attachment as one of the abiding vectors of contemporary life in which multiple "pedagogies" instruct us in the wisdom of identifying "having a life with having an intimate life."[17] Berlant traces the origins of this intimate regime back to a liberal society founded less on separate public and private spheres than on the constant and complex "migration of intimacy expectations between the public and the domestic."[18] While the drive toward intimacy might take many forms, only some of those forms harden off into social conventions. The longest standing and most adaptable of these intimate conventions is the story of marriage since, as Berlant points out, it exactly satisfies the enigmatic requirement that "the inwardness of the intimate is met by a corresponding publicness."[19] That is, of all the things marriage does, it is the way in which it trains us to experience our "internal lives theatrically, as though oriented to an audience" that is key to its social canonicity.[20] While the first to acknowledge that attachments themselves have no preordained utility and are typically marked by contradictory energies and ambivalence, Berlant argues that the story of marriage generates an "aesthetic of attachment" that is normatively promoted "across private and public domains" in a way that stabilizes, clarifies, and cultivates "the couple or the life narrative it generates." Against this "normative" aesthetic of the married couple, she contends, alternative intimacy plots—such as those based in the appetites rather than love, community, and patriotism, the trifecta of emotions uniquely tied up in American notions of marriage—struggle to find a "designated place" in culture and must "develop aesthetics of the extreme" in order to be publicly heard.[21]

Contra Berlant, I will go on to suggest that almost since its eighteenth-century inception the story of marriage has proven capacious enough to harbor nonnormative plotlines and the social publicity they require to thrive. First, however, I would like to return to the presumption that marriage never has, never will provide hospitable ground for the advancement of alternative intimacies. Many have observed that the right to marry may, when awarded, offer no more legal protection or access than gays or lesbians currently enjoy under common-law provisions and in some instances may actually introduce legal vulnerabilities.[22] Coming at this double bind from the perspective of critical legal studies, Katherine Franke has recently pointed out that the extension of rights such as the freedom to marry does not in itself constitute freedom or resolve "complex questions of justice and equality, but rather inaugurates a new set of hard questions about what it means to be liberated into a social institution that has its own complicated and durable values and preferences."[23] Among the durable aspects of marriage that survives its expansion to include same-sex subjects, Franke argues, is its insistently gendered profile: "Paradoxically, gaining rights can have the unintended effect of conscripting the beneficiaries [of marriage reform] into gendered roles they have little interest in inhabiting."[24] I will return to Franke's point about the gendered aspect of marriage below, but I focus first on her decision to approach the legal downsides of same-sex marriage via the historic example of the granting of marriage rights to blacks in the raft of reforms that followed the abolition of slavery in North America. As Franke points out, for many freed blacks this unsolicited equality immediately complicated their capacity to negotiate the ongoing racist strictures of nineteenth-century American life. She documents the many violent injustices visited on black men and women whose sexual alliances did not fit sanctioned models of marriage but approximated forms that were considered criminal, such as bigamy. Rights-bearing citizens, Franke reminds us, are often restrained by the rights they bear and may even become subject to laws from which they previously had dispensation, as when these newly emancipated slaves found their domestic lives subject to state licensure and themselves imprisoned for retrospectively infringing marriage laws that never originally applied.

By framing same-sex marriage through the historic lens of race, Franke cautions those who think of marriage equality as an unmitigated legal advance to be mindful of the unfreedoms and legal liabilities that may follow upon having previously outlawed relationships incorporated in law. But this is not the end of her lesson. As she is fully aware, Franke's critical invocation of the racialization of nineteenth-century marriage law in the context of gay marriage debates runs counter to the more routine political likening of twenty-first-century extensions of marriage law to the overturning of antimiscegenation statutes in the civil rights era. As many have pointed out, this analogy is flawed on multiple counts. Chandan Reddy, for instance, has argued that the frequently drawn connection between same-sex marriage equality and the overturning of US antimiscegenation laws in the late sixties blurs the racially whitening effect of rights discourse itself, a liberal ideology indentured to Enlightenment abstractions notoriously indifferent to structural mechanisms of inclusion and exclusion and their remedy. Reddy argues that the 1967 Supreme Court decision in *Loving v. Virginia*, which specified marriage as a fundamental human right, "does not so much mark the end of antimiscegenation or the racial organization of US kinship or the rise of ideologies of color-blind intimacy and love" but rather "indexes and mediates the shifts in racial meanings conducted through a juridical discourse on interracial intimacy" that is consistent with the wider postwar shift that saw the United States move "from being officially white supremacist to a racial liberal state."[25] Reddy first made this argument in 2008, when the federal recognition of gay marriage was regarded as constitutionally inevitable if still a ways off; then, in 2016, he revisited it in the context of a roundtable on the role of queer theory "after" marriage equality.[26] As part of his update, Reddy points to June 2013 and the proximity of Supreme Court judgments that recognized marriage equality with those that struck down "voting protections for African Americans and other disenfranchised poor communities of color."[27] Reddy insists that, if there is a line of continuity between the *Loving* moment and the recognition of marriage as a fundamental right for homosexuals, too, it is a line that traces their mutual imbrication in a system of biopolitical governance that overlooks structural inequities in favor of categories—such as the rights-bearing citizen, an entity that already presumes layers of state recognition denied to many racialized demographics, such as undocumented migrants, or marriage conceived as a fundamental right or human dignity—that erase the social and racial differences through which injustice operates.

Reddy's argument is representative of a wider field of queer of color critique that targets the racism endemic to neoliberalism and its precursor forms. In general, this strand of social theory has little positive to say about gay marriage, which it tends to sweep aside as the normative proposition par excellence in favor of queer kinship bonds that keep their distance from racially privileged, heterosexist, and gender-normative models of state-sanctioned relationality.[28] Many of these arguments can be traced back to Roderick Ferguson's influential account of the coarticulated "normative ideologies of civil rights, canonical sociology, and national liberation" that serve to pathologize African American culture whenever it departs from the heteronormative models so easily detected in white middle-class family life.[29] In her well-tempered discussion of Ferguson's *Aberrations in Black*, the various chapters of which bind together American schools of sociological thought with exemplary African American literary texts, Amy Villarejo draws out the implications of his methodology and the equivalency it supposes between sociology and literature.[30] Specifically, Villarejo wants to "cleave apart the two senses of *nonheteronormative* Ferguson proposes," on the one hand, nonheteronormativity as a social symptom or pathology understood to be the result of the damage wrought upon African American families by slavery and industrialization that needs be corrected through benevolent social policy, and on the other, nonheteronormativity as a perversion of the American family ideal through which African Americans express social agency outside the normative regime of the expanding black middle class, whose thriving is registered in its capacity to reproduce heteropatriarchal marriage norms. As Villarejo argues, the blurring of these two diagnostics determines that "the politics of African American life and struggle" are "forced to yield their lessons in the same terms in which [they] have been pathologized." As diagnosed by the sociology of race, the nonheteronormative is a sign of ongoing social damage or dysfunction; as diagnosed by the literature of race, the nonheteronormative is an ongoing social resource. Villarejo suggests looking at cinema in order to find a richer "vocabulary for parsing the distinction" between symptom and agency otherwise "collapsed" in the term "nonheteronormative," a strategy that I suggest also yields results in thinking about gay marriage outside the dualism of political poison or political cure.[31]

Although queer marriage critique has rejected the drawing of simplistic parallels between gay marriage and antimiscegnation law, the *Loving* analogy continues to dominate in both popular and legal spheres, where it has become a legal convention in its own right. In an article in 2007 marking the fortieth anniversary of *Loving v. Virginia*, legal scholar Adele Morrison takes up the issue of the case's applicability in the context of same-sex marriage.[32] Morrison points out that, although pro–same-sex arguments freely avail themselves of the *Loving* analogy and the "decision's freedom of choice and anti-discrimination elements," they "rarely incorporate the Supreme Court's antisubordination message, as articulated through its anti–white supremacy stance."[33] So far so good, but in a move that goes against much subsequent queer of color theorizing, Morrison goes on to argue that same-sex marriage subverts white supremacy by undermining heterosupremacy: "The contention is that while heterosexual marriages, as exemplars of heteronormativity, may reinforce the status quo of white supremacy, same-sex intimate relationships challenge white supremacy by being non-normative."[34] Although it is hard to imagine an argument for gay marriage subverting white supremacy getting much traction considering the ongoing persistence of racialized inequality in the era of marriage equality, the symbolic pull of the *Loving* analogy continues unabated in the contemporary moment.[35]

Despite its constitutional specificity, the well-worn *Loving* analogy is not restricted to US contexts but is often invoked whenever advocates wish to lend political gravitas to bids for marriage equality in other legal jursidictions. The international take-up of the *Loving* analogy has been boosted by the release of Jeff Nichols's *Loving* (2016), an earnest melodrama based on the marriage story behind *Loving v. Virginia*. Featuring the Australian actor Joel Edgerton as Richard Loving, the film has been taken as an opportunity for a new suite of well-intentioned but historically wobbly comparisons between US and Australian antimiscegenation law and governance practices. These arguments by analogy get additional celebrity traction from the revelation that Edgerton—near catatonic in the role of Loving but in real life an outspoken supporter of the Australian campaign for marriage equality—has been in a relationship with Cathy Freeman, a Kuku Yalanji and Birri-Gubba woman and Olympic superstar.[36] To be sure, it is not that these transnational analogies are out-and-out wrong or not worth making but that, in striving to establish political parallels, they can obscure the different and contradictory ways in which racialized intimacies have been disciplined and normativized across the postcolonial world.

In the Australian case, for instance, the policing of miscegenation was for much of the twentieth century in line with an assimilationist policy explicitly designed to breed out Aboriginal bloodlines in pursuit of a white Australia. Under this eugenicist order, which ran in one form or another from the 1890s to the 1970s and was stretched particularly thin in sparsely populated northern Australia, where the discouragement of sexual commingling had little effect, the establishment of white paternity could result in mixed-race children being forcibly taken from their indigenous mothers by federal or state agencies and church missions, an occurrence so frequent and extensive that those children are now known as the Stolen Generations. As evidenced in indigenous autobiographies and scholarship, while some white fathers had ongoing relationships with the Aboriginal mothers of their children and sought permission to marry them, others were incorporated into Aboriginal kinship systems as a means of acknowledging these relationships and the children born into them without risking their removal.[37] The complexity of these intimate genealogies, and their departure from state-sanctioned conjugal norms, is often lost within an overall cultural landscape that continues to observe white codes of reticence around the sexual exploitation of Aboriginal women and girls and other generational effects of racism, dispossession, and exclusion.

Manifestations of interracial intimacy that conflict with imperial drives to racial hygiene are part and parcel of the colonial project as it has unfolded in various locations. Their affective byways are always highly specific, however, involving as they do the intermeshing of indigenous and introduced expectations around sexuality, marriage, and kinship.[38] It is well known that different imperial administrations applied different dispensations in relation to interracial marriage or its many corollaries. Ann Laura Stoler's archivally driven work on the Dutch East Indies is the most thorough account of how semisanctioned systems of concubinage, in which colonial administrators and military personnel were permitted to keep indigenous sexual partners in marriage-like relations that bore children, lead to creolized affiliations that ran athwart colonial aims and ultimately assisted the rise of independence movements.[39] In the American context, the social history of Louisiana likewise abounds with instances in which the customary practices of different colonial regimes intersected with the institution of slavery to produce extraordinarily complex systems of sexualized intimacy that continue to unsettle notions of a color-blind polity in present-day America.

Certainly Franke's account of the complications and vulnerabilities that followed the nineteenth-century extension of marriage law to cover emancipated slaves demonstrates not only how much gays and lesbians might learn from historic black experience but also, and more alarmingly, how much the contemporary marriage equality movement has benefitted from the presentation of its cause as an implicitly white concern. Before ending her book with an eight-point manifesto that holds married queers accountable "to the ways in which the same-sex marriage movement has been the beneficiary of a racial endowment, and how some arguments made in furtherance of marriage equality may have amplified the ways in which marriage has not been a liberating experience for many people of color," Franke makes the unsentimental and seemingly contradictory observation that marriage law exists for the requirements of divorce.[40] This legal preoccupation with divorce is a legacy of coverture, or the doctrine by which a woman's rights and obligations were upon marriage subsumed by those of her husband. Yet, long after wives have ceased to be considered their husband's chattels, the state's interest in marriage continues to be most acute at the point of its dissolution, where it exercises control over the distribution of accumulated wealth and the future obligations of alimony and child support. Unsurprisingly, at least in the terms of Franke's argument, it is therefore same-sex divorce that most thoroughly reveals the coercive persistence of gendered expectations in the now expanded domain of marriage law as many gay and lesbian couples discover that laws of divorce devised in support of the financial dependency presumed to be at the heart of heterosexual marriage do not reflect the reality of their same-sex unions, which, whatever inequalities they may harbor, are not founded on sex-based differentiations.

In the final chapter of her book, Franke provides a lengthy example of same-sex divorce that falls somewhere between legal case study and ethnographic anecdote or narrative. Across several pages she outlines the situation of a married lesbian couple who, in the process of legally dissolving their relationship, are differentially positioned as lesbian husband and lesbian wife via a judge's ruling that appears to apply gendered notions of financial dependency that derive from heterosexual templates. Franke's exemplary case has the dramatic richness of a lesbian soap: a history of passionate discord between two women exacerbated by class and economic differences; multiple breakups across a ten-year period and relationships with others established in the periods of estrangement; recourse to counseling and the verbal agreement of ground rules around separate and joint finances prior to reconciliation; marrying out of state on impulse; then a final bust-up followed by one woman filing for divorce and the other demanding her right under the law of the state they resided in to half her spouse's assets and ongoing financial support. In the family court hearing that decided the legal outcome, the judge discounted the verbal premarital agreement as "irrelevant and unenforceable," since state law required prenuptials to be agreed in writing. The coolheadedness of her legal scholarship shot through with a dramatic verve more often associated with scriptwriting, Franke describes how the justifiable distribution of assets that followed "required that the judge determine when the marital clock started ticking." In an unexpected plot twist, the judge "backdated" the marriage to when the two women started dating, even though at that point one was still legally married to her male spouse. The retroactive application of marriage law was justified by the judge's argument that across their lengthy relationship the two women had "functioned as a couple" (a fact narratively evidenced by Franke's account of their ongoing dysfunction) and the presumption that, had they been able to marry, they would have.[41] "In this sense," Franke summarizes, "the shadow of the law of marriage is cast backward as a kind of restitution for a status of injury suffered by same-sex couples," a legal remedy that doubles down on the requirement that same-sex couples resemble their heterosexual counterparts in the making and breaking of marital arrangements.[42]

Whereas Franke uses the case example to caution gays and lesbians against "surrendering the breakup of your relationship to governance by rules set by the state"—either rules of marriage that may reflect long-standing disparities of gender or, as in the example above, rules of divorce responsive to feminist demands that those disparities be addressed at the point they have most consequence, namely the dissolution of marriage—I am interested in the critical leverage that divorce provides in allowing us to rethink the idea of marriage more generally.[43] As evidence of the increasingly complex sociolegal landscape in which marriage exists, Franke cites the now routine adoption of prenuptial legal agreements that were once considered the reserve of the wealthy. These "front end of marriage arrangements," as she calls them, reflect a "new sense of entitlement, or as some call it legal consciousness," that allows soon-to-be married gays and lesbians, like their straight counterparts, to safeguard themselves financially against the failure of a relationship, or in some instances "to treat the rights and wrongs of a relationship," say infidelity or other breaches of marital conduct, "as monetizable claims against one another."[44] In this preemptive imagining, the horizon of divorce repositions matrimony not as a sentimental partnership but as a contractual arrangement similar to any other and thus to be entered into with an equal degree of legal caution. By instrumentally anticipating a retraction of the mutuality considered to be at the heart of companionate marriage for almost two centuries, prenuptial arrangements are considered by some queer critics of marriage to expose endemic skepticism about the longevity and sustainability of marriage as it is nowadays practiced. Amy Brandzel, for instance, insists that one of the "positive effects" of the same-sex marriage movement has been the exposure of "a crack in the facade of heteronormativity," which is no longer a rock-solid social form but a flailing and increasingly irrelevant institution the hegemony of which must be "buttressed" in laws that specify that heterosexuality and heterosexuality alone can be considered "synonymous with marriage."[45] By these lights, queer disparagers of marriage can legitimately support the legal argument for marriage equality since the success of the movement further undermines the institution's increasingly shaky social base.

Other critical attacks on the foundations of marriage, including same-sex marriage, equally involve the dual tendencies to personalized narration and impersonalized abstraction that can be seen in Franke's book. Consider the work of Laura Kipnis, who idiosyncratically adopts the second-person voice to characterize the married couple as the deadening form through which people—straight or gay—bind themselves to the social. Waged initially as an essay-length polemic and subsequently expanded into a trade book titled *Against Love*, Kipnis's project is a kind of thought experiment that presents the widespread practice of adultery as a series of narrative vignettes and conjugal clichés that collectively demonstrate the personal and sexual exhaustion that attaches to the monogamous couple, whether legally married or bound together by common law.[46] Tracing the contours of "the adultery melodrama" with its equal-opportunity cast of cheating wives, philandering husbands, straying domestic partners, suspicious spouses, cuckolds, and bedroom dicks, Kipnis argues that the erotic and affective labor required by the longue durée of coupledom is alienated in the Marxist sense: it binds partners to an object or idea (their coupled happiness) that is irretrievably lost to them.[47] Against this state of bondage, Kipnis poses adulterous disruption as a yearning toward unsanctioned utopias of good feeling, a kind of emotional avant-gardism that carries the force of radical progressiveness.

Although there is much that is beguiling about Kipnis's association of the sexual euphoria and social disturbance of adultery with other sexual subcultures that are not wedded to the couple form as a sexually exclusive unit, David Shumway provides the sobering reminder that adultery can be considered rebellious only within the discourse of romantic love; under the discourse of intimacy that historically superseded romance as the primary framework for marriage, adultery can be considered only pathological.[48] Where Kipnis deploys the insider account of adultery via dramatic vignettes and parenthetical asides that would be funnier if only they didn't ring so true, Shumway engages the omniscient chronological overview of marriage as a historically changing form. To begin, he usefully maps out the three historical phases through which love has been conceived: first, as a social obligation or duty; second, as romance; and finally and most recently, as intimacy. Unlike the discourse of romance in which love is conceived as an involuntary "passion that befalls one," within the discourse of intimacy love is "a condition of a relationship," not of an individual. Further, within the modern discourse of intimacy the love relationship is considered "something that a couple can control."[49] This shift from understanding love as an irrational passion that takes hold of one to understanding it as a shared something that must be collectively cultivated, improved, or healed animates a corresponding shift in the aesthetic forms devoted to love's explication. Although Shumway argues that the rise of capitalism promoted marriage as "a matter of individual choice, rather than social arrangement," he goes on to parse this distinction more finely.[50] In association with the rise of the novel, "nineteenth century marriage became understood as best based on romantic love," whereas "marriage itself continued to be understood as an essential social structure."[51] As a corollary of this implicit tension between the origin of love in romantic passion and the dry social form taken by the institution of marriage, "marriage can be either an oppressive obstacle to true love or its ultimate fulfillment," with both options popularly promulgated through novelistic discourse across the nineteenth and twentieth centuries.[52]

Like Kipnis, Shumway identifies adultery as key to the romantic mechanism of marriage and its narratology. Not only are romantic narratives "triadic in structure, involving at any given moment three desiring subjects," but, Shumway insists, "romance is exclusively concerned with love outside of marriage, either in adultery or courtship." That is, although marriage can prompt stories of adultery or provide closure for stories of courtship, as far as the novel is concerned it cannot tell its own story, or, as he puts it, "marriage itself cannot be represented." Jumping forward from the discourse of romance to the discourse of intimacy, the evidence Shumway gives in proof of the novel's marital nondisclosure clause is the fact that "the marriage manuals of the 1920s advise husbands and wives to maintain separate bedrooms so as not to become too familiar with each other. The model for marriage here is the adulterous affair."[53] Shumway's example anticipates Kipnis's counterlogical argument that to avoid the state of "*surplus monogamy*," in which "monogamy becomes work" and "desire is organized contractually, with accounts kept and fidelity extracted like labor from employees, with marriage a domestic factory policed by means of rigid shop-floor discipline designed to keep the wives and husbands of the world choke-chained to the reproduction machinery," married relationships should be pursued as playfully and purposelessly as if they were affairs, only now the advice given to Edwardian couples on how to avoid exhausting marriage's erotic potential is repurposed in favor of a sexual avant-gardism that would not recognize its place in this lineage.[54]

Not only does the discourse of romance render marriage unrepresentable except as postscript to the story of courtship or prelude to the story of adultery, but the discourse of intimacy seems to model marriage on its erotic surrogates. In Shumway's account the demystified discourse of intimacy does not abandon romance, or the passion and obsession with which romance is associated, but rather relegates these things to an early "stage of love's process." Instead of focusing on "falling in love"—a prospect to be guarded against from the perspective of the established couple since this state can be secured only by what we might call "falling in adultery"—the discourse of intimacy concerns itself with the effort needed to "stay in love." Unlike the romantic narrative that ends or starts in marriage but ignores the marital relationship altogether, the narrative of intimacy that takes its place is concerned exclusively with the relationship, which it comes at from every available temporal position—before, during, and after—in any order that suits. As a prime fictional example of intimate discourse at work, Shumway gives not a novel but Woody Allen's *Annie Hall* (1977), a film that retrospectively explains from the perspective of one half of a failed couple "why the relationship ended, rather than lamenting its end" in the way a romance version of the same story might do. Allen's film, indeed his entire oeuvre, strongly supports Shumway's contention that "as a literary form, intimacy tends toward the case history."[55] The discourse of intimacy produces a new narratological form in which the story of an established relationship, which we may as well call a marriage, can be revisited and revised at the same time in a way that approximates a therapeutic conversation.

According to Shumway, the distinctive feature of the novel of intimacy is not only that it takes as its subject the "troubles" internal to marriage—as can be seen in the novels of John Updike and Alison Lurie—but that this fictional form can be likened to nonfictional forms of marital advice literature that similarly offer instructional vignettes of failing relationships with which readers can identify.[56] This convergence of genres leads Shumway to conclude, "It is in the form of advice that intimacy has achieved it most influential and characteristic expression."[57] This point about the increasing ubiquity of expert and amateur advice directed at ostensibly private relationships has also been made by Candace Vogler in her discussion of the anomalous relations assumed of men and women in relation to intimacy in post-1970s popular psychology and relationship manuals that address those caught in "morbid companionate marriage."[58] Assisted by the deployment of gender-typical case studies that are often rendered in novelistic detail, a form of "case-study heterosexuality" emerges through this discourse that supports the idea that marital discontent can be sourced to the gap between male and female expectations around intimacy: where men regard sex as a means to interpersonal intimacy, women require talk.[59] Rather than accept this Venus/

Mars diagnostic—as complacently heterosexual as it is defeatist—Vogler turns it inside out by engaging a Kantian philosophical critique, although it is the homosexual cast of her philosophy that concerns me here.

Vogler begins by questioning the commonsense understanding of sexual intimacy as "reciprocal self-expression and self-scrutiny" that subtends couple counseling across its various modes of address. Speculating "first, that not all intimacies are affairs of the self and that, second, the fact that some intimacies are *not* affairs of the self is what makes people want them," she argues that while husbands and wives might take different gendered pathways within their interpersonal relationships, they both seek the same outcome, namely "depersonalizing" intimacy or a sense of being made sexually strange to themselves within the familiar orbit of the habitual.[60] To make this argument Vogler has recourse to specifically gay and lesbian representations of the sexual, which respectively address male sex and female talk and can therefore be conscripted to her counterintuitive reframing of heterosexual coupled love. Calling upon Leo Bersani's psychoanalytic account of the profound abdication of the self involved in sexual jouissance conceived as a sublime detachment from both the object-world and its psychic domestications and, less predictably, Adrienne Rich's poetic evocation and complicated disavowal of women's kitchen sink "troubles talk" as the verbal means to attaining a not dissimilar suspension of sexual rationalism and the female-enforced requirement that sexual feeling always be socially accounted for, Vogler outlines the differently gendered but equivalently advantageous pathways men and women take to achieve depersonalizing intimacy: "Now, I want to suggest that what our husbands want from sex is timely self-forgetfulness, rather than an occasion for self-expression, just as I think that what our wives want from talk is likewise self-forgetfulness, rather than an opportunity to express and defend their considered views. Bersani's writings on sex capture something of the spirit of the thing for case-study U.S. *husbands*, not just male homosexuals, just as (I think) a lesbian poet's representation of talk captures something of the spirit of that activity for case-study U.S. *wives*."[61] I am interested in particular in the homosexual source of Vogler's argument about the differently geared but similar sexual needs men and women bring to marriage, since it suggests the necessity to think these forms—not just homosexuality and heterosexuality, but homosexuality, heterosexuality, and marriage—together.

In this context it is worth returning to Shumway, since, in his deliberations on the increasing social acceptability of same-sex marriage, he insists that the contemporary link between marriage and homosexuality is not a novel or unexpected occurrence but merely the crystallization of the longer historical trajectory through which changes in the conception of marriage socially validate homosexual relationships as yet another—perhaps even an idealized form of—companionate coupledom. Drawing on Anthony Giddens's influential account of transformations of intimacy in modern life, Shumway points out that the "shrinking social and economic role of marriage that fostered the emergence of the discourse of intimacy is also one of the preconditions for the social legitimation of homosexuality." But whereas Giddens stresses the sexual innovations that gays and lesbians pioneered outside marriage in the form of open or negotiated relationships that ultimately provide the model of the "pure" relationship based on the assumption of sexual and emotional equality, Shumway places stress on the way that the increasing social visibility of gay and lesbian relationships, however "grudgingly or disapprovingly" acknowledged, began to "relativize marriage" insofar as they were seen to resemble it.[62]

Contra Giddens, whom he thinks overstates the case for the downgrading of marriage to one lifestyle choice among many, Shumway points out that the historical advent of "increasingly acceptable" alternatives to marriage across the twentieth century, including gay and lesbian alternatives, did not produce a "widespread rejection of monogamy" but ensured its continuation as an ideal both inside and outside marriage. While the emerging discourse of intimacy may have "acknowledged that marriage was but one kind of relationship," in practice "the term relationship" meant "the couple." As a corollary of this, practices such as multiple partners, or other arrangements such as those considered "typical of gay men," are regarded "as evidence of the failure of intimacy in the 'primary' relationship." The conclusion Shumway draws from this is worth quoting in full for the clarity with which he identifies how intimacy both softens or weakens the social discourse of marriage and extends its hold over sexual subcultures previously considered outside its purview: "Where under romance adultery was rebellion against marriage, under intimacy it is understood as a pathology of marriage. It is the bias of intimacy discourse toward marriage that leads to the conclusion that marriage is good for everyone, not just heterosexuals. Intimacy allows that a different dyad might be the solution to relationship woes, but it can't conceive, even covertly, that some people might not find happiness in monogamy rightly practiced."[63] The point I draw from this is that, although the social hegemony of the monogamous couple beyond the parameters of heterosexual marriage is now a commonplace point of queer critique, few acknowledge or stay attuned to the historically productive dialogue that has existed between marriage and its homosexual alternates across the twentieth century, or conceptually entertain the idea that marriage (and the couple form with which it remains synonymous) might have been homosexualized long before same-sex marriage captured the public imagination. Rather than consider homosexual engagements with couplehood as contributing to the shifting contours of marriage across the twentieth century, what dominates contemporary critical discussion is the idea that homosexuality has only recently become enamored of marriage as a way of turning its back on its own sexual and social history in favor of the blandishments of married love. This presumption upholds a false distinction between heterosexuality and homosexuality in relation to discourses of marriage that should not be countenanced in a field that is founded on the Foucauldian idea that categories of sexual knowledge tend to interpenetrate rather than stand alone. Alongside the homosexual, the hysteric, and the masturbating child, Foucault explicitly identifies the Malthusian couple as one of the four fulcrum points central to the functioning of *scientia sexualis*, yet many queer theorists continue to quarantine these categories from each other as if they were always, and should continue to be, kept distinct. The interpenetration of homosexuality and heterosexuality is thus another of those key points in queer theory that is upheld in theory but abrogated in practice to powerfully moralistic ends, as Eve Sedgwick first pointed out in relation to the tendency of the field to reproduce the repressive hypothesis in particular ways.[64]

Instead of considering that the evolution of homosexuality and marriage might have mutually entangled histories, much recent queer critique seems designed to get shot of both marriage and the monogamous couple as quickly as possible. For example, while both Warner and Kipnis invoke the queer talent for promiscuous stranger intimacy against the social dominance of the couple within and outside marriage, Michael Cobb has recently targeted the couple from the perspective of the uncoupled. In the "process of theorizing singleness," Cobb takes apart the notion of the lonely crowd, a mid-twentieth-century sociological concept that continues to hold sway in accounts of the bleakness of the social landscape after the eviscerating effects of technological modernization.[65] Cobb points out the surprising longevity of the lonely crowd diagnostic, whose second wind gets a third wind with the advent of each new form of technology that ostensibly brings others closer but only via a network of estrangement that promotes shallow over deep relationalities, novelty over reflection, distraction over commitment. In this account the contemporary embrace of social media is merely the most recent example of a technological modernity that diminishes our capacity for meaningful solitude and underscores the fundamental loneliness of a social sphere that can be alleviated only through the enduring intimacy known as couple love.[66]

For all the inventiveness that Cobb brings to the project of imagining singleness uncoupled from the couple—his dismissal of the apparent paucity of narrative alternatives to the couple form, his disdain for those who celebrate singleness as a form of "antisocial sublime," and his revaluation of abstraction as a mode through which one can experience a "self-horizoned" world more encompassing than that inscribed by the self-absorbed social horizon of couples—his account of the couple is breathtaking for the social and psychic violence said to be at its core.[67] Drawing first on Hannah Arendt's account of totalitarianism and second on Bersani and Adam Phillips's psychoanalytic account of "generic interpersonal relating," Cobb argues that couple intimacy is a compact through which people "destructively overpersonalize and territorialize their relations with each other" instead of pursuing forms of "impersonal intimacy" that are indifferent to personal identity.[68] In this weighted comparison "the single is a *flâneur* figure with an impossible thought project—one who stands in a way of existence that is as unconditional as the vista she surveys, who can tolerate herself for much longer, much larger, than the couple's chopping block ordinarily permits."[69] In the wake of modernity's social insistence "that you should never be on your own, that you must always relate as two," the heroic singleton "is trying to resacrilize itself by removing the face of the other. The single goes to this 'holy' place and doesn't just see the painful, standardizing culture of couple control: instead, she or he sees something very abstract that has only an unspecific language of cliché but nevertheless opens up an extremely important panorama on the grand, distant, oceanic, deserted world."[70] Rather than giving access to a transcendental experience of this order, the mundane "logic of the couple" merely binds one to the foreshortened experience of "the social, otherwise known as the crowd."[71]

Although Cobb associates the couple with romance and the persistence of an idealized form of erotic love, this linking of the couple with the socially anonymous form of the crowd gets closer to the historical conditions through which the heterosexual couple emerges as a sexual and social problem and thus a magnet for biopolitical discourses of improvement. However romantically idealized, the couple form is discursively hemmed in through the constant exposure of its incapacities and limitations relative to the newly transparent standards of modernity, which include not only expectations of romance and intimacy but also new stretch targets of sexual equality as measured by increasingly varied and highly specific metrics. Applying a Foucauldian schema beyond queer theory's usual bandwidth of perversion, hysteria, and onanism, Annamarie Jagose has shown how the well-regulated heterosexual couple is repeatedly required to figure as the solution to the apparent incommensurateness of male and female sexuality through early-twentieth-century marriage manuals that promote simultaneous orgasm as the measure of erotic reciprocity: "Although the two events synchronously brought together in simultaneous orgasm, the husband's orgasms and the wife's, depend on an intimately realized regime of bodily discipline and self-surveillance, this simultaneity is associated with the emergence of a heteroeroticism as a single erotic orientation occupied equally by men and women, the assumed mutuality and coherence of which normalizes, without superseding, older models of gender hierarchy."[72] Jagose goes on to add that "we should not therefore imagine that the efforts of such marital experiments with simultaneity—or even marital ambitions for simultaneity—were limited to the domesticated and private pleasures or frustrations of individual husbands and wives."[73]

Where Cobb points to the idealization of the couple, Jagose points to its normativization, a phenomenon that is concentrated around discourses of marriage but not confined to them, nor, I would suggest, limited to the heterosexual. Rather, operating in concert with other modern impulses to equality, the discourse of sexual reciprocity that begins to penetrate marriage at the beginning of the twentieth century ultimately brings heterosexual and nonheterosexual practices into alignment. Building across the twentieth century, an erotic parallelism is established between heterosexual and homosexual relationships (and their alternates) that might (or might not) take marriage-like form. The perspective afforded by the historical success of the marriage equality movement can only reinforce the idea that this biopolitical expansion does not end here but will continue to extend across the spectrum of the erotosphere pulling others (most obviously the transgendered) into its normativizing orbit.

Massing a huge number of primary sources in evidence, Jagose demonstrates how, across the twentieth century, various biomedical epistemologies increasingly index sex (whether premarital, marital, extramarital, or postmarital) and, in particular, orgasm (which is harder to conceive in marital terms) to "the normative values of personhood" at the same time as they strip personhood from sex.[74] As a result of this contradictory drive to sexual personalization and depersonalization, the "double bind of modern sex" emerges in which "no matter how much sex is imagined as a privileged practice for the alleviation of the anomie that characterizes modern social relations by dint of its being apprehended as an intimate act, both particularizing and privatizing, it is equally available for the experience, whether depressive or euphoric, of the same impersonal intimacies it is normatively understood to counter."[75] Newly available for scientific codification and increasingly severed from reproduction, sexual satisfaction becomes both a personal and impersonal measure of the achievement of interpersonal intimacy, and—as evidenced by the late twentieth-century marital advice literature discussed by Vogler—certainly remains so in the context of heterosexual relationships that are less tightly twined with the institutions of kinship and family than ever before. This "imbrication of personal and impersonal intimacies" in sexual relations that are "more heavily weighted with interpersonal expectation"—including expectation around sexual satisfaction—but increasingly cut free of traditionally mandated social institutions also provides the historical context through which the relation between marriage and homosexuality must be rethought.[76]

In sum, I contend that the relation between homosexuality and marriage is historically richer and more complicated than currently acknowledged in either the specialist domain of queer theory or mainstream same-sex marriage debates. It is the normative detachment of heterosexuality from marriage as a compulsory social form and its complex repositioning as an electively sexual form that permits marriage to attach to homosexuality, a possibility that is further enhanced by the detachment of marriage from marriage, a contradictory state of affairs effected by the rise of divorce, reproductive freedom, gay liberation, and even couples counseling. Responsive to these social changes and all the other things that comprise sexual modernity, marriage continually relaunches itself as sexual, social, and domestic ideal and builds anew appropriate internal and external support mechanisms. In this upside-down world—which has been in place for over a century—gay and lesbian experiments in domestic partnership that both resemble and depart from the conventional couple form have fundamentally reshaped generic understandings of marriage and the principles by which it is defined—namely fidelity, exclusivity, and endurance.

While others have zeroed in on adultery and divorce in order to theoretically dismantle the foundations of marriage, I contend that these challenges are no greater than those posed by the serial media panics generated around marriage across the twentieth century. The idea of a marriage crisis first went into general circulation in the opening decades of the twentieth century in association with an extensive specialist and popular literature dedicated to explicating the difficulty husbands and wives face achieving mutual sexual happiness.[77] A second-wave crisis occurred in the 1960s linked to the convenient provision of reliable birth control, and a third wave followed in the 1990s with the advent of widescale calls for legislative reforms that would see marriage extended to same-sex partnerships. Each of these highly mediatized moments saw marriage reconfigured outside the sacral, contractual, and reproductive obligations with which it was previously associated. It is this constant historical reimagining of marriage that provides the evolving context in which gay and lesbian relationships can begin to appear as leading-edge exemplars of what long-term relationships might look like.

In addition to the specialist analysis and concern generated about the future of marriage across the twentieth century, the changing form of marriage has also been subject to intense popular speculation, particularly in novels and narrative films that take divorce and other social phenomenon, such as female reproductive freedom or the prospect of gay marriage, as an opportunity to explore the stories that can be told in the vicinity of marriage. Rather than challenge the ideological foundations of marriage or lobby for or against marriage equality, my focus in the pages to come is primarily on stories of marriage, or more accurately, marriage as story, a generic form of emplotment that has heterosexual and homosexual manifestations.

Instead of attacking canonic versions of marriage that first had their cultural hegemony challenged at the beginning of the twentieth century, the chapters ahead turn to the archive of popular culture in order to demonstrate that homosexuality has long been integral to the reimagining of affective and erotic horizons within marriage and the wider sociality to which it contributes. Next, chapter 2 briefly considers nineteenth-century literary renovations to the marriage plot before moving on to twentieth-century genres of popular culture that also derive their energy from marriage's susceptibility to change. Although Hollywood cinema in general has been responsive to changing expectations around romantic norms, one genre in particular stands out in relation to investigating explicitly conjugal obligations, namely the Hollywood comedies of remarriage as identified by Stanley Cavell, a clutch of effervescent films from the 1930s and 1940s that originally exercised their popular charge in an era in which middle-class marriage was shaken up by the easy availability of divorce. I revisit Cavell's philosophical discussion of remarriage in the contemporary context of gay marriage. This allows me to set up a theoretical framework through which to address across the course of this book a number of gay- and lesbian-themed melodramas that approach the sexual and social problem of marriage in increasingly explicit ways. Though very different from each other, these films collectively propel a reconceptualization of what same-sex marriage represents as a generalizable social achievement, irrespective of its legal standing.

In order to stress the historical aspect of this reimagining, chapter 3 reads and reads closely a Hollywood film that predates the same-sex marriage movement by several decades but nonetheless anticipates both gay and lesbian alternatives to marriage. The film is Dorothy Arzner's domestic melodrama *Craig's Wife* (1936), in which Rosalind Russell plays a house-obsessed woman who drives her besotted husband away. Drawing on the queer circumstances surrounding the film's production, I begin by offering a biographically enriched account of a film that appeared in an era when divorce was losing its social stigma. Having put this worldly framework in place, I proceed to concentrate (no doubt obsessively) on the cinematic detail of the film in order to show that *Craig's Wife* is simultaneously a critique of middle-class marriage and a validation of the interclass female companionate relationship that exists in its narrative wings. Rather than elevate text over context, or context over text, I use the combination of elements evidenced in and around *Craig's Wife*—lesbian director, gay designer, heterosexual mise en scène—to give more affective texture to the many and varied relationships that lesbians and gay men have historically had to domestic conjugality as a style of life.

Where my discussion of *Craig's Wife* identifies domesticity, style, and celebrity as key rubrics connecting homosexuality and marriage decades before same-sex marriage emerges as a political aspiration, chapter 4 argues for their continued relevance in the contemporary context of the marriage equality movement. Centered on *A Single Man* (2009)—Tom Ford's adaptation of Christopher Isherwood's novel of the same name from 1964—this chapter takes the "Tom Ford" brand as evidence of a wide cultural investment in gay style and emotionality that taps homosexuality's dual personalizing and politicizing effects in order to reinvigorate social forms, including the conventional form of marriage. I show how Ford's film mines both Isherwood's source text and his long-term domestic relationship with Don Bachardy in order to relaunch homosexual style as a universal brand that bestows cultural and emotional capital on its cosmopolitan fans, who, no longer divided in terms of their sexual orientation, class, or race, can be addressed as a single diverse demographic. If Ford's film makes a sentimental case for the legitimacy of same-sex relationships that resemble marriage while at the same time contouring the upmarket consumerist ambitions of a new generation of socially aspirant gays and lesbians, I demonstrate how Isherwood's source text scopes out an alternative conjugal narrative premised on sexual substitution and equivalency.

Where my reading of *A Single Man* engages the queer critique of gay marriage as a homonormative formation, chapter 5 considers the perversity endemic to the couple form via an engagement with Lisa Cholodenko's *High Art* (1998), *Laurel Canyon* (2002), and *The Kids Are All Right* (2010), a trilogy that traces the perseverance of coupled attachments that refuse to dissolve even in the face of their public dishonoring. The persistence of attachment beyond its origins in couple love is generally considered a queer value. Yet, from the perspective of the trilogy—which insists on both the correlation between duration and dependency and the fundamental ambivalence of attachment—things are not so simple. Acknowledging that sexual attachments and the intimate social worlds built on them might not persist, or might persist in ways that cannot be anticipated at their outset, is the condition under which marriage now betokens the uncertainty of happiness rather than its promise. Considered this way, same-sex marriage becomes a rubric for thinking through the terms on which the social and the sexual might be renegotiated in the face of everything we know about sex and its vicissitudes, including the fact that our attachments, which are often formed on impulse but also subject to rigorous social patterning, are mostly resistant to deliberation and will.

Chapter 6 is a concentrated reengagement of Cavell's argument about the Hollywood comedies of remarriage. The popular success of these films, Cavell argues, reflects a complex reattachment to marriage that, in the wake of divorce, must necessarily be approached as remarriage, as a revitalized commitment to a socially de-idealized form. In the present historical moment when the institution of marriage has been once again altered by the social acceptance of same-sex marriage, a cycle of gay and lesbian films has emerged that interrogate the terms on which marriage might be reimagined yet again as a viable social and sexual practice or, as its critics propose, abandoned outright. Where Cavell argues that postdivorce all marriage is remarriage, this chapter proposes that post–marriage equality, all marriage is gay marriage, at least for the popular purpose of renegotiating a general attachment to the form. It does so via close readings of two recent films, Stacie Passon's *Concussion* (2013) and Andrew Haigh's *Weekend* (2011), which both speak to wider conceptions of fidelity than those normally associated with conjugality but also engage notions of the domestic and the everyday, categories homosexuality now makes more public claim to than ever before.

The final chapter turns to *45 Years* (2015), another critically celebrated film written and directed by Haigh that deals with a straight marriage that is faltering under the weight of its repressed past. Haigh's film is an unsolicited endorsement of my argument that the advent or imminence of same-sex marriage has altered the emotional, sexual, social, and ethical framework through which we now encounter marriage in general. The historical arc that ends with *45 Years* corresponds to the timeframe across which marriage has in many jurisdictions been legally redrafted as an institution capable of including gays and lesbians. I argue that the films I have selected for discussion do not simply reflect the social and legal change with which they are coincident but rather run ahead of it in compelling and contradictory ways. Instead of promoting an inclusive model of marriage that accommodates heterosexuals and homosexuals alike, the complex narratives these films inscribe fundamentally alter our sense of what sexual attachment might involve as a social as well as romantic form. Rather than regarding these films as affirmative representations of gay and lesbian couples, I argue for their significance in mediating sexual and social innovation in complex ways. With their capacity to capture the mutability of feelings as they emerge under specific historical conditions, these gay marriage films enable us to re-specify erotic, affective, and ordinary attachments to others and think about their long-term sustainability outside familial frameworks.

Against the tide of the queer critique of marriage, I make a strong argument for the ongoing pertinence of the marriage plot—and the narrative sensibility it cultivates—as generative of the conditions through which we continue to experience ourselves as subjects of feeling and agents of change. While legal histories of marriage barely capture this state of affairs, fictional representations of same-sex marriage and its historical avatars are a significant resource for thinking about the ways in which homosexuality has long been integral to the reimagining of affective and erotic horizons within the couple form. In the chapters ahead, I demonstrate how the narrativization of gay and lesbian relationships that resemble marriages in nature if not in name in a range of popular film texts operates instructionally insofar as it expands notions of attachment and fulfillment to include forms of sexual sociability that are usually thought to be incompatible with the married state. Ultimately, I will argue that the utopian patterns discernible in these fictional gay and lesbian relationships (whether or not they are denoted as marriage) are usefully conceived as perpetual reattachments, or what Cavell would call remarriages. Hence we might begin to think of same-sex marriage as remarriage, or a queer recommitment to marriage as a social and sexual form that has always been radically inclusive of difference. Originally surfacing in the era of divorce and now resurfacing in the era of marriage equality, the idea of remarriage is a resource for thinking otherwise about the impasses of the present. Or so it has proven for me. With the authority bestowed by experience, I offer remarriage as a trope through which to reflect on the full spectrum of disenchantments and deidealizations that have manifested in queer theory over the past several decades. Thus I begin not with social and sexual utopias, nor with the unexpected difficulty attendant on reattaching to marriage as a de-idealized form, but with domestic fiction, the natural home of the marriage plot and all its heterosexual trappings.

2 From Gay Marriage to Remarriage

The fundamental premise of this book is that the queer critique of the marriage equality movement, and the concomitant dismissal of gay marriage as a homonormative aspiration, obscures the long-standing and highly productive relation that exists historically between homosexuality and the couple form. Both theoretically and methodologically, I refuse to concede homosexuality's relation to marriage as signified by its legal profile, just as I call out queer theory's current obsession with marriage as an emblem of the state. In order to better understand how sexual intimacies and social intimacies are historically entwined and negotiated in the vicinity of marriage, we must find other ways to approach marriage as a cultural narrative within which social ambitions, as well as personal desires, unfold and reinvent themselves. Queer theory might ask, for instance, what is the state emblematized by marriage now that it includes gays and lesbians? To answer this we need to bring more than political realism to bear on gay marriage; we need to bring political fantasy and utopian thinking to the scene.

Although the prehistory of gay marriage in the Western world might be traced to the faux weddings enacted in the molly houses of eighteenth-century London and the Boston marriages of nineteenth-century America, in the previous chapter I invoked the early twentieth-century marriage crisis as the more salient historical crux.[1] This moment saw the underpinnings of middle-class marital relationships systematically questioned from a variety of specialist and popular discourses, including sexology, marriage advice literature, and first-wave feminism. As expectations of affective intimacy and erotic reciprocity began to define successful heterosexual couplehood as an expression of sexual as well as social compatibility, the future of companionate marriage become the subject of intense speculation. If marriage between husband and wife did not include mutually satisfying sexual relations as measured against the normative standard of simultaneous orgasm, then those conjugal relationships might be experienced as wanting in ways not previously articulated. The expectation of erotic normalcy, or what we might think of as the social drive to feel sexually normal, emerged as an objective criterion for gauging conjugal health and happiness. Bolstered by science and cut loose from moral precept, the idea that the viability of a marriage might be calculated sexually coincided with the growing acceptance of divorce across the class spectrum. The popularization of divorce—a practice previously confined to the socially entitled and indexed to the accumulation and distribution of inherited wealth—both disturbed the ideological foundations of marriage and allowed the couple form to be reimagined as a sexual and domestic ideal within the context of emerging gay and lesbian subcultures that were increasingly apprehended through sociological frameworks concerned with objectively mapping behavioral patterns, norms, and deviations across populations rather than specifying pathologies.

It is my contention that, coincident with the broader evolution of sexual modernity, gay and lesbian experiments in living that approximate or refurbish the couple form had, by the end of the twentieth century, conclusively reshaped marriage and the notions of fidelity and exclusivity engaged in its vicinity. The recent call for marriage equality tends to obscure this extended history and, instead of acknowledging that same-sex marriage understood as an informal or customary practice already exists and has done for decades, promotes the conventional understanding that marriage is something gays and lesbians want to borrow from straight culture. Despite the attention given to the recent successes of the marriage equality movement, gay and lesbian marriage has tended to emerge not as a full-blown state-sanctioned ideological apparatus exercising hegemony across all the crisscrossing private and public planes that comprise the social sphere but as a practice of living that is more or less quietly absorbed into common law across time through a variety of processes and informal mechanisms that are tuned to changes in cultural practice and what is or is not considered appropriate social conduct. Witness the now common phenomenon by which a marriage-like status adheres to nonlegalized same-sex relationships via the provisions of de facto law, which tends to find analogies to marriage everywhere, even in relationships explicitly excluded from that legal state. As any unmarried middle-class gay or lesbian couple living in a socially liberal jurisdiction knows, when it comes to dissolving your estate either while you live or in the event of you and your partner's separate or simultaneous deaths, de facto law raises the ghost of marriage everywhere. Although you may jointly consider your estate as separable from your partner's, the law may consider them inextricably combined or only extricable through the framework of marriage, which is to say divorce. We might also add to this observation the further twist by which de facto marriage is now so ubiquitous it is all but impossible to legally distinguish the same-sex couple from its seeming opposite, the heterosexual couple, who may also have elected not to legally marry but are considered to have done so in common law. If marriage law now throws a nondiscriminatory shadow across de facto straight and gay couples, it is worth observing that the classical novel is likewise guilty of promoting marriage as a sexually inclusive institution while seeming to do the opposite.

It is a truism of literary studies to say that the cultural evolution of marriage and that of the novel are linked. Since the late 1950s, when Ian Watt first argued for the rise of three inseparable phenomena—the middle class, literacy, and the novel—literary criticism has increasingly finessed its account of the role played by marriage in the emergence and evolution of domestic fiction and argued for the centrality of the form to modern life, at least as it is lived in the increasingly industrialized context of nineteenth-century England.[2] Watt's account of the rise of the novel speaks of marriage as a negotiated social contract that brings together romantic and economic concerns, thus collapsing marriage and market in a way that prefigures recent criticism of same-sex marriage as a normative extension of the neoliberal state. In the late 1980s, however, Nancy Armstrong abruptly shifted critical focus away from classical notions of the social market to the way in which the female-centered discourse of the novel is central to the benign systems of power that are considered distinctive of modernity. Influenced by Michel Foucault's account of disciplinary power, Armstrong argues that the real project of the novel is domesticity and the bringing to prominence of an indicatively female desiring subject who is "independent of political history" but recognizable to the emerging psychological, therapeutic, and regulatory discourses of power that operate through gender rather than class.[3] In the process of making this argument about the feminization of disciplinary power, Armstrong singles out Watt as one of many major critics of the novel who "at some point capitulate to the idea that sexual desire exists in some form prior to its representation and remains there as something for us to recover or liberate. It is this dominant theory of desire," she goes on, "that authorizes domestic fiction and yet conceals the role such fiction played in modern history."[4]

Consistent with their different approaches to romantic love, Armstrong and Watt zero in on different kinds of marriage stories within the broad span of the English novel at its height. Whereas Watt emphasizes the novel of courtship that ends in marriage and leavens out different class-based attitudes toward sex and morals along the way (as in the novels of Samuel Richardson), Armstrong favors plots in which marriage is not the resolution of "social competition" but the means by which class conflict could be "sexualized and therefore suppressed even while it was being experienced."[5] For Armstrong the simultaneous incitement and suppression of female desire is evidenced by the many madwomen and protohysterics that populate the pages of late Victorian domestic fiction and the Freudian case study that is their logical progression. Her book-length working through of this argument terminates with the assertion that the authority to represent sexuality ultimately passed from domestic fiction understood and embraced, however ambivalently, as "writing for, about, and by women" to the male-dominated profession of psychoanalysis, a normative development consistent with other regulatory impulses in the gendered regime of modernity.[6]

Although Armstrong's revisionist account of domestic fiction and the role it has played in specifying gender and sexuality has been hugely influential, she has far less to say about the fate of marriage under this new discursive regime. Not only does she more or less agree with Watt that Richardson's sexed-up novels represent class tensions as gendered struggles that can be resolved in terms of the sexual contract (by which she means the contract of marriage) but she also presents the more "respectable" novels of Jane Austen as mere modifications to an already established narrative formula that depends on marriage for its resolution. While Austen's novels are said to partake of a new drive to define "an alternative basis for desirability" on affective rather than social grounds, Armstrong nonetheless agrees that they continue to rely on "the figure of sexual exchange" in which the "union" of men and women deemed eligible for marriage "miraculously transforms all social differences into gender differences and gender differences into qualities of mind." As Armstrong quickly points out, for all the apparent difference between Austen's novels and the novels that preceded them, Austen's version of the marriage plot simply changes "the nature of the social conflict that marriage appeared to resolve."[7] Although derived from a Foucauldian starting point, Armstrong's account of the role played by domestic fiction in tempering social differences to the point that they are misrecognized as sexual differences is exactly congruent with Watt's account, which is shored up by the statistically fuelled, narratively driven work of Lawrence Stone, a social historian and staunch anti-Foucauldian.[8] Despite seeming to be at loggerheads, both Armstrong and Watt emphasize the emergence of companionate marriage as a middle-class ideal that does not exclude erotic passion but balances its claims with additional aims and objectives, such as compatibility, comradeship, practical need, and the alignment of the married couple with other forms of social organization.

In the critical vicinity of marriage, it seems as if the more things change, the more they stay the same. Whether marriage is conceived as an affective alignment between women and men who live in a literate, middle-class world in which gender splits their area of operation between public and private, political and nonpolitical spheres (Watt), or is better thought of as part of the new machinery of power by which women and men are productively disciplined through the highly gendered discourse of feeling (Armstrong), the ideal of companionate marriage that undergirds these two arguments is not itself disputed, nor is its heterosexual profile. Although they might bicker about the details, Watt and Armstrong tend to agree on the basics, which are, first, that marriage functions as an effective switch point between social and sexual contracts, public and intimate worlds, and second, that the marriage plot serves as a heterosexual training program for future companionate husbands and wives. More importantly, in the general affective swirl that is the English novel, marriage is not treated in any sustained manner but rather invoked in the service of narrative closure. Whether approached from the Foucauldian or anti-Foucauldian perspective, it is a truth universally acknowledged that the marriage plot concerns itself with the grounds on which companionate marriage should be contracted, not with the sexual and social complications that result from conjugal intimacy of the companionate kind.

For a compelling articulation of the idea that what is English about the English novel is its structuring reluctance to represent marriage except as a means of shutting down the story of sexual attachment, one need only turn to Tony Tanner, who in 1979 deployed the emerging lingua franca of poststructuralism to give an account of the European novel as perversely invested in the narrative pull of not marriage but adultery. Refreshingly unconcerned with a general theory of the novel and notoriously selective in relation to prior scholarship, Tanner recasts the marriage plot from the vantage point of its transgression. While never disputing its centrality to the bourgeois novel, Tanner more or less turns inside out the novel's putative relation to marriage by insisting that the eighteenth- and nineteenth-century novel is a "paradoxical object" that "may work to subvert what it seems to celebrate."[9] Since in the novel, as in nineteenth-century middle-class life more generally, the marriage bond stands for the ultimate social contract—"the all-subsuming, all-organizing, all-containing contract" in which passion, property, and loyalty are braided together—and, since adultery threatens this pact—both the pact of marriage and the more general social pact that marriage represents—Tanner contends that marital transgression must also be a central theme of the novel.[10]

Drawing a parallel between bourgeois genre and bourgeois theme, Tanner goes on to argue that not only is the novel of marriage a mirror image of a world newly founded in contractual relationships, as advanced by the political philosophy of John Locke and Jean-Jacques Rousseau, but "contracts *create* transgressions; the two are inseparable, and the one would have no meaning without the other."[11] Thus the French novel, in particular, "does not show a simple *contest* between marital fidelity and adultery" but rather demonstrates how one generates the other."[12] It is from this paradox, Tanner argues, that the nineteenth-century French novel draws its power, an assertion for which he finds latter-day apologists in Georges Bataille, Foucault, and Roland Barthes, for whom "the model of a good contract has become, not marriage—but prostitution," a transparently monetary pact that figures forth not "the bourgeois ideal" of marriage as "a good contract" but its "reverse mirror image" in which we can see "the very structure of its bad conscience."[13] In this distorting French lens, which tells a marital truth that remains hidden in the prudish tradition of the English novel, the "adulteress" emerges as "a wife who is not a wife, a prostitute who is not a prostitute, the keeper and breaker of the insecure security of the contract of marriage."[14]

Somewhat unexpectedly, in the final pages of his book Tanner goes on to state that "by definition you cannot transform transgression" into "a regular way of life," since, as Emma Bovary finds out, the adulterous transgressor of marriage simply reenters "the vicious downward spiral of devaluation through repetition, and the loss of difference engendered by habit. Which is why, for Emma"—and in some sense for Tanner—"to rediscover in adultery all the banality of marriage, is one of the most disturbing discoveries in the history of the novel."[15] As this citation suggests, female adultery in the novel acquires a special significance for Tanner over and above other sexual contraventions, such as infidelity, seduction, or rape, because it "introduces an agonizing and irresolvable category-confusion into the individual and thence into society itself." Unlike the lover, mistress, or whore, categories that although denigrated are nonetheless "recognized as having an existence and a definition that is not incompatible with the social terminology and economy within which they live," the unfaithful wife "is an unassimilable conflation of what society insists should be separate categories and functions." In confirmation of this argument Tanner asserts that "the very word *adulteress*," with its implications of pollution and contamination, "is close to a contradiction in a single term" and "points to an activity, not an identity."[16] Although Tanner here invokes the Foucauldian distinction between sexual acts and sexual identities, he does not pursue what I take to be its implication, namely that adultery understood as a gendered act pitted against the contract of marriage (and the more fundamental social contract that marriage represents) is in some sense unassimilable to modern sexual discourse and the social world of sexual contract it implies. As I will go on to argue, in the postadultery world that same-sex marriage ushers in by loosening contractual notions of fidelity in favor of negotiated systems of sexual association, marriage is no longer a bad thing that must be rejected as, in Tanner's terms, the "structure that maintains the Structure," but a place of perpetually insecure security that is nonetheless subject to a complex de-idealization and re-idealization of marriage-like dimensions.[17]

In terms that resonate with Jacques Lacan and his more recent interpreters, such as Leo Bersani and Lee Edelman, Tanner goes on to call the adulterous woman "a paradoxical presence of negativity within the social structure." In this sense, adultery is not just a source of narrative conflict that brings "the wrong things together in the wrong places (or the wrong people in the wrong beds)" but a full-scale philosophical assault that reveals the social contract to be "arbitrary rather than absolute." Given the epistemic force attributed to it, it should come as no surprise that "the actual adulterous act (the initial act that makes of the woman an adulteress) is not described" in the novels Tanner discusses but rather "becomes a silence and an absence in the text that gradually spreads, effectively negating what *is* made audible and present."[18] For Tanner, that is, adultery appears to be a problem primarily of signification and, perhaps for this reason, necessarily kept separate from the more pragmatic world of modern divorce in which there are no bad women, or even bad men, just bad marriages with built-in escape clauses. As many others have pointed out, Tanner values the transgressions of adultery because he sees them as ultimately leading to a crisis in the realist novel that ushers in the modern novel or "what might be called the novel of metaphor."[19] Neither English nor French, the modern novel of metaphor finds its trans-Atlantic apotheosis in Henry James's *The Golden Bowl* (1904), in which an American woman's muted response to her European husband's adultery proves the making of her marriage. Identifying with neither adulterer or adulteress, still less the father and daughter patsy pair the adulterers collectively betray, Tanner assumes the full height of the Jamesian perspective in order to reject divorce—"the main way in which society came to cope with adultery"—on purely novelistic grounds: "It is as if the novelist realized that divorce was a piece of surface temporizing, a forensic palliative to cloak and muffle the profoundly disjunctive reverberations and implications of adultery."[20]

As Kimberly Freeman argues, Tanner's formal dismissal of divorce as an easy option almost as tedious as the novelistic marriage it would dissolve relies on the assumption that all divorce is the result of adultery, as opposed to allowing that divorce might be the result of the normal wear and tear of companionate marriage.[21] In her book-length discussion of divorce in the American novel from 1881 to 1976—the timespan running from the publication of William Dean Howell's *A Modern Instance* to John Updike's *Marry Me: A Romance*—Freeman identifies not just adultery but a full range of personal-political triggers leading to bust-ups between fictional US husbands and their increasingly feminist wives. Although Freeman reads the American novel's high divorce rate as symptomatic of irreconcilable differences between romance and realism, her account of the Americanization of divorce is useful for clarifying that in Tanner's perspective the French divorce plot is simply another version of the English marriage plot insofar as it is hell-bent on closure against the novelistic energies represented by adultery. Like an antidote to Tanner's archformalism, Freeman's critical pragmatism ends up divorcing itself from divorce and pitching toward an entirely speculative sociosphere in which "conflicting ideologies of property, nation, ethnicity, marriage, divorce, and even gender have all been dissolved, giving these survivors the chance to divorce themselves from those ideologies, and, true to American idealism, to start again."[22] In a literary critical world made increasingly fraught by the alignment of heterosexual marriage with divorce, and in an actual world newly aligned to the possibility of same-sex marriage, the more oblique relation that exists between homosexuality and marriage opens up narrative space for approaching notions of conjugality in less absolute terms.

The idea that heterosexual marriage is a rote or tired story surfaces in the context of post-structuralist accounts of the novel that favor increasingly self-reflexive narrative forms. If Tanner promotes the adulteress—less frequently the adulterer—as someone who "effectively 'renarrativizes' a life that has become devoid of story," others go further by arguing that marriage is all plot and no story to begin with.[23] In his highly influential *Reading for the Plot*, Peter Brooks brilliantly articulates the distinction between the order of discourse (the literal plot events that comprise a text in the order narrated) and the order of story (the overarching narrative that can be distilled from plot points and their various delivery mechanisms). Brooks is interested in the ways in which these two orders switch-hit in a process he calls emplotment (or plotting) that engages the competent reader's almost instinctive capacity to move between plot and story in the drive to achieve complete narrative understanding. Much easier to do in practice than in summary, this narrative facility—our more or less conscious way of "seeking through the narrative text as it unfurls before us a precipitation of shape and meaning, some simulacrum of understanding of how meaning can be construed over and through time"—is buoyed along by our confidence that, once the end is reached, the relation between the orders of discourse and story will be satisfactorily resolved, as in the exemplary case of the detective novel that blatantly propels both its hero and its reader on the forward-directed, backward-looking path of emplotment.[24]

Although Brooks does not directly address the marriage plot in his account of narrative reflexivity and its activation in "the anticipation of retrospective narrative understanding" that drives the compulsion to read, the connection between the two will be taken up by D. A. Miller, who will be known to readers in film studies through his tightly wound formal unravelings of the work of Alfred Hitchcock and the highly personal columns he contributes to *Film Quarterly* on the occasion of DVD releases that speak to the sex and class pedagogy of his early informal immersion in film.[25] Miller was trained in literary rather than film studies, as am I, and his first book on problems of closure in the traditional novel begins by taking issue with Brooks's emphasis on the paradoxical priority of plot endings, arguing that "closure never has the totalizing powers of organization" claimed for it. Without disputing that nineteenth-century novels build toward closure—and neither disputing that the form that closure takes is frequently enough marriage—Miller argues "that they are never fully or finally governed by it."[26] In a classic instance of having it both ways, Miller first accepts that closure is the be-all and end-all of novelistic narration and the backward-forward form of reading it supports, then acknowledges that his actual interest is in the regulatory mechanisms the classical novel develops in order to contain the diverse erotics of story within the heterosexual marriage plot. This highly complicated investment in the narrational strictures by which the story of heterosexual marriage constrains itself to a topic at odds with its own internal energies seems reflected in the real-life conundrum Miller discretely signals when graciously acknowledging his untellable debt to his wife at the end of his book's prefatory remarks. In a final demonstration that he has earned his critical stripes in relation to both the general impulse inscribed in the marriage plot and the specific impulse inscribed in his own marriage, Miller posits that "the narratable is stronger than the closure to which it is opposed in an apparent binary" that is better understood as a "principle of vaccination" in which the novel or story of marriage incorporates "the narratable in safe doses to prevent it from breaking out."[27]

For Miller—who in the preface recalls himself as the soon-to-be-gay husband not yet broken out of a marriage which is real in all the ways that count—it is the classically executed novels of Austen and George Eliot that exemplify this prudently inoculated condition insofar as they are oriented toward "a 'utopic' state that is radically at odds with the narrative means used to reach it." In the case of Austen's novels, he argues, this idealized end-state of "absolute propriety," which is conjugally glossed as "proper understanding expressed in proper erotic objects and proper social arrangements," is constantly threatened by all the wayward instabilities of "desire, language and society" that make up the flirty story that has to get us to "this definitive 'finalizing' state of affairs."[28] Although Miller does not argue that the marriage plot is the only plot of the novel, or even the only plot discernible in Austen, he does insist that the narrative offer of a perfect union or ideal marriage like the one posited between a Darcy and an Elizabeth is a false or at least misleading promise insofar as the state of coupled perfection is, as he frames it, nonnarratable. In this account of the marriage plot, marriage functions as the almost abstract point at which plot and story are finally laminated together and there is nothing left to say in either the register of event or the register of reflection on event.[29] In this respect conjugal closure comes at a heavy price, since marriage can neither sustain the ongoing crossing of the codes of discourse and story that comprise novelistic narration nor sustain their activation in reading for the plot (as Brooks terms it). At best, it is the plotting of marriage—the desire for its emplotment rather than its narrative achievement—that forms the narratable, a category that Miller privileges above both closure and the deconstructive narratology practiced by both Tanner and Brooks, which merely shifts the stabilizing effects of closure from marriage onto narrative itself.

What Miller values—and what he thinks all nonspecialist readers of marriage plots value whether they know it or not—is everything that stands between the desire for marriage and its consummation. This everything can be thought of as less the discontents of marriage (or the sort of thing that might prompt adultery) than the discontents of the marriage plot: its compellingly dilatory way of deferring its heterosexual rationale in favor of everything that queerly stands in its way.[30] Two decades later, in his monograph on Jane Austen's style, Miller—who has by this time finessed his own late-gay style— takes apart the narrational mode through which Austen appears to serve "the marriage plot as its aging maid of honor" while effectively blotting it.[31] Once Miller unravels this narrational logic, Austen's marriage plot is revealed as a complex front for promoting the unmarriageable, a kind of same-sex marriage equality strategy before the fact. Through his rhetorically flawless recasting of Robert Ferrars's foppishness as an "unheterosexual effeminacy that shrinks the bachelor pool" available to the women in *Sense and Sensibility*, Miller launches the notion that the heterosexual marriage plot—even at its nineteenth-century height, let alone the ravaged state the twentieth-century popularization of divorce delivers it to—already accommodates everything it is by definition set against, a recognition that might also apply to marriage as a broader cultural story.[32]

Even in an exclusively textual context, Miller's argument is agenda setting insofar as it traces a feedback loop between marriage and not-marriage, heterosexuality and homosexuality (or at least their precursor forms), positing both sets of terms as narratively dependent formations that occupy the same discursive landscape. As odd as it seems, this straightforwardly Foucauldian observation runs counter to the gay-positive tradition in novel criticism that prefers to keep the marriage plot as an exclusively heterosexual concern that needs to be formally broken with in order to liberate alternative narratives that we recognize as gay or lesbian to the degree that they are implicitly or emphatically against marriage. It is to that gay-positive tradition that I now turn.

The most high-profile advocate of this countertradition is Joseph Allen Boone, who names it thus in his book-length account of the conventional strictures of the marriage plot and the many counterplots set against it in literary history's unswerving drive toward modernism. Tracing the emergence of the marriage plot as a signature of social order in eighteenth- and nineteenth-century middle-class culture, Boone considers the marriage plot both sexually and aesthetically conservative. Within the novel, he contends, "ideological structures of belief—of which the ideal of romantic wedlock is the primary example—are translated into narrative structures that at once encode and perpetuate those beliefs."[33] Boone goes on to accuse the traditional novel of knotting together wedlock and narrative closure, thereby "protecting the text's ideal vision of unchanging love by strangling the possibility of more narrative at the very juncture" of marriage.[34] Against this vision of the marriage plot in which the story falls victim to the rough handling of conjugal closure, Boone uncovers a tradition of pushback that unleashes what he thinks of as the sexually radical potential of the novel. Representing a "small but subversive attack upon the evolving hegemony of the marriage tradition in Anglo-American fiction," the countertradition blossoms into a full-blown modernism that dismantles the formal structure of the marriage plot and undermines the ideological force of marriage as a social ideal.[35] So far, so exciting, until it is revealed that the modernist countertradition critiques marriage-oriented culture by either exposing "wedlock to be a state of impasse, of irresolvable tensions and conflicts," or elaborating alternative possibilities centered on sameness and repetition (or a better kind of impasse).[36]

Many of Boone's narrative alternates to marriage are gender separatist in orientation. They involve plots of masculine quest or female friendship and the same-sex communities that support these kinds of stories, whether it be the rough-and-tumble world of a whaling ship (Herman Melville's *Moby Dick*) or the vegetative surrounds of a pastoral retreat (Sarah Orne Jewett's *The Country of the Pointed Firs*). Presented as masculinist and feminist ethical alternatives to the cross-gendered complementarity posited in the heterosexual marital ideal, Boone ultimately ends up idealizing same-sex relationships as unmarked by internal tension or ambivalence of any kind. Same-sex relationships are presented, that is, as re-idealizations of the ideal of marriage cut free of the obligation to smooth over the gendered inequities manifested by marriages contracted between a husband and a wife. As Elizabeth Abel notes, where Boone "anatomizes the antagonisms of marriage, he celebrates autonomy and same-sex friendships without acknowledging the loneliness of the single life or the hierarchies and opacities that can operate in friendship" thereby "foreclosing analysis of the aggression unleashed and sometimes masked by identification and writing conflict out of same-sex bonds."[37] Certainly the bachelors and spinsters that make up Boone's same-sex communities enter into anodyne relationships about which there is little left to say, just like the beyond-the-ending marriages these relationships are supposed to narratively supplant. Rather than being a same-sex counter to marriage, the same-sex bonds and communities that Boone celebrates appear to offer up a more benign version of marriage than the kind that heterosexual culture has been able to achieve in the two centuries since the novel began its conjugal rise.

A more productive approach to the written and lived tradition of same-sex bonding can be found in the work of Sharon Marcus, who, unlike Boone, insists from the get-go that Boston marriages need to be read as akin to marriage, not as an alternative to it. In her account of Victorian marriage culture (as opposed to the Victorian marriage plot), Marcus starts out by upturning the gendered coordinates of what we have previously taken to be the heterosexual compact of marriage. Like a good new historicist, Marcus begins by citing the 1844 diary entry of a ten-year-old girl, Emily Pepys, who, in a journal intended to be read by others, bemusedly recounts a dream in which she is to be married to another girl. Far from representing a break in the gendered protocols of Victorian sexual culture, Marcus argues that "Emily's dream was in fact typical of a world that made relationships between women central to femininity, marriage, and family life." In the typical Victorian world in which Emily lives, marriage is already a same-sex phenomenon, "not only a Victorian dream but also a Victorian reality."[38] This reality is evidenced in the massive amount of historical documentation Marcus collates in order to demonstrate that relations between women, including sexual relations, are integral to the overall social project of marriage that, in its Victorian iterations, does not understand same-sex intimacy as opposed to cross-sex relationships but frequently posits them as mutually reinforcing, both socially and sexually. Putting a straight twist on the old-school erotic continuum model that presumes a "lesbian potential of all relationships between women," Marcus is drawn not to the separatist communities applauded by Boone but to commonplace female friendships that are the erotic exercise ground for similarly conceived relationships with men.[39]

By "just reading" a number of Victorian courtship novels for what they show about relationships between women at the manifest level of plot rather than plumbing their depths for the things they cannot say, Marcus demonstrates that "female friendship was neither a static auxiliary to the marriage plot nor a symptomatic exclusion from it, but instead a transmission mechanism that kept narrative energies on track."[40] She then goes on to demonstrate, via a similarly shallow reading of Charles Dickens's *Great Expectations*, that this "transmission mechanism" involved both the homoerotic training of women and the disciplining of men whose eligibility for marriage depends in part on their sloughing off the traits of working-class masculinity in order to present as a more appropriately feminine object of female desire. Toward the end of her book, Marcus convincingly maintains that the Victorians in general, and Victorian feminists in particular, appreciated what contemporary debates around marriage equality forget, namely the fundamental plasticity of marriage as a social and erotic institution. In her account of the marriage debates set in train by the legalization of civil divorce in the English Divorce and Matrimonial Causes Act of 1857, Marcus reveals that "many involved in those discussions were either women in female marriages or knew women in female marriages," but instead of making of this a countertradition to marriage, as Boone might, she argues that these same-sex relationships provided the model for marriage as we now understand it: "Familiarity with those conjugal partnerships shaped feminist reformers' vision of marriage as a plastic institution that could be reformed into a dissoluble contract based on equality, rather than an irrevocable vow that created a hierarchy."[41]

This observation prompts me to issue a spoiler alert for folk wrapped up in current marriage equality debates: marriage equality arrived at least a century and a half ago when advocates of heterosexual marriage wanted to claim parity with same-sex models. Marcus insists that the legal unfurling of "the notion of marriage as contract"—a process kick-started by the legal advent of divorce and subsequently accelerated by its popular acceptance across the social bandwidth—made it possible to "define marriage in nonheterosexual terms and to posit increasing equality and similarity between spouses as progress towards modernity."⁴² Based in notions of parity and equivalence, the Victorian version of marriage equality looks mighty contemporary in the way it declines to distinguish between its coupled civilians on grounds of gender or sexuality. While Marcus gives only a handful of paragraphs to the discussion of the gay marriage debate circa 2007, the moment in which she is writing, she is unequivocal in her assertion that, "just as the 'homosexual' is a recent invention, so too is the opposition between marriage and homosexuality." Indeed, it is "only once medical writers and social thinkers in the 1880s began to equate inversion with the infantile, the primitive, and the undoing of a civilization premised on monogamous, heterosexual marriage did homosexuality come to seem antithetical to marriage."⁴³ Marcus's argument aligns with mine insofar as she claims not only that marriage has always accommodated homosexuality but also that same-sex couples have been innovators across the conjugal field. Indeed, from the historical perspective articulated in *Between Women* it can be argued that, to the extent that marriage has survived as a viable social form into the twentieth and now twenty-first century, it has done so thanks in part to nineteenth-century female marriages that were "conducted openly and discussed neutrally in respectable society," whatever form they took (and they took many).⁴⁴

According to Marcus, these nineteenth-century same-sex arrangements stretched and exercised the innate cultural adaptability of marriage, a malleableness that is also demonstrated in the sheer "heterogeneity of public opinion" generated around the question of what form the institution of marriage should take. Surveying Victorian marriage reform debates, she identifies a welter of perspectives as "antic" as any proposed at the end of the twentieth century or beginning of the twenty-first.⁴⁵ Surveying Victorian same-sex marriages that were never incorporated in law, Marcus detects yet more signs of conjugal innovation: "Forced by necessity to construct ad hoc legal frameworks for their relationships," the women coupled in nineteenth-century female marriages were not only "precursors of late-twentieth-century 'same-sex domestic partners,' but also anticipated forms of marriage between men and women that were only institutionalized decades after their deaths." Just as importantly, Marcus insists that these "female marriages had their share of troubles and were as plagued by infidelity, conflict, and power differences as legal ones," a point she demonstrates through her acquaintance with the nineteenth-century celebrity culture that surrounded the world of theater and, in particular, the sexual career of the actress Charlotte Cushman.⁴⁶ No more exempt from ambivalence than any legal attachment between people and no less caught up in principles of financial restitution and care, these same-sex "unions exemplified the features that British activists fought to import into marriage between men and women: dissolubility, relative egalitarianism, and greater freedom for both spouses."[47]

Marcus is unique among literary and cultural historians in arguing not that the road to marriage is the road to divorce (as Laurence Stone has already put it) but that the road to divorce is the road to same-sex marriage. Although I cannot match the historical data Marcus marshals in support of her argument, I will go on to argue that in the twentieth century it is the road to remarriage, an odd detour on the road to divorce first mapped out by Stanley Cavell when rifling through Hollywood's back catalogue of marriage comedies, that ultimately points to the road to same-sex marriage. Although Cavell is concerned with film rather than literature, and with philosophy rather than cultural history, like Marcus he is drawn to scenes of gender instruction within an overall marriage plot that features surprisingly mobile couples—some of them coupled with other couples in star-crossed foursomes—who seemingly infringe all our established expectations of conjugality. In the feature-length marriage films discussed by Cavell—all of them as popular in their day as the great marriage novels of the nineteenth century were in theirs and, like those novels, retaining their audience appeal decades after they first appeared—the many impediments to married love thrown down by the mechanics of plot ultimately serve to make the shaky institution of modern marriage stronger by including in it things often said to be against it, such as feminism.[48]

In 2004, over twenty years after the publication of *Pursuits of Happiness,* Cavell explicitly makes the connection between his interest in the Hollywood comedies of remarriage and the contemporary expansion of the institution of marriage to include same-sex couples but immediately slides out from under the obligation to think the two forms together on experiential grounds: "While same-sex marriages, or unions, have become common enough to force a consciousness, and elaboration, of the economic and legal consequences for partners and for children reared in such marriages, it is too early yet to know (or I am too isolated in my experience to tell) what new shapes such marriages will discover for their investments in imaginativeness, exclusiveness, and equality."[49] The more obvious point that generations of gays and lesbians have grown up watching exactly the same Hollywood remarriage films as Cavell, many of them indelibly marked by gay and lesbian talent both above and below the line, suggests to me that we already have in both studio-era film and the independent cinema that followed it an archive deep and rich enough to explore evolving conjugal "investments in imaginativeness, exclusiveness, and equality" relevant to everyone.

The seven remarriage films discussed by Cavell in *Pursuits of Happiness*, then rediscussed in *Cities of Words*, repeatedly recast particular stars as husbands and wives, most notably Clark Gable, Cary Grant, and Katharine Hepburn, who, when they were not remarrying each other, were remarrying others, such as Claudette Colbert, Irene Dunne, Rosalind Russell, Barbara Stanwyck, Henry Fonda, and James Stewart. As well as being a self-declared fan of these dialogue-driven comedies, which he thinks of as the epitome of Hollywood popular filmmaking circa 1934–49 (a span of years that runs from Frank Capra's *It Happened One Night* to George Cukor's *Adam's Rib*), Cavell is interested in what these films represent as a sustained philosophical engagement with marriage. Ultimately interested in building a rhetorical bridge between American popular culture and Western philosophical thought, Cavell kicks his project off by pointing out that Hollywood's technological advance to cinematic sound in the 1930s more or less coincided with the maturation of the first generation of women to be born after the advent of first-wave feminism. That is, for the first time in history there was a mass population of women (and men) who had grown up with the feminist expectation that women's lives would be different from those of previous generations, in particular in the area of marriage, which was no longer considered the mandatory fulfillment of female destiny but merely an elective option, one among many personal and professional pathways a woman's life might now take. Given this profound shift in lifeway expectations around what might comprise a good life for a woman, it is hardly surprising that—as Cavell puts it—when Hollywood finds its voice it also finds that the first "conversation" it needs to have is about marriage.[50] To Cavell's way of thinking, it is also no surprise that the classic Hollywood conversation about marriage takes the form of the plotting of remarriage, since these films are coincident with an era that saw in America the social acceptance and destigmatization of divorce.[51] Significantly, Cavell posits a break between the cycle of remarriage films that appear in the late thirties once the talkies had hit their stride and the somewhat earlier wisecracking comedies of divorce, many of them adapted from English sources, such as the stage plays of Noel Coward.[52] Unlike the comedies of divorce, which ridicule marriage and its ridiculously wealthy exponents, Cavell's signature comedies of remarriage are tonally and narratively in accord with William Shakespeare's late romances, a group of plays that share courtly or dreamlike settings, themes of redemption, and an interest in paternalism, especially as it is exercised in the vicinity of daughters and wives or daughters about to become wives.[53] Perhaps most like *The Winter's Tale* (1611), the remarriage comedies tend to take as their romantically mature subject the tribulations of an established relationship and spread their plots across culturally urbane and pastoral settings in order to demonstrate love's redemptive qualities. As opposed to the world-upturned, helter-skelter plots of Shakespeare's early comedies—such as *As You Like It* (1594) or A *Midsummer Night's Dream* (1595)—in which young lovers encounter and misrecognize each other before their worlds are set to right, the lovers in the Hollywood variant of Shakespearean romance are not only known to each other from the outset but are usually on the verge of annulling their love through divorce or the act of marrying someone else.

Although Cavell has been criticized for the sexism inherent in his account of remarriage insofar as his scenes of conjugal education typically position the woman as the beneficiary of husbandly or fatherly instruction, his philosophical musings about modern marriage as the knowing reaffirmation of sexual and social reciprocities that have a dual basis in exclusivity and commonality are strangely fruitful in the contemporary context of gay marriage.[54] Drawing from John Milton's tract on divorce, in which it is argued that the effects of an ill marriage and household unhappiness are visited upon the commonweal so that it is in the state's interest to free husbands and wives from conjugal bondage, Cavell advances the idea that the sexual union of marriage cannot thrive without social support. He finds exemplification of this idea in George Cukor's *The Philadelphia Story* (1940), a film in which the divorced couple "are evidently unable to *feel* themselves divorced." This state of failed divorce is readily observed in the fact that "the conversation between the divorced pair"—in this case the affectionately dreamy dialogue that Grant and Hepburn share as the legally separated C. K. Dexter Haven and Tracy Lord—"is continuous with the conversation that constituted their marriage." As Cavell goes on to identify in his distinctive philosophical voice, the problem of the film is that "the bondage in question is not in these cases to an isolating unhappiness but to an isolating happiness, or to a shared imagination of happiness which nevertheless produces insufficient actual satisfaction."[55] As generations of viewers can testify, that Dexter and Tracy should be together is quickly apparent to anyone with eyes to see and ears attuned to screenwriter Donald Ogden Scott's ramping up of Phillip Barry's stage play dialogue. As Cavell elsewhere argues about the remarriage genre more generally, the talkiness of theses films—a quality they share with other films of the era—finds its clearest frequency in the singular back and forth between "the principal man and woman," who, when speaking, sometimes appear to "invent each other's language" and thereby "seem a mystery to the world around them."[56] But, as beguiling as this shared language is for both the couple and the viewer, it is not shared with anyone else, which is the problem the film must resolve. The lesson of *The Philadelphia Story* is that the once-married, not-ever-really-divorced pair cannot secure the pursuit of happiness that the adventure of marriage represents unless their private erotic conversation is supportively nested within a wider and distinctly American public, specifically the paternalistic world of rights and allegiances founded in the city that gives the film its name.[57]

For Cavell, the dependency of sexual privacy on social publicity is demonstrated in the wedding that gives *The Philadelphia Story* a second shot at marital closure. This ending entails not just the act of marriage, or even the act of remarriage, but the act of remarriage as captured by the flashbulbs of the society press. Cukor's film closes, Cavell reminds us, with photographic stills that present the scene of remarriage in images of the kind that might be found either in a wedding album or in the pages of Sidney Kidd's *Spy* magazine—the institution that gives the journalist Mike Macauley Conner (James Stewart) and photographer Liz Imbrie (Ruth Hussey) reason to join the film's plot—but here stand as "the document, or official testimony, that a certain public event has taken place, and that the event is essentially bound up with the achievement of a certain form of public comprehension, of the culture's comprehension of itself, of meet conversation with itself, the achievement, in short, of a form of film comedy."[58] The media sophistication that Cavell finds at work in this wedding scene is both amusing and unsettling for the film's viewer, who is suddenly pitched from the status of "illusory participant to that of observer," a position from which it is far harder to "arrive at a conclusion about the narrative" and the nuptials that end it. The formal closure of *The Philadelphia Story*, he argues, marks a shift from mise-en-scène to something resembling a production still that reasserts the movie star status of Grant (who is dressed as if casually in a bespoke collarless jacket rather than the formal attire demanded of grooms) and Hepburn as they disport in front of a camera playing husband and wife: "Shall we say that the film ends with an embrace, betokening happiness? I would rather say that it ends with a picture of an embrace, something at a remove from what has gone before, hence betokening uncertainty."[59]

For Cavell, the effect of this uncertainty is insufficient to undermine the postdivorce utopianism at work in the Hollywood comedies of remarriage; rather, it makes their utopianism (or what he will elsewhere define as their drive to moral perfectibility, a journey best undertaken through the vehicle of married life and a jalopy of a ride if you are lucky enough to get on board) all the more exquisite. The remarriage of Dexter and Tracy tops their marriage—

2.1
Remarriage: the culture of marriage comprehends itself
(*The Philadelphia Story*, George Cukor, 1940).

which foundered on his drinking and her judgment of it—insofar as it "fantasizes" a morally perfect "balance between Western culture's two forces of authority," spontaneity (his) and strictness (hers). The philosophical insight that Cavell discovers in these Hollywood comedies can be summarized in the truism that what was lost in marriage can be found in remarriage, although he puts it in more Emersonian terms. In these films, Cavell writes, "American mankind can refind its object, its dedication to a more perfect union, toward the perfected human community, its right to the pursuit of happiness."[60] Of course, "American mankind" is a hard act to live up to, but then so is Cary Grant.

Through his sustained readings and rereadings of these remarriage comedies, Cavell turns Hollywood's conjugal conversation into something approaching a general philosophical theory that posits that the self is best pursued in the company of married life, an imperfect but perfectible institution within which one person learns that none but the other will make them feel other than alone in their human separateness. In keeping with the Shakespearean logic that magically bestows second chances on the humanly error-prone, Cavell's version of marital perfectionism (a quirky derivative of the moral perfectionism for which he is more widely known as a philosopher)

From Gay Marriage to Remarriage · 45

is more strongly advanced in *Contesting Tears: The Hollywood Melodrama of the Unknown Woman*, which identifies a subgenre of female melodrama that is the perfect foil to the comedies of remarriage.⁶¹ Where the comedies validate marriage through the utopian articulation of remarriage, the melodrama of the unknown woman—a Cavellian designation that catches up *Blonde Venus* (Josef Von Sternberg, 1932), *Stella Dallas* (King Vidor, 1932), *Now, Voyager* (Irving Rapper, 1942), *Gaslight* (George Cukor, 1944), and *Letter from an Unknown Woman* (Max Ophüls, 1948)—provides tragic glimpses into cursed or confined marriages that prompt women to pursue their perfectionism in other ways.

In his introduction to an anthology of Cavell's writing on film, William Rothman notes that the arguments of *Pursuits of Happiness* and *Contesting Tears* are connected by an "operation of negation" that goes largely unexplained. In order to tease out the negative relation between the two books and their counterset arguments about marriage, Rothman points out that between writing them Cavell turned his attention to Hitchcock's *North by Northwest* (1959), a film in which Cary Grant, in the persona of Roger O. Thornhill, undergoes death and revival, a process previously reserved for female protagonists in the comedies of remarriage.⁶² In the course of his discussion, Rothman cites a lengthy passage from Cavell's essay on *North by Northwest* that effectively puts Grant in the position of the woman in remarriage comedy:

> The goal of the comedies requires what I call the creation of the woman, a new creation of a new woman. This takes the form in the comedies of something like the woman's death and revival, and it goes with the camera's insistence on the flesh-and-blood reality of the female actor. When this happens in Hitchcock, as it did in *Vertigo*, the Hitchcock film preceding *North by Northwest*, it is shown to produce catastrophe: the woman's falling to her death, precisely the fate *averted* in *North by Northwest*. Here, accordingly, it is the man who undergoes death and revival (at least twice, both times at the hands of the woman) *and* whose physical identity is insisted upon by the camera. Hitchcock is thus investigating the point that the comedies of remarriage are least certain about, namely, what it is about the man that fits him to educate and hence rescue the woman, that is, to be chosen by the woman to educate her and thereby to achieve happiness for them both.⁶³

Perhaps what fits Grant for the rescuing role of husband is his ability to take up the role of wife in relation to the new woman created by these films, a proposition that allows us to imagine an ideal marriage predicated on two wives, or perhaps two husbands, no matter the gender they happen to be.⁶⁴

As I suggested at the outset to this book, all marriage is gay marriage, whenever it is redone right.

While I could take up Cavell's discussion of melodrama and marriage for queer purposes, it seems unnecessary since his ideas are already foundational to the field. Although he is not mentioned in the usual roster of influential sources for queer theory, Cavell's ideas are central to the work of Lauren Berlant—like Miller, another literary theorist whose conceptual breakthroughs take on a second life when they migrate to the theater of film—from her first book on Nathaniel Hawthorne's *The Scarlet Letter* and American everyday utopianism to her work on intimate culture and female complaint, right up to her recent article on humorlessness and its role in defending objects, scenes, or relationships from change, which might be related to Cavell's speculation about the sound of a happy marriage and the paradox that conjugality is both deeply embedded in the habitual repetitions of dailiness and fundamentally premised on change.[65] While the influence of Cavell's philosophy on Berlant is not widely countenanced, the idea that it might be has surely been incentivized of late by her own insistence that her work engages his to the degree that no one could miss the connection unless determined to do so. This sentiment is voiced—more accurately, double-voiced—in the context of Berlant and Lee Edelman's spirited rejoinder to Tim Dean's review of their co-written book *Sex, or the Unbearable*.[66] "If you haven't read the book," write Berlant and Edelman, clearly at the end of their co-authorial tether, Dean's "assessment would lead you to believe that we address ourselves solely to Bersani and Freud. Our engagements with Sedgwick, with Lacan, with Badiou, with Bollas, with Cavell, with a swathe of feminist and antiracist critique—all of that is moot here."[67]

For those who do not immediately recollect the extent of Berlant and Edelman's engagement with Cavell, the index to *Sex, or the Unbearable* handily points the re-reader to two sentences seventy-five pages apart, both of which are attached to the initials "LB." In the first reference, which appears in chapter 1, LB writes that she takes "cues from Lacan and Cavell to see sex as part of a comedy of misrecognition at the same time as it also can be a tragic drama of inflation and deflation."[68] So far, so straightforward. In the second reference, which occurs in chapter 3, LB acknowledges her indebtedness to Eve Sedgwick and Cavell on the matter of "acknowledgment." In so doing, however, she confusingly directs the reader (and therewith the re-reader) back to chapter 2, a chapter in which neither Cavell's name nor his ideas explicitly or implicitly appear.[69] At the risk of over-reading things, LB seems to over-and underacknowledge Cavell on the precise issue of acknowledgment. While it is true that Cavell does appear in *Sex, or the Unbearable*, it is also true that he disappears or becomes a citational blur insofar as the in-text and other bibliographic signposts that point to him are slightly but consistently off the mark. Someone trying to trace a line of critical influence between Berlant and Cavell, for instance, might be put off the scent by the dates given for his monographs in her and Edelman's list of references. For *Pursuits of Happiness*, which appeared in 1981, the year given is 1984, which is neither here nor there. People make mistakes. But some mistakes are more interesting than others. The date given for *Contesting Tears* is 1997, or the same year as Berlant's *The Queen of America Goes to Washington: Essays on Sex and Citizenship* appears, although Cavell's book, which is largely comprised of essays from as early as 1987, actually came out in 1996, the year before Berlant's reputation-setting volume. Again, this mistake is neither here nor there, but it does has the effect of drawing attention to the surprising omission of Cavell's name in *The Queen of America*, a volume of essays that explicitly address the themes that obsess him, namely America, citizenship, the nature of community, intimacy, publicity, gender politics, and the mediating role of popular culture in all of the above.[70] The name Cavell covers, that is, everything we think of when we think of Berlant. And vice versa. This "comedy of misrecognition" indicates to me—and I hope to her—that Berlant is so obliged to Cavell that the only acknowledgment sufficient to the task would be a nonacknowledgment of the kind that, in her words, "can extend a nonmastering relation to the enigma of that object," the enigmatic object being in this case his work and its relation to hers. Paradoxically this comic scene of misrecognition becomes apparent only when, goaded by Dean, Berlant (with Edelman in her corner) steps into a critical "drama of inflation and deflation" played out in the accommodating pages of *American Literary History*. Like a jaded couple brought together by outside adversity, Berlant and Edelman make their rejoinder a team effort in a way that is harder to detect in their co-written book. In the joint response, Berlant can dress down Dean in a performance that also makes bearable the task of correctly acknowledging her debt to Cavell, since only a mistake of this order would live up to Cavell's peculiar philosophical demand that an attachment (conjugal or critical) must first be publicly denied before it can be reaffirmed. Cue *The Philadelphia Story*, reset in the green world of Hyde Park, Illinois, with a bunch of wisecracking literary critics comically playing out dramas of influence that ultimately testify to, in Cavell's words, "the importance of importance" and the human need to make and admit mistakes.[71]

As anyone who has read Cavell will know, this sequence of errors and forgettings would not be out of place in any one of the seven Hollywood

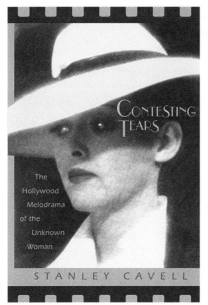 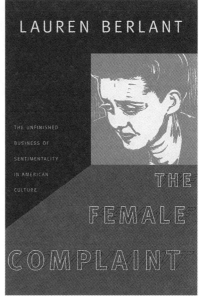

2.2–2.3
The ambivalence of acknowledgment. Stanley Cavell, *Contesting Tears* (Chicago, IL: University of Chicago Press, 1996). Designed by Joseph Alderfer, featuring a photograph of Bette Davis in *Now, Voyager*. Lauren Berlant, *The Female Complaint* (Durham, NC: Duke University Press, 2008). Designed by Heather Hensley, featuring original artwork by Micha Mae Melancon, "Now Voyager," 2000.

comedies of remarriage that he has written not one but two books about, as if he understood the need for getting things wrong before you have a shot at getting them right.[72] Berlant's critical indebtedness to Cavell's work on genres of attachment catches her up in the workings of an open secret, the epistemological mechanism that turns understatements into overstatements, and overstatements into understatements, no matter the intention. How else to describe the graphic homage the cover of *The Female Complaint: The Unfinished Business of Sentimentality in American Culture* pays to *Contesting Tears: The Hollywood Melodrama of the Unknown Woman*, both of which sport representations of Bette Davis, in character as Charlotte in *Now, Voyager*, staring down the diagonal amid a dispersed arrangement of titles and subtitles in differently weighted sans serif type?[73]

The conceptual progression between Cavell's account of moral perfectionism and female inaccessibility and Berlant's interest in the laminating of sentimentality and complaint in various forms of melodrama is made so visually patent by this in-your-face resemblance that the further snuggling up that goes on behind these covers seems to escape notice. Even when Berlant explicitly says her work draws from Cavell's—as she does in *Female Complaint*, as she does in *Cruel Optimism*, as she does in the essay with Edelman—even her closest readers can still miss the connection between her work and his. *Female Complaint*, for instance, carries five footnote references to Cavell, only one of which is wrong. The index directs the reader looking for Cavell to page 308, note 30, which actually appears a page earlier and comprises a backhanded dismissal of Cavell's reading of "Charlotte's homosexuality" in *Now, Voyager* via the recommendation of Teresa de Lauretis's "quite right" argument that the thing we "mainly learn" from Cavell's reading—which by the by is said to have "a lot in common with Elizabeth Cowie's psychoanalytic universalization of feminine/lesbian/homosexual spectatorship"—is "the will involved in misrecognizing the heroine's experience as emotionally identical to one's own." This note about the willfulness of misrecognition ends with Berlant willingly acknowledging, "I learned to think about broken circuits of attachment from Sedgwick," just in case anyone had any residual doubts about where these ideas about attachment, detachment, and reattachment were coming from.[74]

In another of the *Female Complaint*'s references to Cavell, Berlant acknowledges that her troping on Agamben's "whatever community" with the idea of "whatever optimism" is also "cognate, I think, with Stanley Cavell's argument in *Contesting Tears*, that love ideally involves a commitment to a mutual continuity without guarantees," which, in this context, seems to be a major acknowledgment manifesting as a minor one.[75] In *Cruel Optimism* the acknowledgment to Cavell comes early in the piece and relates to yet another big-ticket Berlantism: "This ordinary is an intersecting space where many forces and histories circulate and become 'ready to hand' in the ordinary, as Stanley Cavell would put it, for inventing new rhythms for living, rhythms that could, at any time, congeal into norms, forms, and institutions."[76] A serial case of hiding in plain sight, all Berlant's work on the attachment to attachment—a Cavellian formulation if ever there was one—has its origins in her attachment to him, which manifests as a detachment, specifically a detachment from his work on the Hollywood comedy of remarriage, a genre that at first and even second glance seems an unlikely match to feminist or queer theoretical interest, which is more comfortable in the terrain of melodrama and female disappointment with marriage. Interestingly, in her recent foray into comedy theory, Berlant cites Cavell as an exception among comedy theorists, most of whom insist on humorlessness as key to comedy. Cavell's interest in romantic comedy and specifically the Hollywood comedy of remarriage with its "binding of lovers to a scene of demonstration" reveals that "romantic-comic love is a test of the conditions of freedom in relation."[77] Although confined to a footnote, Berlant's reference to Cavell on the comedies of remarriage resonates with the case I am making for queer reengagement with marriage as a utopian proposition that teaches and tests the conditions of social and sexual freedom.[78]

While utopianism seems a lot to lay on any marriage, let alone a same-sex one, Cavell's philosophical engagement with the genre of remarriage comedies makes clear the massive amount of work popular entertainment has done in allowing broad publics to renew their attachment to romantic forms that are elsewhere showing signs of social attrition. To return to *The Philadelphia Story* a final time, it is not just that the remarriage plot allows Dexter to demonstrate he has stopped drinking or assists Tracy down a peg or two by confronting her with her own drunken mistakes, but that the film—along with the six other hugely successful Hollywood films Cavell discusses—resynchronizes public expectations of marriage to the times. Helmed by stars such as Grant and Hepburn who exercise their popular powers of attraction across the full spectrum of sexual possibility, these films remake the story of marriage as an accommodating vehicle for expressing a general ambition for sexual and social happiness that is not restricted to one sexual orientation or another but is fueled by the possibility of their crossing and coinciding in attractively renovated institutional forms.

As I will go on to demonstrate in the pages ahead, popular narrative films that deal either obliquely or directly with the trope of same-sex marriage do heavy lifting of the kind that only light entertainment can do as they reimagine the terms on which conjugal happiness might be pursued by everyone, not just the lucky gays and lesbians for whom marriage has never been a particularly weighty social burden to bear. Before I go on to discuss films that revivify the marriage plot for queer purposes, I want to return briefly to the novel to identify what I think is really at stake in queer critical maneuvers around marriage. In a discussion of Bram Stoker's *Dracula*, a novel that I suspect does not appear on many syllabi devoted to the marriage plot in either its traditional or countertraditional iterations, Barry McCrea has suggested that the ongoing queer investment in the dissing of marriage may simply be because queers are afraid to let go of the comfort of critique. If queers are not against marriage, he argues, then they must be for it, a normative prospect that is hard to accept given the antinormative cornerstones of the field. In McCrea's account, *Dracula* is an exemplary queer marriage text since it presents "a nightmarish embodiment" of bourgeois marital relations and sentimental love.[79] It is a form of heterosexual horror, a gothic representation of the kind of married world it would terrify many queers to wake up in. Arguing that Stoker's novel is best understood as a "vampirized resurrection of the marriage-plot," McCrea insists on reading *Dracula* against the novels of Jane Austen in a kind of post-*Twilight* critical exercise that yields stunning insights: "*Dracula*'s subtle but persistent focus on marriage, and the uncanny continuity between Castle Dracula and the happy English home both suggest that the horrified fantasy is about life outside, not inside, the closet. *Dracula*, I want to suggest, is a novel about heterosexuality as it is viewed from inside the gay closet—as an exotic foreign world, at once alluring and frightening."[80]

Arguing against the rising critical trend that regards Stoker as a closeted homosexual wracked with anxiety by the trial of his contemporary, Oscar Wilde, McCrea contends that "the panic of which the lurid gothic imagery is surely a sign" is not traceable to the author's queer "fear of exposure but almost the opposite: a horrified conjecture of what it would be like to be heterosexual in an officially heterosexual world, how it would feel if one's innermost desires were coopted by official discourse."[81] And how would it feel if there were no gap between one's private desires and their public face? It would feel normal, is how it would feel. To those beholden to a politics of antinormativity, to feel normal must be a very scary prospect indeed.[82] Dracula—who for present purposes can stand in for any number of queer opponents to marriage— "imagines with terror the abolition of the buffer of queerness between one's private self and the official world" of social legitimacy. What all this gothic agitation produces, concludes McCrea—though to be fair he is writing about Stoker's novel and not the queer critique of the marriage equality movement— "is, above all, a giddy, gruesome conjecture about what it might mean to be a well-married, lucky wife."[83] So, let the faint-hearted reader be warned, the pages ahead fully engage giddy, gruesome conjecture about what it might mean to be well-married in a world, such as the one in which we live, in which gays and lesbians are leading exponents of coupled happiness.

3 Dorothy Arzner's *Wife*

Before I go on to discuss the first of the feature-length films I have selected in support of my thesis that gay and lesbian innovation has been integral to the revivification of the marriage plot for at least a century and a half, I return to the novel a final time in order to ask why it is that the marriage plot changes when it migrates to sound cinema and why we might predict further changes ahead in sync with other format shifts, such as the rise of quality television, the renewed popularity of the serial form, and the advent of small-screen viewing. The nineteenth-century marriage plot has been an oddly elastic form from the moment of its novelistic inception. The idea that the English novel conventionally promotes a hegemonic form of heterosexual courtship that ends in a companionate marriage about which there is nothing left to say has been thoroughly contested from many quarters, including queer ones. These contestations can be usefully separated in relation to whether they take a narratological or a sociological approach to the novel and the marriage plot with which it is considered conjoined. In the previous chapter I discussed the narratological chastening of the marriage plot at the hands of the poststructuralist triumvirate of Tony Tanner, Peter Brooks, and D. A. Miller. I now turn to the sociological end of things, where a considerable amount of energy has gone into identifying the many variants and alternates to companionate marriage that can be found within the nineteenth-century British novel and its modernist successors.

To those of us outside the field, the secondary scholarship on the marriage plot can seem almost as large as the body of literature on which it draws. Within this crowded critical landscape I am invariably drawn to arguments that seem to anticipate or contravene my own. Talia Schaffer has recently argued, for instance, that the Victorian novel, long thought to be the crucible of modern marriage, is as adept at undoing the notion of companionate love as it is at advancing it.[1] While it is generally agreed that companionate love combines or balances the passionate drive to romance (sexual compatibility) with a more pragmatic or rationally based sense of partnership that serves the inclination for financial or professional advancement (social compatibility), Schaffer points out that the late Victorian novel often sets these two impulses in opposition to each other in the form of two suitors between whom a choice must be made. In Schaffer's account, the rivalry plotted between romantic marriage (the new and still controversial practice of marrying a person for whom one feels passionate love) and familiar marriage (the more established practice of marrying a trustworthy friend) is simply the most routinized of the many deviations of which the Victorian marriage plot is capable. Engaging wider discussion around the issue of consent, Schaffer argues that the two-suitor marriage plot is related to what Wendy Jones has termed the Victorian novel's "repetition compulsion," the self-soothing process through which it plays out the problem of marriage via a shifting cast of characters and scenarios.[2] In opposition to romantic marriage, the anxiety-prone novel tries out four primary nonromantic alternatives: neighbor marriage, cousin marriage, disabled marriage, and vocational marriage. As Schaffer goes on to argue, through this period the notion of familiar or nonromantic marriage "underwent multiple mutations" in response to the demand that it provide certain kinds of life choice that romantic marriage failed to guarantee.[3] Following Sharon Marcus's insistence that we should under- rather than over-read Victorian fiction, Schaffer argues that literary criticism—particularly in its feminist iterations—has neglected to engage the socially aspirational and expansive nature of Victorian marriage on its own terms. Instead of taking the marriage plot at its word, feminist criticism has tended to approach Victorian novels on the assumption that all marriage is based on sexual desire, hence marriage to a cousin, friend, physically impaired person, or professional helpmeet is legible only as sexual perversion: incest, asexuality, masochism, or frigidly self-interested ambition. By adopting the opposite and more Victorian presumption that familiar marriage should be approached at the level of social surface rather than sexual depth—"a choice that consolidated a useful future in a social nexus rather than a transformative state of private bliss"— Schaffer draws attention to the way that the practicalities of familiar marriages could also provide a polite beard for "a range of feeling among its participants beyond conventional heteronormative orientation."[4] For instance, she suggests, "one could achieve proximity to one's real object of desire by marrying his or her relation," a mutually enabling situation in which familiar marriage and a romantic relationship with a new in-law could both thrive.[5]

Schaffer's argument is obviously in alignment with Marcus's more general account of the social and sexual openness of Victorian marriage culture, which I canvassed in the previous chapter. As convincing as these accounts of marriage are, however, they tend to keep in place the idea that the marriage plot, understood as a novelistic rather than a sociological device, encounters a formal roadblock in modernism. There is a general consensus, that is, that modernism is marriage's break point in narratological terms. Brooks speaks for many when he launches *Reading for the Plot* with the statement that "the advent of Modernism" is marked by "a suspicion toward plot, engendered perhaps by an overelaboration of and overdependence on plots in the nineteenth century."[6] Since there is general agreement that chief among the overelaborated plots on which the nineteenth-century novel depends is the marriage plot, it is only to be expected that capital-M modernism set its sights against marriage in an avant-garde enterprise that disrupts its conjugal modus operandi at the level of discourse. But while Gertrude Stein's prose experiments and the wider emergence of "lesbian modernism" are sometimes cited as evidence of a Sapphic breakaway from the conventional novel form and the marriage plot to which it is considered indentured, one only has to look past the page to see that the domestic lifeways of gay and lesbian modernist writers frequently engaged forms of companionate coupledom that are as responsive to female and male homosexuality as to anything else.[7]

The disconcerting alignment between marriage-like relationships, such as that established between Stein and Alice B. Toklas, and a narrative avant-gardism opposed to the conventional marriage plot continues to agitate many discussions of queer literary modernism. In Elizabeth Freeman's recent account of Djuna Barnes's *Nightwood*, a novel that sets its modernist course by beginning, not ending, with a marriage proposal, Stein and Toklas are identified as inhabiting a "couple-centered domestic arrangement" that serves to sharpen the novel's radical renunciation of the two religious sacraments associated with the regime of sexuality: confession and marriage. In explicit opposition to the fuddy-duddy world of coupled love, Barnes's "sexual worldview," writes Freeman, "may have drawn less from the sexological model of the lesbian, the Sapphic Left Bank's protofeminist revaluation of women's culture, or the ideal of the Boston marriage than from her spiritualist grandmother's influence, her own father's bigamy, and her nonconsensual, quasi-incestuous first marriage to her father's second wife's brother."[8] This opposition between a formal avant-gardism considered corrosive to conventional coupledom and a marriage-like domesticity considered inconsistent with queer aspiration is further reinforced by the ongoing diversification of the twentieth-century literary marketplace and its various brow formations. Elizabeth English, for instance, has recently argued that the highly publicized banning of Radclyffe Hall's *Well of Loneliness*, which made the lesbian into an identifiable and offensive figure, impelled many gay and lesbian writers to crime, fantasy, and history as popular genres within which they could explore homosexual desire—including the desire for marriage or its same-sex approximation—more freely.[9] As a result of these evolving and interconnected literary taste formations and censorship codes, gay and lesbian marriage plots have tended to appear in the vernacular guise of popular paperback fiction, particularly in the pre-Stonewall era. The lesbian pulp of Ann Bannon deserves special mention in this tradition. Although Bannon's work is usually associated with the twilight world of Greenwich Village and its gay and lesbian bar communities, Julian Carter has recently mined *Women in the Shadows* (1959) for its inclination toward marriage. Carter argues that precisely because "conventional affects"—among which he includes the "culturally normative motives for marriage" such as "romance; desires for social inclusion, personal support, and children; concerns about comfort and companionship in old age"—are "both everywhere and nowhere, embodied in behaviour but rarely fully articulated," they achieve "their purest documentation in mass cultural representations that do not strive for sophistication."[10] The ambivalent assignation of the gay marriage plot to a degraded literary form that is considered minor to the extent that it has mass appeal motivates my parallel turn to the twentieth-century arena of film. Unlike the literary tradition, which continues to separate its gay and lesbian content into high and low forms until the emergence of a gay middlebrow print culture in the 1960s, in the emerging tradition of Hollywood cinema, gay and lesbian marriage plots—and remarriage plots—represent the leading edge of genre without having to carry the cultural baggage of the modernist avant-garde.

Like Stanley Cavell, I regard Hollywood cinema as a form of lowercase "modernism" in which the marriage plot is sustained and transformed through the popular vehicle of narrative film. Though Cavell distinguishes the comedies of remarriage from preceding comedies of divorce, he makes no mention of earlier silent films that deal with the renewal of marriage, particularly the trilogy of films studio head Jesse L. Lasky instructed Cecil B. DeMille to make all of whose titles hint at marital discord: *Old Wives for New* (1918), *Don't Change Your Husband* (1919), and *Why Change Your Wife?* (1920). Capturing a wider popular audience than the respectably middle-class audience that Lasky's studio had previously gone after, the success of DeMille's films launched a wave of similarly named features: *Trust Your Wife* (1921), *Rich Men's Wives* (1922), *Too Much Wife* (1922), *His Forgotten Wife* (1924), and *How to Educate a Wife* (1924). Though these films are not remarriage comedies in Cavell's sense of the term, what is interesting about them in this context is that they use the story of marriage to recalibrate the respective value of literature and film as different forms of narrative capital. According to Sumiko Higashi, the first film in DeMille's trilogy is remarkable for establishing cinema as aesthetically on par with literature, an equivalency asserted in the opening credits, which specify David Graham Phillips's novel as the source material for *Old Wives for New*. Although the director is credited as the author of the overall production—a hierarchy DeMille underscored in the third film of the trilogy with the addition of a trademark medallion bearing his name and profile—Higashi's discussion is useful in drawing attention to Lasky's astuteness in "recognizing the importance of the novel" to the development of the series. Although Phillips was a best-selling novelist "ahead of his time in contemplating the impact of modernity upon the upper-middle-class family," it is not the originality of the story behind *Old Wives for New* that is valuable but its replicability in both the film that bears its name and the many that follow it in something approximating a "Wives" franchise.[11]

As well as identifying the durability of the marriage renewal plot in early film, Higashi also anticipates Cavell in drawing attention to its ontologically ambiguous nature. "DeMille begins *Old Wives for New*," she tells us, "with a didactic intertitle that could be construed as a quote from the novel but was not even a paraphrase and, moreover, could not be attributed to any character in the film."[12] Proceeding from an authorial no-place that is neither novel nor screenplay and addressed to the slovenly middle-aged wife whom the plot finds in need of renewal, the bizarre intertitle that inaugurates the silent film is worth quoting in full: "It is my belief, Sophy, that we Wives are apt to take our Husbands too much for granted. We've an inclination to settle down to neglectful *dowdiness*—just because we've 'landed our Fish!' It is not enough for Wives to be merely virtuous anymore, scorning all frills: We must remember to trim our 'Votes for Women' with a little lace and ribbon—if we would keep our Man a 'Lover' as well as a 'Husband'!"

While Higashi interprets this as "a legacy of Victorian pictorialism, addressed to female spectators enjoined to embrace the delights of the consumer culture if only to retain their marital status," I am tempted to see the intertitle less as a readable "sermon" than as a discursive switch point between the established novel of marriage and the nascent cinema of remarriage.[13] Entertaining this premise allows me to posit a Cavellian conundrum: if the rise of the novel is linked to marriage and the rise of cinema is linked to remarriage, what is it about film that lends itself to reimagining marriage as remarriage? To begin answering this question I turn to an early marriage film directed by a lesbian director whose career encompasses the shift from silent cinema to sound.

In 1936, at the height of her career in the Hollywood studio system, Dorothy Arzner directed *Craig's Wife*, a domestic melodrama featuring Rosalind Russell as Harriet Craig, a woman whose obsessive preoccupation with maintaining the immaculate interior of the marital home eventually drives away her adoring husband. Frequently credited as the vehicle that lifted Russell from bit player to star, *Craig's Wife* is equally significant in marking the eclipse of another acting career—that of William Haines, who specialized in smart-talking rather than romantic roles and peaked as a star 1930, when he was voted Hollywood's number-one box-office draw in the Quigley poll.[14] By mid-1931, Haines's career was already in decline, with Louis B. Mayer cutting his salary and announcing he would not renew his contract, decisions influenced in part by the MGM star's disregard for the protocols of public discretion by which Hollywood managed homosexuality and other publicly unacceptable behaviors. Although the trade magazines continued to hint at the reasons behind his perennial bachelorhood, Haines made the transition to Mascot Pictures in 1934 and continued acting until 1936, when in late June and early July he was involved in a sexual scandal in which his partner, Jimmie Shields, was alleged to have molested a six-year-old boy at El Porto beach. Despite the local police investigation determining there was nothing on which a legal indictment could stand, the incident made national headlines because of the mob assault it precipitated on Haines, Shields, and their gay guests at their summerhouse in El Porto.[15] In the same month the El Porto scandal broke, Arzner, who was always discrete about her own lesbian relationships, approached Haines to work on *Craig's Wife*, which had already entered production. Seen only in the interior sets Arzner informally commissioned him to redesign, Haines's uncredited contribution to *Craig's Wife* completed his transformation from leading man to interior designer, a professional role in which open knowledge of his homosexuality would prove less of a career impediment.[16]

Haines's talent for interior design, which he had been offering as a paid service through Haines Foster, Incorporated, since 1933, was confirmed by the look of the film, securing him an off-screen position as a celebrity designer whose gayness was a foregone conclusion.[17] In stark contrast to this biographical narrative of sexual notoriety and professional success, the fictional Harriet Craig's talent for interior design (also confirmed by the look of the film) spells the end of her middle-class marriage and leads to her ultimate isolation within the empty family home. The suggestion that homosexuality and heterosexuality have different relations to the spatial and narrative coordinates of domesticity and publicity is not a new one, but the particular combination of elements evidenced in *Craig's Wife*—lesbian director, gay

3.1
William Haines at home.
MGM publicity photograph, 1926 (Photofest).

designer, heterosexual mise en scène—invites critical inquiry because it has the potential to break open a number of accepted truths around Hollywood melodrama and the marriage plot assumed to thread through it.

Though hardly substantial, the archive of writing on Arzner punches above its weight in critical terms. Since the publication of a pamphlet of essays to accompany a British Film Institute retrospective of her films in 1975, Arzner has frequently provided the rubric through which a feminist rethinking of both film practice and the masculinist paradigms of film criticism has occurred.[18] Now over forty years old, the essays by Claire Johnston and Pam Cook that read Arzner's films as evidence of a feminist countercinema practice resistant to the dominant system of classical narrative film continue to provide the starting point for many discussions, not just of Arzner's oeuvre but of feminist film theory more generally. Both are included in Constance Penley's landmark anthology *Feminism and Film Theory*, alongside later essays by Jacqueline Suter and Janet Bergstrom that reengage with Arzner's films in order to contest the subversive function of rupture and contradiction within the classical Hollywood romance narrative and its consequences for female representation as put forward by Johnston and Cook.[19] As Judith Mayne has pointed out, the proponents of both sides of this unresolved debate have in common an inability to focus on Arzner's lesbianism, despite a fascination with her butch professional persona at the level of image. Arguing that feminist film criticism's high circulation of photographic images of a crop-haired, besuited Arzner—masculinized by her proximity to either the usually invisible machinery of Hollywood production (oversized cameras and tracking equipment) or its familiar on-screen fetish, female stars—amounts to a disavowal of her lesbianism, Mayne has scrupulously documented details of the director's professional and private life in order to argue that her sexual orientation has critical implications for readings of her work, as well as concepts of auteurship more generally.[20]

In her 1994 monograph on Arzner, Mayne emphasizes the director's consistent representation of strong, resourceful female characters and the women-oriented communities that feature in many of her films. As Mayne recognizes, the girls' dormitories, women's boarding houses, dance studios, and dressing rooms that serve as backdrops in films such as *The Wild Party* (1929), *Working Girls* (1931), and *Dance, Girl, Dance* (1940) assist the profiling of relationships other than those mandated by the conventionally dominant heterosexual romance plot. If not precisely lesbian, these story spaces nonetheless articulate the emotional and physical ambitions, intimacies, and rivalries that exist among unmarried women in close quarters that are not those of the conjugal or familial home that is the usual setting for melodrama. Moreover, these alternative fictional settings or chronotopes have real-world counterparts in the institutional architectures of the 1920s and 1930s, which were specifically designed to house the aspirations of a generation of newly independent young women otherwise adrift in the urban centers of prewar America. Frequently commissioned by philanthropic organizations or professional women's clubs, these actual women's hostels, gymnasiums, and sorority houses gave mutual emphasis to female ambition and companionship, intellectual pursuit and physical recreation, all elements that were amplified in the Arzner films set in similarly feminocentric or homosocial locations.[21] Yet the feminist orientation of space, whether real or fictional, is not the same as the lesbian orientation of person. If criticism is increasingly comfortable designating Arzner as a lesbian director, it has yet to address the question both raised and occluded by Mayne's line of inquiry: what is the relation between homosocial space and homosexual narrative, particularly in its lesbian iteration?

For Mayne, the connection between homosociality and homosexuality is clinched tight biographically, but shifting the critical focus away from Arzner's sexual identity to questions of film form allows for more detailed mapping of their interpenetration. Taking a formalist approach is unexpectedly productive when considering *Craig's Wife*, Arzner's most sustained foray into domestic melodrama, a genre in which there is a seemingly tight fit between the heterosexually aligned story and its definitive setting in the marital home. Unlike other Arzner heroines, who are located within the sex-segregated environments of unmarried life and establish relationships with other women even as they pursue romances with men, Harriet Craig scarcely ventures beyond a home in which she is no more pleasant to her female relatives and domestic help than she is to her husband, Walter (John Boles). If Arzner's single girls are found inside homosocial spaces that retain an oddly tangential relation to the heterosexual romances that occur on their periphery, Harriet faces the opposite problem: despite the emotional distance she maintains from her husband throughout the film, as a married woman she is sexually contiguous with the house in which she resides, a relation condensed in the term "housewife." In this sense, domestic melodrama, even when it explores the insufficiency of married life, nonetheless upholds the principle of conjugal intimacy. This melodramatic convention by which heterosexual femininity and domestic location, identity, and place are metonymically linked has no same-sex parallel: a wife who does not sleep with her husband is still considered to be heterosexual, whereas two men or two women who share a college room—both situations exemplified in critically ignored scenes from *Craig's Wife*—cannot be presumed gay.

One suspects the flamboyantly homosexual Haines, who passed for a playboy Southern gentleman in Hollywood, delighted in designing the pretentious yet hollow look of the Craig house sets, scornful as he was of professional and amateur interior decorators alike who lacked his knack for pulling together discriminatingly elegant, intensely social rooms. By the mid-1930s Haines had already established a reputation for designing in the open modern style of Elsie de Wolfe, whose well-known advocacy of white walls became a signature of his own developing style.[22] White walls—and not only white walls but white rugs, white curtains, white furniture—are certainly much in evidence inside the Craig house, where they are aesthetically correct but symbolically wrong. As Kathleen McHugh notes in a historically minded essay on the film's representation of housekeeping, the stage directions for the Broadway play on which the film is based "call for dark greens and deep browns livened by canary yellows and golds, all against 'dark, highly polished wood,' but Arzner stresses Harriet's fastidiousness by decorating the Craig home primarily in white. White rugs cover the floor, white curtains hang in most of the windows. All of the walls in the interior and exterior of the house are beige or white."[23]

Not quite all, since in an early scene in which Walter Craig and his live-in aunt, Miss Austen (Alma Kruger), share a meal in the dining room, the rare sociability of the event, filmed in a classic two shot, is accented against the hand-painted wallpaper, which depicts a pastoral landscape that wraps around the entire room, an effect Haines would repeat in numerous designs he devised for his elite client base of Hollywood stars, directors, and executives. Harriet, however, rarely enters either this room or the intimate shot composition it is associated with, being more typically positioned against a flat background, looking not at the person who speaks to her but past the camera into an empty middle distance that never succumbs to a reverse shot.[24] Both architectural and cinematic elements of the mise-en-scène advance the viewer's perception of Harriet's inadequacy to a domestic backdrop that is usually considered heterosexuality's conventional, if not natural, framework. Unlike her domesticated husband, Harriet is not visually incorporated into the scene of married life but dramatically set off from it, an effect exacerbated by other elements in Haines's design repertoire that also work against the conventional gendered ideologies of hearth and home.

Credited with ending the West Coast commitment to pseudo-Spanish colonial motifs, Haines's early Hollywood Regency style, as it became known, involved an elegant and eclectic mix of antiques, chinoiserie, and modern art deco, all of it deployed to create interiors fit for movie stars and their sometimes unconventional lifestyles. Haines developed his style remodeling the Spanish colonial property on North Stanley Drive that he and Shields moved into in 1926 and where they stayed until 1964, when they moved to a more modest, but equally lush, house on Larna Lane, Brentwood. As an interior designer, Haines's first significant clients were Joan Crawford, Carole Lombard, and Constance Bennett, but his most obviously gay commission came in 1935, the year preceding *Craig's Wife*, when his close friend George Cukor asked him to work with architect James E. Dolena on the interiors of his residence at 9611 Cordell Drive. In 1937, the year following *Craig's Wife*, Jack and Ann Warner engaged Haines and architect Roland E. Coate to transform their Spanish-style estate into a Georgian mansion with period antiques and many of the neoclassical flourishes displayed on a far smaller scale in the Arzner-commissioned sets. Signature components of Haines's Hollywood style to be found within Harriet's diegetic East Coast home include a richly upholstered

3.2–3.3
Supine husband and upright wife
(*Craig's Wife*, Dorothy Arzner, 1936).

chaise, a canopy bed, elaborate moldings, and Georgian architectural details, as well as the novel placement of a telephone in a bedroom, an innovation Haines took to extremes in the Cukor residence, where even bathrooms and poolrooms had telephones. In thematic terms, however, these stylish furnishings register not the social cachet of the Hollywood insider but a specifically conjugal incompatibility: when Walter Craig rises from where he has been

Dorothy Arzner's *Wife* • 63

sitting on his wife's bed, she moves forward to smooth out the indent he leaves in the counterpane; when he finally makes use of the inviting daybed in the living room it is only because he has realized his marriage is over and so lying down fully clothed is a way of relinquishing any claim he may have had on the private spaces and intimate relations of married life.

Far from being a distortion of Hollywood style enacted for the specific requirements of the film, this ability to imbue domestic interiors with a quality of heterosexual estrangement was already recognized as Haines's peculiar talent, particularly by female clients who frequently called him in to redesign their houses after they divorced their husbands. In 1933, for instance, after Lombard and William Powell divorced, Haines undertook a pro bono restyling of their formerly shared Brentwood home. Reviewing the altered interior, *Motion Picture* magazine commented that it contained "no place for tweeds or slacks" before concluding that the home's "femininity is so unmistakable that your first glance tells you that it is occupied by a single woman—a woman, moreover, who has no intention of marrying," as if sexual status could be determined by domestic setting alone.[25] In Crawford's case three failed marriages meant three interior makeovers by Haines in twenty-five-years. As these real-life examples of divorce and serial marriage suggest, the more glamorously feminine the interior scene achieved within the narrative film, the less likely it is to fix the fashion plate Harriet within the stable coordinates of married life.

Although the rooms of the Craig house recall Haines's other residential commissions and even include furniture from the house he shared with Shields on North Stanley Drive, their fictional attribution to Harriet Craig means that their scale and conjunction of elements is deliberately skewed. As in a modern McMansion, the oversized rooms dwarf the inhabitants, and the interiors, insofar as they are credited to Harriet, everywhere betray the mark of cultural aspiration. In particular, the historical references embedded in the reproduction furniture and Grecian ornaments do not sit well with the middle-class values and aesthetic neutrality typically animating domestic melodrama. Classical statuary abounds within the public spaces of the house, most of it isolated in space as if the figures were of museum quality and not off-the-shelf household bric-a-brac. A suburban residence on a monumental scale, the center of the Craig house is dominated by a full-height marble-columned entrance atrium from which a curved stairway leads to an open landing in a manner that suggests pretentiousness and grandeur rather than practicality. Downstairs on either side of the vast entrance hall are steps down to dining and living rooms that, crossed by the line connecting the

3.4
Wife as domestic statuary
(*Craig's Wife*, Dorothy Arzner, 1936).

front door and stairway, form the central dramatic axis of the interior action. Although cinematically tight, this open-plan configuration of interior spaces is physically stretched, with the distance between rooms requiring almost athletic stamina from the actors as they track back and forth, up and down, in a deep field that remains technically out of focus yet thematically sharp.

The set and furnishings would be more at home on a Broadway stage, on which the distancing perspective of the fourth wall might make their dimensions appear less obtuse. Within the less rigid perspective of a camera shot, objects are frequently larger than they seem and tend to take on a dramatic life of their own, a feature commonly noted of melodrama's mise-en-scène, whereby background elements are never neutral but reflect otherwise unacknowledged aspects of character, such as duplicity or ambivalence. In *Craig's Wife*, however, this tendency of inanimate objects to come to symbolic life in the vicinity of the camera is reversed in the climactic scene of the film in which a flesh-and-blood character takes on the quality of stone. In the scene that marks a crisis point in her marriage, Harriet Craig appears in the living room in an unstructured evening dress that resembles the stone draperies worn by the ornamental female figures that populate the house in the absence of actual female friends. Designed by Lon Anthony, the belted toga dress with gilt-wreathed dropped shoulderline reinforces the climax of the film more convincingly than the overweight dialogue, much of it retained

Dorothy Arzner's *Wife* • 65

from George Kelly's 1926 Pulitzer Prize–winning stage play, as Mrs. Craig, her hair braided Grecian style, simply leans against the oversized mantelpiece displaying the emotional flexibility of a stone caryatid.[26]

Untouched by any of her husband's sentimental arguments, Harriet merges with the interior fittings of the house, simultaneously instantiating the spatial principle of domestic melodrama that equates femininity with its setting in the home while evacuating it of its customary narrative and ideological intent: the endorsement of heterosexual normativity as expressed in the satisfactions of married life. Visually embodying the classical ideal of femininity, Harriet stonewalls her husband before the hearth that would ordinarily function as the heart of the marital home. Alongside her on the mantelpiece stands the Attic shape of the black urn overwrought with marble men and maidens familiar to us from the opening scene, a fake antiquity that has pride of place within the complex aesthetic code of a film that everywhere asserts the domestic incompatibility of men and women while preserving the glamorous veneer of heterosexuality.

The static theatrical staging of scenes inside the Craig house extends to the way actors make entrances from off-screen space then stand and deliver their lines as if unassisted by cinematic projection and sound recording, or the way dramatic dialogue invariably dictates camera action. Rather than being a weakness of the film, this is entirely consistent with the overall spatial design of the film and the drive to bestow on Harriet the quality of alabaster until she is finally indistinguishable from the place she calls home, an empty monument to married life.[27]

Harriet's association with the house is underscored in an essay by Giuliana Bruno, who in the context of a more general discussion of gendered identity and space makes a brief reference to Arzner's film. "As Harriet Craig's obsession with the house intensifies," writes Bruno, "a narrative shift occurs: Craig's wife is becoming a *house*wife. Wrestling with the topos of the term, Harriet works from within its confines toward her goal of freedom." All Harriet's manipulations of domestic space are, for Bruno, motivated by her attempt to free herself from her status as Craig's wife. While this reading of Harriet's motivation is not an untypical one, Bruno's essay productively departs from previous readings of the film in her frank acknowledgment of the problem the end of the film poses to feminist recuperation. By the final scene Harriet "has, *tout court*, become the house." This transformation is "epitomized in a long shot in which Harriet Craig looks like a column as she stands in front of the staircase of her home. She has become the pillar of the house." Shot from below, elements of the cinematic mise-en-scène, including dress and decor, combine so that the willowy figure of Russell becomes another of the architectural features that make up the set in made-to-order Hollywood style with its abundance of columns, pilasters, pediments, and niches: "For Harriet the housewife, 'house' and 'wife' have been incorporated to such an extent that the wife has *become* the house." But, as Bruno is forced to conclude, this visual conflation of character and space "is not a happy ending. As Harriet Craig sits alone in her home, having conquered ownership of herself and her house . . . the walls appear to be closing in on [her], as if there were too much space and yet not enough. A house devoid of motion, and with closed doors, is as much a prison as the marriage it was built to contain."[28] Leaving aside the question of Harriet's happiness since it inevitably returns us to matters of character and plot, identity and sentiment, or the usual terrain of melodrama, Bruno's brief account of the film is particularly useful for focusing the relation between occupied space and vacant space within the film. After all, the house that Harriet takes possession of is bestowed on her not by the title deed that her lawyer husband assures her will be transferred to her name as part of their divorce settlement but by a visual distortion of figure and background, an effect intensified by the sheer emptiness of the final scene, all other characters having left for an elsewhere that claims no further screen presence.

If *Craig's Wife* visually entraps Harriet within the architectural coordinates of a finally empty house, that point is reinforced by the film's prior and unexpected insistence on the expanded social world in which her domestic separatism makes tragic sense. While Arzner's conscious decision to maintain theatrical continuity of time and space in *Craig's Wife* can account for the theatrical staging of the domestic scenes, it cannot account for the frequent cross-cutting between different locations and the doggedness with which the film visualizes spaces that are not essential to the viewer's comprehension of the heterosexual marriage plot. Ostensibly included to open out the stage play's single setting and convey the simultaneity of events, transitions to scenes outside the house are managed via a virtual compendium of cinematic devices: dissolves, fades, blackouts, and horizontal and vertical wipes, often appearing in quick succession.[29] Less than subtle, these techniques are backed up by equally heavy-handed dramatic mechanisms for story advancement, particularly the repeated reliance on the arrival of newspapers to deliver plot information and telephone calls to motivate shifts in location, all of which reveal the artificiality of the space-time continuum they nonetheless promote. Firmly established within the diegesis, these peripheral locations—such as the hospital in which Harriet's sister Lillian Landreth (Elizabeth Risdon) lies dying, or the brief telephone exchange and police station scenes that clumsily advance the complicated subplot in which Walter and Harriet

3.5
Advancing the plot through female-centered space
(*Craig's Wife*, Dorothy Arzner, 1936).

become tangentially involved in a murder investigation—confirm the film's refusal of the usual hierarchies of classical narration that conventionally assist the viewer to distinguish between necessary and incidental information and scenes. Far from being a failing in cinematic technique or an inability to achieve classical continuity style, this refusal to rank diegetic elements is key to the film's advancement of a counterplot that would otherwise recede behind the conventional scenic dominance given the heterosexual story. The almost obtrusive depiction of ancillary locations in *Craig's Wife* implies that all story spaces are equal, including those that are never represented on screen.

These editing techniques are at their most concentrated when called on to propel the somewhat leaden murder subplot involving Adelaide and Fergus Passmore, which takes up the central section of the film and functions to instill in the naïve and trusting Walter the skills of a detective, since nothing less is needed for him to see what to everyone else is patently obvious: that his love for his wife is not reciprocated. Slotted between melodramatic soft-focus close-ups of tear-filled eyes, one sentimentally assigned to Lillian at the beginning of the film, the other given more ambiguously to Harriet in the final scene when she receives news of her sister's death, the Passmore murder investigation uses hardboiled clichés, such as the close-up scanning of directory pages and back-and-forth wipes between the female telephone exchange operator and the tough-talking police precinct. Standard in police procedural films, these ancillary locations and associated narration techniques, whereby objects and information isolated within the visual field can be used to signal causal relations of plot and resolve questions of character motivation with forensic certainty, are eventually transferred across to the marriage plot in a gesture that makes a man, or at least a suspicious husband, of Walter Craig. The generic transfer of the narrational structure of detection to the domestic melodrama is demonstrated in an otherwise gratuitous scene transition executed on a close-up of the murder weapon. Cued by a phone call interrupting a police detective's interrogation of Mrs. Craig in the living room, the scenic introduction of police headquarters, filled to the brim with uniformed officers who will not see celluloid again, merely provides an excuse for the plainclothes cop to vacate the Craig house so that Walter can return to it and assume the authoritative role of wife questioner. The melodramatic content of the subsequent confrontation scene between husband and wife, which earnestly contemplates masculine bewilderment and feminine justification, is of so little dramatic value that Arzner twice interrupts it with the entrance of the housekeeper, whose only concern is getting Mr. and Mrs. Craig to sit down to dinner. By this point in the film, procedural methods are so in the ascendant that dialogue, particularly highly emotive dialogue of the kind that husbands and wives freely exchange, is less important than the visual close-up on the overstuffed ashtray by which Walter signals, and Harriet understands, that their marriage is over. Once again, *Craig's Wife* overturns the classical rule that centers story development on strongly defined characters in favor of a more free-ranging capacity to locate the story of marriage anywhere at all, in an ashtray, for instance, or outside the house that otherwise dominates interpretation of the film.

The Passmore residence on Willow Avenue is key to establishing the cinematic coordinates by which Harriet is unforgivingly positioned inside the conjugal home but outside the marriage it normally connotes. If the reasons behind marital estrangement in the Craig household remain oddly obscure, the Passmore residence is the setting for open—and openly sexual—hostilities between husband and wife. Once the camera follows Walter through the wrought iron gate that secures the Passmore townhouse from the street, the interior set suggests a form of cultural entitlement against which all Harriet's domestic riches are awkwardly and pretentiously nouveau. From the moment the crumpled Fergus Passmore (Thomas Mitchell) opens the front door, drink in hand, throws Walter's coat aside, and takes him through to a den filled to the point of cliché with masculine accessories (an open bar, cigar boxes, books, and architectural drawings), Walter finds himself in a domestic milieu in which the differences between men and women, however fraught, are a constitutive element of the household design. When the beautiful but evasive Adelaide Passmore (Kathleen Burke) glides across the room, adjusting her jewelery and refusing her husband's invitation to stay home, her presence endorses an explicitly sexualized aesthetic that has as its loudest critic not Mrs. Craig but the straight-talking Craig housekeeper, Mrs. Harold (Jane Darwell), who on subsequently learning of the location of the Passmore murders responds instantly: "I know that Willow Avenue kind with their high steppin', loose livin' friends, their cocktails and their meals at all hours and their dirty oil paintings." The artistic nudes that, in Mrs. Harold's imagination, line the walls of the Passmore residence reflect a heterosexual sexual culture, whereas the naked breasts on the faux Grecian statue that stands on the upstairs landing in the Craig house are just another externalization of Harriet's aggressive femininity, heterosexual in cast but freestanding insofar as it evidences no necessary relation to men.[30] Although Harriet has no time for the Passmores alive or dead, they nonetheless serve to precipitate the crisis in her own loveless marriage when Walter subsequently defends Adelaide's extramarital affair and Fergus's murder-suicide. Speaking as both husband and lawyer, Walter lends his sentimental and professional authority to the notion that heterosexual romance, here a literal crime of passion, is its own justification. Yet it is precisely this entrenched assumption—the assumption that the story of marriage belongs to heterosexuality—that Arzner's film systematically undoes in its highly mannered visualization of Adelaide's adultery. Operating within the constraints of a Production Code that overdetermines both homosexual and heterosexual representation, *Craig's Wife* can confirm the rocky state of the Passmore marriage only obliquely. Cut loose from his wife for the night and looking for adventure, Walter's friend Billy Birkmire (Raymond Walburn) sits with his wayward father in a theater bar, where he observes Adelaide Passmore meeting an unknown man. Arm in arm, the handsome couple cross the scene in an eloquent right-to-left movement that is all that is needed to establish Adelaide's infidelity and the compromised state of the Passmores' marriage. The sexual significance of this action—nothing more than a wife passing through a scene with a man who is not her husband—is reinforced by a seemingly deliberate instance of stilted editing: the reaction shot given to Birkmire when he sees Adelaide's arrival recues the film so that the wayward wife stepping down the final few steps of a staircase arm in arm with a handsome male stranger is seen not once but twice, an impossibility in the real world as great as the impossibility of showing an actual sexual infidelity on-screen in the context of the Motion Picture Production Code of 1936.

In comparison to Adelaide, whose every cool move references the well-known script of adultery, Harriet is most content when left alone in her glamorous boudoir with its satin covers and walk-in wardrobe filled to excess with dresses and hats and high-heeled shoes, the wearing of which provide her only reason for going out. As compelling as Harriet is to behold in her Lon Anthony gowns, she exercises no narrative claim to sexual agency, being upstaged in that arena by both the sexy Adelaide and her overly earnest niece, Ethel Landreth (Dorothy Wilson), whose aptitude for romance provides the film's other subplot. About Harriet, who is coiffed and groomed to the edge of feminine perfection, there is simply no sexual story to tell.

Precisely because Harriet instantiates the trophy wife so well—a heterosexual figurine who represents the ideological form of domestic melodrama while draining it of its conventional lifeblood of affective content and generic storyline—Arzner can, in her ice-cold vicinity, cinematically validate other sexual possibilities conventionally denied narrative legibility. If, for instance, in the chill and stilted scenes between Mr. and Mrs. Craig, all of which occur within the pristine environment of the marital home, Arzner deliberately eschews camera movement, it is so she can reserve the sense of intimacy a mobile camera can bestow for those scenes that occur elsewhere, in locations more typically associated with homosocial, not conjugal, relations.[31] Consider the three scenes that occur in the peripheral location of Northampton College, Massachusetts, where Harriet's independent young niece has, in events that precede the opening of the film, fallen in love with her instructor in romance languages, Gene Fredericks (Robert Allen). Traveling by train back from the Albany hospital in which her mother is dying, Ethel conveys to her disappointed aunt the news of her engagement, thus precipitating Harriet's comments on marriage as a contract to be engaged in without sentiment, a speech many interpretations of the film cite at length since it complies with their sense of the film as a feminist analysis of the gendered inequities of marriage.[32] At the conclusion of this exchange, after Ethel has distanced herself from her aunt's rationalization of marriage by requesting to send her fiancé a telegram, the film cuts from the train carriage to Fredericks's college rooms. This gives significant screen time to a new location that is unnecessary to the plot, the conversation on the train being sufficient setup for the young man to ring the Craig house and inquire after his girlfriend, which is all that the marriage story requires. The transition from train carriage to college, conveniently effected on a close-up of the telegram sent from one location to the other, yields to a more expansive frame that reveals Fredericks, telegram in hand, standing before his faculty colleague, Ted. While the two men read the telegram, the mobile camera discloses that the desk at which Ted sits abuts another desk in a face-to-face arrangement more intimate than anything glimpsed in the Craig household, in which husband and wife keep separate bedrooms. Determined to speak to Ethel, Fredericks rings her "dizzy roommate" Bunny to obtain her aunt's address, which is reason enough for Arzner to explore yet another single-sex domain, the sorority house at which the phone is answered by a pajama-clad girl who is required to provide the name and address of Ethel's aunt, once again information the film scarcely needs. Redundant to the story, Bunny's screen presence serves to establish a second location in which sheer proximity, unassisted by backstory or the other lumbering devices needed to establish heterosexual relations, breeds an easy physical familiarity between single girls, evidenced by the joshing and elbowing Bunny gets from her sorority sister at receiving a call from a man.

Both scenes—one in male college rooms, the other in a female dormitory—reveal a productive tension between the heterosexual marriage plot and peripheral same-sex details that advance the straight action even as they point up its almost mechanistic nature. Involving only incidental persons and places, but aided by mobile figures and camerawork, the homosocial scenes are spatially energetic in comparison to the preceding scene on the train, in which the only indication of mobility is the back projection of an unfurling landscape glimpsed through the carriage windows across which married woman and affianced girl converse.[33] Although Mayne's account of *Craig's Wife* includes a lengthy discussion of the significance of the spatial composition of the scene in the railway carriage, in which she notes that the blocking of actors requires the feminine tête-à-tête to be transacted across the visual impediment of an anonymous male figure situated in the background, she ignores the relationships put on display between men and men, women and women, in the college scenes through similar mise-en-scènic devices.[34] Unlike the scene on the train in which the discussion of marriage between the two women is visually triangulated by the presence of a third masculine figure, the college scenes spatially quarantine the two genders. A textbook example of the kind of same-sex community that Mayne elsewhere celebrates, it remains unclear whether or not the homosocial space of the college has homosexual significance.[35] While it is hard to read much into the nearness of office desks, when *Craig's Wife* returns to Northampton College later the same day, the college study the two young male faculty members share is surprisingly revealed as a bedroom. Second time around, the camera picks up Fredericks as he bursts into the room and follows him as he circumnavigates the desks. Strictly centered on the frustrated young man who feels denied access to his girlfriend, the

3.6
Nothing to hide in male homosocial space
(*Craig's Wife*, Dorothy Arzner, 1936).

camera pan allows us to glimpse—as if unrelatedly—his friend lying in bed reading.

Caught lounging around in the daytime by a roommate who doesn't bother to knock, Ted has nothing to hide, unlike the faceless man on the train whose male silhouette must carry the blame for the gendered inequalities of marriage. Ted's bedroom scene adds nothing to the story until Fredericks once again takes up the telephone in an action that visually reconnects the shared twin room to Harriet's conjugal suite, where she has just finished defending herself against the intrusion of her husband, who insists on sitting on the nuptial bed despite her admonishments against it. Once the temporal connection between homosocial scene (college rooms) and heterosexual set (marital bedroom) is made, the two locations can be read against each other in a way that makes clear that only one scene—Harriet's boudoir—has sexual implications, albeit negative, since we have already seen Walter bound ardently into Harriet's most intimate space to embrace his wife, only to be met by physical coolness and reproach. No sooner does Walter leave the room than Harriet removes any lingering sign of his presence, restoring the conjugal scene to its sexually immaculate state.

With the mere stroke of a hand across a bedspread, Arzner can both reveal and rescind the presumptive relation between heterosexuality and conjugality. Alternatively, the homosocial college scene, in which homosexuality is neither suggested nor denied, ends with Fredericks rummaging for traveling clothes in a dresser weighted down by an oversized photograph of Ethel, who looks as out of place in this institutional interior (an appealing amalgam of professional and domestic space) as Ted looks at home. By visually reaffirming the heterosexual coordinates of life beyond the sex-segregated precincts of college, the film puts on display not the naturalness of that progression but the inexplicable gap between the institution of Northampton College and the institution of marriage, whose architectural exemplar remains the Craig home.

What makes a marriage is, of course, the question posed by Kelly's original playscript, where it is clunkingly answered in the portentous dialogue that Mary McCall's screenplay retains for Miss Austen and Walter Craig, most of it defending historically emergent ideas of companionate marriage between men and women that could be found in numerous marital advice manuals from the same period.[36] On another purely cinematic level, however, Arzner's film restages the question of marriage and its gendered coordinates in ways that are not available to stage drama or the novel form that lies further in the historical background. Rather than being the misogynistic exposure of a frigid wife whose hard-edged distrust of men is manifest in the sterile environment she has created, Arzner's film explores the sexual potential of companionate relationships primarily as an effect of the cinematic manipulation of space, where space is understood both scenically and in terms of a diegetic story world that extends beyond the edges of the screen.

Contemporary reviewers clearly detected something amiss in the configuration of the Craig household, finding Mrs. Craig's love for her home symptomatic of an emotional insufficiency that is pathological. Russell, who had to be persuaded by Arzner to take on such an unsympathetic role, is congratulated by Muriel Babcock for her portrayal of "the horrid, frigid Harriet Craig, who beneath a beautifully velvet exterior, extended so much malevolent selfishness," but other reviewers explicitly link Harriet's feminine perversity not to her repressed sexuality but to her overt materialism. Things, not men, are what Harriet craves, according to Harold Barnes, who diagnoses her as "a vicious and selfish wife, almost neurotically in love with her house and its objet d'art." Mrs. Craig, Frank Nugent notes in the *New York Times*, can only respond to a husband once he has been made over "into just another bit of house furnishing." Robert Garland, in *New York American*, agrees that the housewife is "sick with the poison of possession, watches every lamp, every table, every chair. She keeps her eye on them, as, in a presidential year, a politician keeps his eye on Maine. The four walls and the goods and the chattels to be found therein obsess her. They are like drink to a chronic alcoholic."[37]

Given the misogyny implicit in these responses—a misogyny that extended beyond the reviewers to include those audiences reported to have cheered when Walter Craig finally stands up to his wife and deliberately smashes her most precious vase, an action overdetermined by the rules of domestic melodrama where one empty vessel stands for another—it is hardly surprising that clearing Arzner from the charge of misogyny remains one of the central preoccupations of feminist critical writing on the film.[38] Yet what is equally remarkable in these contemporary responses is that from the moment the film premiered, reviewers recognized the importance of stage properties and set to a story in which a childless wife values her showcase house more than the conjugal relationship it is meant to protect. In *Craig's Wife*, the popular press concedes, background elements take a foreground role.

According to a story that ran in *Modern Screen* in December 1936, the *Craig's Wife* set "was undoubtedly one of the most artistic and complete interiors ever constructed on a lot. A ten-room house was built in its entirety, with an estimated cost of $60,000 in furnishings."[39] Diegetically located at 39 Benton Road, Rye, New York, the exterior façade of the Craig dwelling, provided by an actual colonial-revival house in suburban Beverly Hills, is first glimpsed through the estranging gray wash of day-for-night shooting. Judged from the street, the Craig house has all the overblown grandeur and strict formality that marks its interior, its clipped and constrained topiary and hedges contrasting with the romantic garden next door where the neighbor, the perpetually breathless Mrs. Frazier (Billie Burke), stands in the misty half-light watering her roses. Dwarfed by the Craigs' mock-Palladian mansion complete with double-height entrance portico, Mrs. Frazier's frame house in physical and thematic comparison seems held together by nothing more than the roses that cover its exterior.

Without any evident interior, Mrs. Frazier's house is at a glance recognized as more of a home than the dwelling next door, the rooms of which the camera relentlessly measures. Within the Craig home the draughty emptiness of Harriet's interior scheme is similarly offset by Miss Austen's bedroom with its canopied four-poster bed, across which the camera shoots in an awkward setup that exaggerates the snugly confined nature of the space. Given free access to public and private domestic space, the camera also roams into the servants' quarters, both the well-appointed kitchen and the tiny maid's room directly adjacent to it, the better to point out the sentimental imbalance of a middle-class house in which compassionate relationships are limited to a subclass of live-in domestics. The maid Mazie (Nydia Westman), for instance, is seen inside her bedroom packing her things to leave having been sacked by Mrs. Craig for inviting her boyfriend through the kitchen screen-door that, unlike the architectural centerpiece that is the Craig front door, inadequately barricades the house against male intruders. Effectively ejected from the Craig house on grounds of her heterosexuality, Mazie is shown removing a photographic pinup of Gary Cooper from her bedroom wall. Although her actual boyfriend bears no physical resemblance to the Hollywood star, Mazie's taste in interior decoration is nonetheless a direct reflection of her sexual orientation and the incidental gesture of removing the Hollywood pinup underscores the socially pretentious aspect of Harriet's decorative penchant for Greek nudes and Roman busts, evenhandedly male and female, and its disregard for popular standards of heterosexual romance.

As Mazie prepares to leave a house that has no room for her commonplace version of heterosexuality, the housekeeper Mrs. Harold stands by ready to take over the role of representing an alternative to Mrs. Craig's version of sexual and spatial propriety. Frequently heard before she is seen and absolved from the politeness of knocking by her status as a domestic, the comings and goings of the widowed Mrs. Harold, like the comings and goings of the unmarried Miss Austen, are key to understanding Arzner's capacity to reshape the marital storyworld. With her claim to marriage confined to the honorific, Mrs. Harold exercises a spatial license throughout *Craig's Wife* that is ceded her in the opening shot, a closeup of her face that precedes a pan movement across to the Grecian urn that it would be easy to mistake for the inaugural image and dominant symbolic figure in the film. Ultimately broken, as dictated by Kelly's playscript, the screen life of the urn is less important than the mirror it sits before, since it is in that visually complex surface that Mrs. Harold's meaty face is brought into cinematic alignment with the more patrician countenance of Miss Austen. In separate scenes in the downstairs living room, both women are seen conducting difficult conversations with Harriet Craig, whose two-faced nature is confirmed by her screen image being doubled in the mirror into which she gazes. In both cases, Harriet is filmed from behind, the low-angle shot capturing both the reflection of her face and, elevated above it in the depths of the mirror, the face of her female interlocutor. Harriet's duplicitous nature is captured by her appearance in both the room and its reflection, whereas the integrity of Mrs. Harold and Miss Austen, who stand physically behind the camera's forward scope, is confirmed by the unitary nature of their image as it appears solely in the mirror. Disembodied by reason of camera-angle, the two women's reflected faces are positioned in exactly the same visually recessive spot in a compositional setup that attests to the capacity of film to carve out new spatial dimensionalities. Separated by the temporal gap between the two scenes, the faces of the two women

3.7–3.8
Mrs. Harold and Miss Austen align in cinematic space
(*Craig's Wife*, Dorothy Arzner, 1936).

appearing in the same purely cinematic space nonetheless implies a superimposition that will subsequently become the signature gesture of a number of films that deploy female facial doubling to explore the possibilities of lesbian story and the conditions of cinematic narration to which it invariably relates.[40]

Already linked by their mise-en-scènic doubling, it is hardly surprising that Miss Austen and Mrs. Harold eventually depart the film together for other adventures, circumnavigating a story world that is far larger and more inclusive than the chillingly heterosexual set designed by Haines. Despite being dependent residents of the Craig household, the two unmarried women, a widowed housekeeper and a spinster aunt, are more spatially autonomous throughout the film than its nominal head Walter, a thoroughly domesticated man who always behaves as if his wife can see his every move. Free to come and go whenever Harriet is not about, the two women simultaneously inhabit the same on-screen space twice, once when they make Mrs. Frazier welcome inside the house, and a second time when they arrange Miss Austen's departure from it. The second task requires the two women to enter the previously unexplored realm of Miss Austen's bedroom, where they are soon interrupted by the lummox of a removal man who manages to scar the otherwise adamantine surface of the house on the way to taking Miss Austen's trunk out the symbolically loaded front door. While this disfigurement of the polished floor is given a scene of its own in which Harriet bemoans the stupidity of the hired man to his face, there is no filmic representation of the more delicate transaction in which two women of a certain age agree on a companionate relationship beyond the marital home. Presumably not limited to the pay-and-notice clauses repeatedly invoked by Harriet in the context of hiring and firing her own domestic staff, the understanding achieved between Miss Austen and Mrs. Harold is unspoken, negotiated outside the literal orders of both marriage and the Production Code circa 1936. The only elaboration of their companionate relationship exists in the later bitchy exchange between Harriet and Mrs. Harold, who is already dressed in her traveling clothes and set to depart the heterosexual house once and for all. Arguably the dramatic climax of the film, certainly for a gay and lesbian audience, the brief scene between house servant and housewife fully establishes that whatever it is that Miss Austen has engaged Mrs. Harold to do for her, it is not "keep house."

Not yet lesbian, neither are Miss Austen or Mrs. Harold evidentially straight. Destined for the Ritz Carlton, New York, before a shared passage around the world, Miss Austen and Mrs. Harold circumvent the rules of heterosexual melodrama, rules that at this point in time make it impossible to imply a lesbian couple any less obliquely. Not for them the front-door exit of the engaged couple, Fredericks and Ethel, who evacuate the house as if being in it one second longer would threaten their marital prospects. But no sooner than Walter ushers the affianced pair out the front door, he is forced to reopen it to let past Miss Austen's trunk, an apt visual signifier for the cinematic closet and a queer stage property more mobile than the nailed-down components that make up the extravagantly heterosexual set.

With the Craig house emptied of both the heterosexual and nonheterosexual couple, all that remains is for the titular owner to abscond, a departure registered off-screen by the sound of a closing door. Once Harriet has confirmed Mr. Craig's leaving with a look through the venetian blinds, she crosses the living room to adjust the two male busts on the mantelpiece. The decorative gesture compensates not for the loss of the husband but for the loss of the ornamental urn, which might prove harder to replace.[41] As in the Lombard interior designed by Haines in 1933, the exquisitely heterosexual veneer is perfected when the vestigial sign of any former husband is finally removed. No longer encumbered by Walter and the stolid narrative outcomes he represents, Harriet's domestic freedom is now compromised only by the lingering claims of familial allegiance, which the film efficiently cancels with the arrival of a telegram from Albany bearing news of her sister's death. Like the earlier aggressive entrance of Fredericks, this final sentimental challenge to Harriet's emotional containment requires an exterior shot in which an anonymous delivery boy stands four-square to the house, back to the camera, drawing the woman of the house out of the front door for the first time in the film. Standing on the cusp of the house in her monogrammed housecoat, Harriet, now technically an abandoned wife, signs for the telegram before reentering a home that is no longer a conjugal space. Neglecting to close the door of this newly defined house, the estranged wife becomes vulnerable to anything that blows in from outside, which in Harriet's case is the woman from next door.

What happens next has been the subject of much critical conjecture. According to Julia Lesage, Harriet is left materially "well off" by the departure of her husband and emotionally enriched by the receipt of the telegram informing her of her sister's demise. Rather than fulfilling the conventional requirement of narrative closure, the telegram that ushers in the final scene opens up the female protagonist to "emotional life through the direct and cathartic experience of grief." Emphasizing that moment when the statue that is Mrs. Craig throughout most of the film slowly begins to weep, Lesage points out that Harriet "has for a neighbor a warm, sympathetic widow" who at this point stops by "to leave off flowers and thus hears about the sister's death." Although "previously rejected" by Harriet as an unwelcome intrusion in her house, "with the breakdown of her previous, rigid domestic routine, the film's final mise-en-scène leaves it open for us to assume that the neighbor, an emotionally willing source of support, will return."[42] Entirely imaginary, the scene of womanly empathy anticipated by Lesage is then thematically aligned with the companionate relationship previously established between Miss Austen and Mrs. Harold, as if all relationships between women were comparable. This assumed continuum of same-sex connection seems at odds with the way *Craig's Wife* determinedly keeps the older women's oblique partnership separate and different in kind from any relationship Harriet achieves with another women, be it her sister or her niece, let alone a female neighbor she has previously imagined to be flirting with her husband.

Writing from the perspective of lesbian studies, Mayne similarly accepts that the arrival of the neighbor in the final scene represents Harriet's "one last chance at connection with another human being," interpreting the ending of the film as leaving open possibilities—presumably including erotic possibilities—for female bonding.[43] Linking the "potential coupling" between Harriet and Mrs. Frazier with the "distinctly not heterosexual" relationship established between the maiden aunt and the widowed housekeeper, Mayne goes further than Lesage in neglecting to mention the not insignificant detail that Mrs. Frazier withdraws from the house having failed to obtain any sentient response from the visibly distracted Harriet.[44] In a reading of the film that is otherwise intensely attuned to the nuances of mise-en-scène, Mayne implies that Mrs. Frazier, who has withdrawn from sight, remains in the house with Harriet, although her off-screen departure is signaled by the sound of the front door closing, the exact mechanism that earlier signals Walter's conclusive departure from the marital home: "Whatever else one might say about the conclusion of the film, when virtually everyone except Harriet and Mrs. Frazier have been evacuated from the house, one thing remains true—the chance to sustain and extend a conversation among women has finally been made possible."[45] Not so, or at least not under these terms.

Arzner's film makes clear that if any conversation between women is to take place, never mind take on a sexual aspect, the one place it can never straightforwardly occur is the screen setting of domestic melodrama.[46] While Arzner has the technical capacity to reanimate the cold-as-stone wife with the simple device of an extended soft-focus close-up, she does not yet have scenic access to the lesbian story except by suggesting everything the heterosexual set cannot contain. This observation should not lessen our interest in Arzner's renovations of domestic melodrama and the marriage plot with which it is associated, renovations that begin at the level of the homosexually designed set and end in entirely speculative lesbian scenes. In the last moments of *Craig's Wife*, when the generic aspects of melodrama assert closural dominance over the rigorously unsentimental mise-en-scène supplied by Haines's glamorously stylized heterosexual set, Harriet Craig finds herself trapped in a space that is not of her making. But Miss Austen and Mrs. Harold, two female companions better practiced in evading the restrictions of narrative closure, are already safely exiled to a homosocial somewhere that has yet to find its exemplary scenic space in the way that heterosexuality lays cinematic claim to the marital home. As I will go on to demonstrate, although the longue dureé of the Production Code and its representational aftermath means that homosexuality's centrality to the marriage plot will often go unnoticed, the recent emergence of the marriage equality movement shifts the burden of representation in ways that continue to invigorate cinematic imaginings of coupled life.

4 Tom Ford and His Kind

In the previous chapter, I suggested that feminist readings of Dorothy Arzner's *Craig's Wife* overstate the case against marriage by concentrating on the middle-class husband and wife at the titular center of the film. To the extent that they cannot see past heterosexuality, even when arguing against it, they neglect the far more appealing couple: Miss Austen and Mrs. Harold. Neither is the marrying kind, but nonetheless they model companionate marriage, going so far as to depart on something like a honeymoon at the end of the film. How is it, we might ask, that so many accounts of Arzner's film, most of which tether themselves to the fact of her lesbianism, cannot see the woods for the trees when it comes to a same-sex relationship that is like marriage in all but name? Is it that they cannot envisage a relationship between the well-bred Miss Austen and her uneducated housekeeper despite their blatant butch-femme complementarity? Or is it that they cannot imagine a marriage-like relationship between two postmenopausal women, despite Alma Kruger and Jane Darwell delivering the two most vibrant performances in the film?

As Patricia White has argued, lesbianism, in particular, has often been smuggled into Hollywood films of the Production Code era by supporting actors whose roles are incidental to the main romantic plot.[1] These queer outsider roles often bring a perverse or cynical perspective to the heterosexual proceedings that nonetheless command the narrative drive of the film. As White points out, generations of viewers have come to identify with these outsider figures and the queer possibilities they signal in the periphery of straight romance narratives that imply the closure of marriage or some related form of social coupling. So too have generations of critics, as the archive of Arzner criticism confirms, however this investment in sexual outsiderness and the concomitant disidentification with stories of marriage-like attachment has its edge sharpened now that same-sex marriage has become a horizon of social possibility. As I will go on to demonstrate, once gay and lesbian content lays a direct rather than oblique claim to the erotic implications of domestic melodrama, all kinds of tensions arise between established queer critical formations, many of them to do with genre and its capacity to capture or distort gay and lesbian styles of living.

Consider, for instance, *A Single Man* (2009), Tom Ford's adaptation of Christopher Isherwood's novel of the same name from 1964, a film that conveniently takes up the question of cinematic style and the question of gay marriage as if they were the same thing. In terms of the film's reception, both Ford's fans and his detractors agree on one point: the film's claim to attention rests on its style. Whether they run hot or cold, his critics are uniform in regarding the film as an exercise in cinematic mannerism or mood. "All art and no direction" is how Stephanie Zacharek dismisses the film on *Salon*, "less a finished, fleshed out movie than it is a mood board, one of those collages of images and colors that designers sometimes use to help define and fine-tune the vibe they're going after in their creative ventures."[2] In the *New Yorker*, Anthony Lane finesses the same point: in Colin Firth and Julianne Moore, Ford's film reveals "two strong actors refusing to be tight-laced by a director's exercise in style: here is a mood piece looking for a fight."[3] Although the subdiscipline of film-philosophy has recently taken up the issue of mood from a phenomenological perspective, in the less reified discourse of film reviewing, mood is not a desirable cinematic quality but the kind of thing that gives a film a bad name.[4]

To put it succinctly, mood has gone to market. The term "mood piece" currently designates any sonically wrapped montage of images designed to convey the emotionalism of a brand, product, or service provider. Initially big-budget productions associated with luxury goods and high-end fashion houses such as Gucci, where Ford was creative director for most of the 1990s, mood films are now ubiquitous in the world of corporate identity and client communications. To call Ford's film a mood piece, therefore, gets straight to the heart of its stylistic ambivalence and the tension it performs between the personalization of feeling—gay feeling in particular—and the framing of that feeling within a larger aesthetic and commercial system marked by impersonality and the extension of creative property rights into intimate domains, namely the Tom Ford brand.

This tension is not exclusive to Ford's film but indicative of a wider cultural investment in gay style and emotionality, which, in the charged contemporary context of marriage equality, taps homosexuality's dual personalizing and politicizing effects in order to reinvigorate established social conventions, representational genres, or commodity forms.[5] By uniquely combining the personalized discourses of character, biography, and celebrity engaged by the film, Ford's mood piece relaunches homosexual style, once a coterie fashion, as an aspirant brand that impersonally bestows cultural and emotional capital on its cosmopolitan fans, who, no longer divided in terms of their sexual orientation, can be addressed as a single diverse demographic. Rather than being simply another exercise in heritage cinema, a style of filmmaking Richard Dyer has identified by its capacity to evoke, "especially through clothes," the "utopian pleasure of a vision of integration even in homophobic societies of the past," Ford's celebrity-driven film successfully retools homosexual feeling into an on-trend sensation hovering on the brink of mass identification and uptake, like self-carbonated water or reuseable shopping bags.[6] Unlike these two ecoexamples, however, which both involve the retraining of everyday habits as part of a general swerve toward green, homosexual feelings tend to remain in the ambivalent order of emotional responsiveness, somewhere between personal experience and impersonal trigger. An always nebulous thing, the contemporary gay mood that *A Single Man* participates in spans the full breadth of the intimate public sphere, a field of artistic and commercial operation that Tom Ford has profitably made over in his own gay image since at least 2004, when he left Gucci to launch his namesake brand "Tom Ford by Tom Ford."

I approach the question of film style and its relation to gay marriage through a discussion of Isherwood, not only the author of Ford's source text but also an early prototype of the high-profile gay creative now epitomized by Ford. Isherwood was no stranger to celebrity culture in either its elite or populist forms. In 1938, when he and W. H. Auden were photographed departing Victoria Station for China to report on the Sino-Japanese War, they were already recognizable as the public face of a generation of left-leaning intellectuals, more so together than apart. From 1940, when Isherwood took his first writing job with MGM, his American diaries record encounters with Hollywood stars, many of whom would subsequently become frequent guests at his home. From the late 1950s on, established celebrities and other media-emergent figures, many of them gay, would visit Isherwood's Santa Monica house to pose for, and autograph, the portraits and nudes for which his domestic partner, Don Bachardy, is now recognized. Almost three decades after his death, Isherwood's celebrity no longer depends on his literary fame or his connections with Hollywood royalty but resonates within the broader framework of gay lifestyle and media. As the many feature reviews given to *Liberation*—the most recently published volume of Isherwood's private diaries—indicate, Isherwood's present-day gay figurehead status is often established by invoking Bachardy's name.[7] Although the circumstances of their getting together continues to rivet attention, the current media angle on the Isherwood-Bachardy relationship seems to be that, however they met or whatever the age difference at the time, the more significant fact is that they stayed together as domestic partners for thirty-three years.

Beginning with the welter of trade and academic publications that followed Isherwood's death in 1986, the coupled names Isherwood and Bachardy, or, just as frequently, Chris and Don, have come to signal the possibilities of gay long-term relationships across an increasingly wide cultural band. Initially referred to in the alternative press as the "first couple" of gay liberation, Isherwood and Bachardy are nowadays more likely to be hailed as proponents of gay marriage before the fact.[8] Many of the promotional taglines accompanying the DVD release of the feature-length documentary *Chris and Don: A Love Story* in 2009, for instance, vouch for the marriage-like status of the relationship between the two men and conveniently forget Isherwood's prior relationship with photographer William (Bill) Caskey, with whom he also lived and collaborated, if turbulently, in the late 1940s and early 1950s.[9] The *San Francisco Chronicle* applauds a "portrait of a marriage as full and enviable as the greatest unions in literature," whereas John Boorman more pragmatically notes, "Of all the people I came to know in Hollywood, their marriage was the only one that endured." In explicit contradiction to these marketing statements, the DVD extras include an interview with Bachardy in which he states that he can't believe that anyone would think that he, let alone Isherwood, would have a bar of marriage. While filmmakers Guido Santi and Tina Mascara do not edit out the nonmonogamous aspect of the Isherwood-Bachardy partnership, the sexual and emotional jealousies recorded by Isherwood in his diaries secure no visual registration in *Chris and Don*, which is buoyed along by luminous home-movie footage and cute animation sequences based on Dobbin and Kitty, the two animal avatars that Isherwood and Bachardy respectively adopted in their private correspondence.[10] Although Bachardy candidly refers to the rules agreed between the two men for negotiating casual affairs and briefly mentions the fraught period in which he was seriously involved with someone else, the live-action camera that tracks him through the light-filled Santa Monica house he shared with Isherwood manages to convey a relationship without shadow.

The documentary's airbrushing of the Isherwood-Bachardy relationship it is at odds with Isherwood's sustained experiments in sexual self-disclosure through the personalized formats of autobiographical fiction, biography, and memoir. With so much of his writing fusing biographical content with fictional form and his repeated deployment of namesake narrators, not to mention the sheer volume of his memoirs and diaries, Isherwood is now acknowledged as a pioneer in gay autobiography and life writing, a genre with a pulp as well as a literary pedigree.[11] While it would be hard to underestimate the talismanic appeal of his memoir *Christopher and His Kind* (1976) to the post-Stonewall generation, Jaime Harker has recently pointed out that Isherwood's career has always troubled those critics who associate literary merit with cultural exclusivity rather than popular dissemination.[12] Rather than cordoning Isherwood off from the West Coast gay culture that drew him to Los Angeles, Harker demonstrates that Isherwood's American writing career was crucially indexed to middlebrow publishing and involved "mainstreaming gay content for heterosexual audiences" while covertly "encouraging identificatory reading practices and constructing a symbiotic relationship between reader and writer" that would eventually transform into a mass gay readership.[13] As Harker demonstrates by tracking his literary correspondence with editors and publishers, Isherwood's publicity-friendly form of success was built on his capacity to engage both straight and gay readerships in the years leading to gay liberation and the sexually explicit print landscape it helped usher in. In the wake of marriage equality it is possible to find similar instances of broadening straight interest in gay or queer creative content delivered in newly hospitable media formats, such as Jill Soloway's Amazon series *Transparent* (2014–), which kicks off its second season with a gay marriage, or the 2017 reboot of *Will and Grace* (1998–2006), in which the lead characters return childless from the hinterlands of marriage in order to retake Manhattan and the single sex-life with which popular culture associates it.[14]

If American Isherwood broke new ground in being transparently gay to a broad audience, it is worth remembering that the popular accessibility of his writing style had previously been critically disparaged. In 1938, Cyril Connolly famously grouped Isherwood with Ernest Hemingway and George Orwell as one of the chief proponents of the "new vernacular" style while also declaring the simplicity of his diction "impoverished" and the overall effect of his writing one of "fatal readability." While Isherwood's manuscripts reveal his prose style to be the result of endless authorial revision, the trick of its final form is to cast off the literary and disappear into the colloquial.[15] It would therefore appear that Isherwood's increasingly explicit homosexual subject matter, and its acceptance by gay and general readerships alike, is crucially linked to its deceptive presentation as a literary nonstyle that amplifies the effect of personal intimacy and uninhibited revelation even as it slips the usual conventions of first-person narration.[16]

Typically regarded as his fictional masterpiece, *A Single Man* is often cited as evidence that Isherwood—who had long experimented with various "ironic" distances between himself and his narrative others, many of whom carried the name Christopher—had finally achieved stylistic maturity.[17] Linked to the eradication of the personal perspective and, more specifically, the removal of the author's nominal trace from the story world, the narrational style of *A Single Man* is a highly complex affair. As Jonathan Raban identifies, the novel engages "three varieties of tense and four of person" in order to capture the "emotional movements of the narrative."[18] Famously gearing its narration through the neuter third person ("That which has awoken then lies for a while staring up at the ceiling and down into itself until it has recognized *I*, and therefrom deduced *I am, I am now*"), Isherwood's novel excludes the first-person singular but otherwise uses the full range of grammatical pronouns available in English to position his protagonist within an extremely supple net of personal and impersonal identifications that attract or distance the reader across a range of temporal coordinates.[19] From its initially detached perspective on a body waking into the "*now*" of consciousness followed by the "*here*" of spatial recognition, the narration assembles the gendered personal pronoun as carefully as "the creature we are watching" assembles "itself" in front of a mirror in which "there isn't so much a face as the expression of a predicament" (2). The subsequent introduction of the second-person pronoun establishes an intimate spatial bond between the newly denoted character and the implied reader, who, having tracked George's shambling movement from bed to bathroom, now steps into his skin and experiences the peculiar dimensionalities of his world: "He crosses the front room, which he calls the study, and comes down the staircase. The stairs turn a corner; they are narrow and steep. You can touch both handrails with your elbows and you have to bend your head—even if, like George, you are only five eight" (3).

As many commentators have observed, in its style and structure *A Single Man* anticipates cinematic adaptation. Isherwood's narrational capacity to shift from a detached to an embodied perspective that nonetheless shuns the first person seems tailored to cinematic treatment in which objective and subjective camera setups work to place actors and actions within three-dimensional space. At the point at which he was writing *A Single Man*, Isherwood had put in over twenty years as a contract Hollywood screenwriter, so it is hardly surprising to see these cinematic devices on display alongside direct speech that reads so well as dialogue that much of it is taken across verbatim into Ford's film. Unimpeded by conventional chapter breaks and seamlessly unfurling across a grammatical landscape of dashes and semicolons, Isherwood's literary nonstyle—his unfailingly transparent prose and indirect handling of focalization—is, it seems, already made for cinema's systems of continuous visualization.

But the cinematic ripeness of Isherwood's technique is not what makes the novel attractive to Ford. Although he maintains Isherwood's restriction of present-tense events to a single day, Ford and his coscriptwriter, David Scearce, dramatically reorient the plot around the invented device of an intended suicide in order to meet the emotional needs of melodrama.[20] Just as importantly, in reworking the source material into a feature-length film, Ford abandons the novel's free indirect framework. Redeploying Isherwood's opening sentence as the first words uttered by a voice-over visually synchronized to the character George (Colin Firth), Ford enacts a stylistic shift away from impersonality toward a subjectively marked style. Whereas in the novel, narrational authority and readerly identification accrue to the impersonal framework that pinpoints the character's personal point of view but remains removed from it, the personal voice-over heard at the beginning and end of the film channels and intensifies spectatorial identification through the lens of character. In presenting the story through this form of bespoke narration, Ford's text would seem to establish from the outset what Isherwood's does not: a gay perspective on the diegetic world, as opposed to the novel's impersonal perspective on a gay character. Yet, although it explicitly elevates homosexuality from the order of story to the order of discourse (or framing of story), Ford's cinematic handling of the novel simultaneously raises the question of to whom the gay story belongs. This is not simply a case of an introduced narrator invariably raising the specter of unreliability but more to do with Ford's signature mood. The way the visual style of the film encloses the embedded character voice-over forces us to ask, in a way that Isherwood's free indirect style does not, whose story is it?

By evidence of the many reviews and interviews generated around the film's release, this question of to whom the gay story belongs, which I am posing as a question of personal or impersonal style, is more often approached as if it were a question of genre: is the film fiction or biography?[21] Little attention is given to how the film's narrational technique departs or corresponds to the novel it adapts since Ford is considered most faithful to Isherwood in adopting the hybridized format of autobiographical fiction and embedding in the film text numerous real-life reference points. Like the novel, the film includes many solicitations to be read as in some way connected to the coupled lives of Isherwood and Bachardy. Preserved from the novel are those aspects of George that correspond to Isherwood's experience as an adjunct professor loosely affiliated to a number of college literature and writing programs. Preserved from life is Bachardy himself. Untypically dressed in a jacket and bow tie, Bachardy sits in the Brooks College staff room in a scene that briefly

4.1
The enclosed and exposed narrator: whose story is this?
(*A Single Man*, Tom Ford, 2009).

4.2
Richard Buckley and Don Bachardy in character
(*A Single Man*, Tom Ford, 2009).

captures his true-to-life English stammer.[22] Though Bachardy is credited with a creative consultancy role, his influence is hard to detect at the level of style. Unlike any of the overhung domestic spaces revealed in *Chris and Don*, the interior spaces Ford associates with George and his architect boyfriend, Jim (Matthew Goode), tend to be minimally furnished with books or art but maximally furnished with academic citations of midcentury modernism. George's campus office, for instance, comprises a clean-line credenza and desk with a state-of-the-art electric typewriter never once put to diegetic use.

Stretching more thinly the period-perfect setting of the film, however, are those instances in which elements before the camera reference Ford's celebrity biography and its contemporary corporate coordinates. That is Richard

4.3
Pink is in the air (*A Single Man*, Tom Ford, 2009).

Buckley, Ford's partner of twenty years, sitting at the opposite end of the sofa while sharing the paper with Bachardy. That is Tom and Richard's smooth-haired fox terrier stealing the scene in the liquor store parking lot prior to the arrival of an equally sleek, long-faced hustler sniffing around George, his cantilevered cheekbones set to catch the setting Los Angeles sun. The invented figure of the emotionally astute hustler, an Iberian James Dean look-alike played by Spanish supermodel Jon Kortajarena, the face of the Tom Ford menswear and eyewear campaigns of spring 2009, elegantly conflates characterological, biographical, and celebrity identities in what registers as the most intimate transaction between men in the entire film. Art directed within an inch of its life, the beautiful scene between Firth and Kortajarena effortlessly slips the plot implications of rough trade to convey a corporatized gay feeling that simply hangs in the air like pink smog over the city.

Though the visual effect of pinkness can be traced to the use of light filters, the scene between the two men remains a precise indicator of the way Ford's film tailors the gay mood into a more generally accessible style that registers as both everywhere and nowhere, streetwise and elite, historically specific and ubercontemporary. The poignant diffusion of gayness across characterological, biographical, and celebrity domains broadens its aesthetic appeal in the here and now of audience reception while presenting homophobia as a historical artifact with which no one, or at least no one who counts themselves as up with the times, can identify.

Throughout the film, an aimless, unmotivated homosexual desire is repeatedly loosened from the hold of present-tense action the better to saturate other levels of discourse and their primarily affective registers, most of which are intensified in relation to personal melancholy and nostalgia for a painfully beautiful past. This is not just a matter of all George's interactions with Jim being linked to flashback and fantasy, or the more obvious objection that the film is inaugurated and achieves closure on kisses between men premised on one or other of them being dead (Firth kissing Goode's frozen corpse in the dreamy aftermath of a road accident; Goode kissing Firth as the character he plays lies dying on the bedroom floor), but is also registered in other sentimental deferrals of gay action: think of Carlos the beautiful hustler paid to go away, or the chaste intimacy established between George and his might-be-straight/might-be-gay student, Kenny (Nicholas Hoult). Whereas novel-George is brought back to animal life the moment his and Kenny's "bodies rub against each other, briefly but roughly" (131), when Kenny presents his naked body to film-George in another scene completely invented by Ford, nothing happens at the brute level except a briefly held glance that measures the emotionally foreshortened but physically inviolable distance between two men. While Ford's direction restricts his actor's movements within the scene so as not to distract us from the symbolically overloaded dialogue they are made to deliver—"We're invisible, don't you know that?"—Isherwood's freewheeling narration makes clear that it is physical contact between the "drunk-trustful" professor and his student that breaks the "electric field of the dialogue" so that "their relationship, whatever it now is, is no longer symbolic" (131). In the filmic world created by Ford, homosexuality is the delicate—some might say inhibited—sensibility through which everything is apprehended, a fragile ecosystem sustained by nothing more than the color tone of a room and the nonassaulting warmth of a minimalist score.

As if aware that the universal appeal of homosexuality might be diminished by the spectacle of gay sex, Ford maintains the stylistic and thematic foregrounding of emotion even in scenes that seem animated by other possibilities. Take the scene in which George dances with Julianne Moore's Charley. With his jacket open and shirt unbuttoned, Firth inhabits his body as if for the first time in the film. Initially centered on Moore but widening to include Firth, the scene of dancing instantly energizes the screen and ties the viewer to the on-screen figures in a rush of kinesthetic identification whose only precedent is the sidelong glances George cuts at the bare chests of the tennis players who earlier distracted him from the ponderous conversation of his campus colleague. Recalling George's spontaneous mention of "Elvis Presley's hips" in his otherwise dreary seminar on Aldous Huxley, the dance scene's thematic significance is not fully felt until Ford reprises it late in the film at the point at which George has decided against killing himself and burns his suicide notes. As George walks through the dark house, the personalized voice-over resumes to spell out what the golden firelight already

4.4–4.7
George inhabits his body
(*A Single Man*, Tom Ford, 2009).

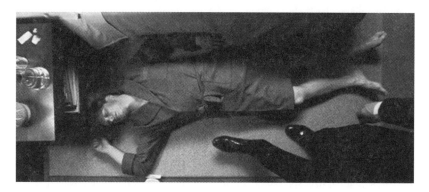

4.8
Jim's suit steps into frame
(*A Single Man*, Tom Ford, 2009).

indicates—that George has returned from the abstracted space of thinking to the "sharp . . . fresh" moment of feeling: "I have lived my life on these moments: they pull me back to the present." At the word "present," the image track briefly cuts to a replayed shot of Firth's swinging hips in a flashback that belongs less to him than to us.

In activating the viewer's memory of the earlier scene and linking it with the voice-over's affirmation of the present, the film lays down the aesthetic conditions in which George's character might be experienced as passing out of story time into some other discursive register. When George falls to the floor during a heart attack, Ford audibly stops the clock before an immaculate Jim steps into the overhead shot. Having bestowed an uncorrupted kiss, Jim's face is seen to withdraw from his boyfriend's point of view before the voice-over delivers the film's last line: "And just like that it came." The camera slowly pans the length of Firth's classically draped body before pausing on a close-up of his face. Firth's mouth relaxes to indicate George's release from time and place before the camera telescopes all the discursive levels of the film into a high overhead shot that holds on the lifeless figure below. With the out-of-body perspective attained, the scene bleaches out before the screen fades to white, then black, as the theme music associated with George ushers in the haptic vision of a naked Firth (although who could say for sure) swimming in the homosexual afterlife, a no-place of feeling that succumbs to neither the demands of gay character nor those of gay narration but is experienced as an amniotic wash of sound and image, an effect further exaggerated if you find yourself weeping in the clutch of emotions that might not stand the critical light of day.

These gay mood effects are not simply the sentimental tripwires we expect of melodrama in its closing frames. They are not specifically linked to gay themes or the exclusive domain of gay characters. Rather, Ford's film insistently places homosexuality in an arena of style and sensual apprehension that is hypertuned to ambient feeling but almost indifferent to the arcs of character and story. As George moves through his day, for instance, Firth is scarcely required to register responsiveness to others or to his environment since Ford executes this in postproduction via the flooding of color into otherwise monochromatic scenes.[23] The digital enhancement of the image carries the full force of period detail and a nostalgic mise-en-scène that frames the past as a series of sensual encounters or memories that momentarily arrest the teleology of the gay suicide story: the color of the carpet in a bank in which customers are known by name, the blue of a dress reflected in the eyes of young girl, the tone of a lipstick matched to a head scarf, the audibly muffled interior of the car George leans into while inhaling the scent of the terrier. While the film links these melancholic effects to George as a homosexual man apprehending the world on the day he has determined to leave it, this subjectively customized style remains the conduit for a gay mood that, while holding tight to the personal name, extends its market reach into otherwise straight terrain.

The moody idiosyncratic filter through which film-George sees everything around him is strikingly at odds with Isherwood's narration, which avoids George's perspective the closer it nears the moment of his death. Framed as pure speculation, the last pages of the novel record the expiry of a gay character whose personal sensibility was always less than the temporal and cognitive limits of the indirect narration, which now attains new levels of impersonality: "Thus, slowly, invisibly, with the utmost discretion and without the slightest hint to those old fussers in the brain, an almost indecently melodramatic situation is contrived: the formation of the atheromatous plaque" (151). Apprehended with clinical precision, the "body on the bed stirs slightly, perhaps; but it does not cry out, does not wake. It shows no outward sign of the instant, annihilating shock." As the narration goes on to report, "Cortex and brain-stem are murdered in the blackout with the speed of an Indian strangler" before the neurological cells of the homosexual body, not its subjective memories, shut down like lights across an electricity grid. Without any call on emotion, the novel extinguishes personal consciousness and puts in its place a collectively attained perspective on the "non-entity we called George," a bag of bones now "cousin to the garbage in the container on the back porch" (151–52).

Capable of this level of detachment, Isherwood's narration is also adept at pinpointing George in a gay subcultural milieu that has no equivalent in Ford's film, not even in the bar scenes shot on location in Santa Monica. Consider when, in the novel, George, preparing to have dinner with Charley, "changes out of his suit into an army surplus store khaki shirt, faded blue denims, moccasins, a sweater. (He has had doubts from time to time about this kind of costume; doesn't it give the impression that he's trying to dress young? But Jim used to tell him, No, it was just right for him—it made him look like Rommel in civilian clothes. George loved that.)" (91–92). Rather than the bespoke suit Firth takes from Ford's wardrobe, novel-George puts on the sixties' gay leisure uniform in order to be seen for what he is: a gay man of his generation, not one but one of many.

In her discussion of Isherwood's American career, Harker not only makes a strong case for reading *A Single Man* alongside the conventions of gay pulp, but also sets his later work in the context of a post-Stonewall print culture that will eventually see *Christopher and His Kind* excerpted in *Blueboy: The National Magazine about Men* surrounded by advertisements for gay commercial services.[24] Harker also reminds us that the years immediately following the publication of *A Single Man* saw the appearance of two books that would transform the public conversation around homosexuality, race, and the undersides of mainstream American culture: James Baldwin's *Another Country* (1962) and John Rechy's *City of Night* (1963). Ford's preference, however, is not for queer sociological veracity but other vintage effects, such as Julianne Moore's updo hairstyle and Cleopatra eyeliner, which recall the Taylor-Burton film under production in 1962, the year in which the film is set.

Similarly, although *A Single Man* abounds in cinematic citations of Alfred Hitchcock in the late 1950 and early 1960s, this visual and aural homage cannot obscure Ford's creative credentials uniquely asserting themselves in a personally branded mise-en-scène and proprietary film style. Just as Ford literally penned the handwritten notes that George leaves in his house as instructions for those who will find him after his suicide and threw off the Ellsworth Kelly–like abstract that hangs above Charley's fireplace, Ford's designer marque is everywhere across the film. As if it were already a screenplay, Isherwood's novel rarely attaches adjectives to objects or space, but the descriptors applied to George's novelistic house are remarkably consistent in the picture they draw: "narrow," "tightly planned," "small" (3), "dark and low-ceilinged" (6), "low damp dark," and "tiny" (9). Isherwood's George "feels protected" by the "smallness of his home" (3), but in its cinematic iteration the house that George wakes in is a carefully choreographed structure of brick, wood, and glass planes that angle off each other expansively. Recognizable to some as the Schaffer house in Glendale designed by John Lautner in 1949, the relatively intimate scale of the house was an impediment to Ford insofar as its redwood paneled volumes, though everywhere enhanced

4.9–4.10
George confined in the Schaffer house
(*A Single Man*, Tom Ford, 2009).

by clerestories and floor-to-ceiling windows, were too small for the needs of a location crew. Instead of filming within the Lautner-designed spaces, Ford had the living room enclosed with false walls that were continually redressed in order to meet the various requirements of the diegesis by set designer Dan Bishop, who made his name on the purpose-built sets of *Mad Men* (2007–2015), yet another sixties-style melodrama that interleaves the story of marriage and homosexuality.[25] Whether Lautner originals or those provided by Ford and his design team, the immaculate domestic spaces seen in the film offset George's investment in personal grooming and his adoption of a tailored Tom Ford silhouette that restricts itself to blacks and grays. Of course, Firth's narrow-lapeled suits and square-framed spectacles are Tom Ford originals, but when Jim fleetingly appears in morning flashback, dressed California-style in plaid Bermuda shorts that command a whole colorway of oranges and tawny browns banished from George's wardrobe, the overall effect is the same: if Tom Ford did leisurewear, this is what it would look like circa 2009.[26]

As though in accord with theories of auteurship that claim every frame of a film is marked by the visual signature of its director, all the other commodity objects in the film—the Rambler Cross Country in which Jim meets his death, the Mercedes-Benz 220S coupe with its customized sunroof and whitewall tires, Charley's Princess phone and Sobranie cigarettes, the Tanqueray that drops to the pavement outside the liquor store and has to be replaced, the monogrammed stationery exclusive to Smythson of Bond Street—seem also to carry Ford's invisible imprimatur. From this perspective—the perspective of homosexual style—carrying Ford's name can seem George's primary cinematic function: in the novel George is known only by his first name, but in the screenplay he is additionally saddled with both Ford's mother's name, Carlyle, and Falconer, the name of Ford's first lover and a line of Tom Ford sunglasses, as if to close the pact between fictional figure, trademark brand, and homosexual celebrity.

Ford's extraordinarily continuous brand-name style is maintained across George's home and work environments and all the spaces in between. The wooden veneer that abounds in George's house also manifests in the walnut dashboard and detailing of George's car and the many vintage clockfaces on which Ford effects scene transitions and temporal ellipses. The redbrick walls and green canopy first seen in the Schaffer house are also found in the scenes set at Brooks College, a campus-sized instantiation of Ford's midcentury modern aesthetic. As if to make George's right to this space visually patent, Ford has Firth slowly walk from bucolic car park to modernist office while all the pedestrian extras that make up the college community divide around his elegant form as though he were solid and they merely liquid. In this diegetic world, and perhaps the self-funded bubble in which it was produced, everyone defers without complaint to Tom Ford style as the beacon of gay feeling.

In his unchallenged occupancy of beautiful spaces that seem to exist solely for him, Ford's slow-driving, slow-walking fashion-plate hero is completely unlike Isherwood's hyperagitated protagonist, who, as he goes about his day, is constantly irritated by transformations in the architectural landscape of Los Angeles, which offer him and his gay kind less and less room to move. Whereas film-George moves through a built environment that seems the physical extension of his own good taste, a world in which any of us—gay or straight—might like to live, novel-George knows he is part of a homosexual demographic being squeezed out by heterosexual interests: he backs his car onto the streets of Santa Monica Canyon, the former expat and bohemian colony now turned into a "breeding-ground" by families abandoning the city as, "one by one, the cottages which used to reek of bathtub gin and reverberate with the poetry of Hart Crane have fallen to the occupying army of coke-drinking television-watchers" (8). Uninterested in family space and the all-American activities that attend it, novel-George reserves his "patriotism for the freeways" and the feeling he gets from merging and speeding that "he can still *get by*" (20). Through the seemingly effortless technique of flexible focalization, Isherwood's novel unreels a surprisingly tight critical overview of Los Angeles in the early 1960s as prompted by the view through George's windshield. After navigating the freeway entrance, George, as though under "autohypnosis," relaxes into the body memory of driving while Isherwood confidently steers him through the ten pages of free indirect narration that comprise his commute: "And George, like a master who has entrusted the driving of his car to a servant, is now free to direct his attention elsewhere" (22). With the character carried along by the indirect vehicle of narration, the novel is free to unburden itself of a series of impassioned rants against the spatial degradation of Los Angeles as triggered by a variety of civic and corporate initiatives that appear on cue through the fictional car window: the explosion of new high-rise apartments blocking established views of the coast, wave after wave of campus expansion, and the relentless sprawl of identikit tract housing that constitutes "the nowadays of destruction-reconstruction-destruction" (27).

This increasingly normative landscape future-geared to reproduction, education, and upward mobility depresses the hell out of George, who buoys himself up with the "easy-going physical democracy" (87) of the gym and, as he looks at himself naked, the reassurance that "despite his wrinkles, his slipped flesh, his greying hair, his grim-lipped strutting spryness, you catch occasional glimpses of a ghostly someone else, soft-faced, boyish, pretty. The combination is bizarre, it is older than middle-age itself, but it is there" (83). Reconnected with a homosexual present in which "no-one is perfect and no-one pretends to be"—even the "godlike young baseball player confides to all his anxiety about the smallness of his ankles" (86)—George impulsively takes the scenic route home. When he stops his car on Mulholland Drive to take a leak, he again becomes "thoroughly depressed" at the spectacle spread out before him of a city dying of "over-extension" (88). But as he zips up his pants and drives on, "the clouds close in low on the hills, making them seem northern and sad like Wales" (89). The melancholic observation of space as touched by personal memory and grief—which the film sustains for its entire duration—is here merely held for the beat of a semicolon before the narration glides on in its impersonal mode: "and the day wanes, and the lights snap on in their sham jewel colours all over the plain, as the road winds down again on to Sunset Boulevard and he nears the ocean" (89). As this visualization of landscape indicates, Isherwood's unsentimental style captures exterior space as a symbolic extension of homosexual character, then, without breaking the effect of continuous montage, puts in place a nonsubjective perspective that continues to register gay presence: George's unfeigned reverie of Wales segues into the "sham" city of the plain, the personal gay memory into the impersonal gay city, each image as beautiful as the other and more beautiful still for their unforced conjunction.

With his creative stripes attained in the fashion industry, it is not surprising that Ford's capacity to invest both people and products with a cinematic aura recalled for many the wave of fragrance films in which the houses of Chanel, Dior, and Prada, among others, engaged contemporary auteurs such as David Lynch, Martin Scorsese, and Ridley Scott to conceive short mood pieces to promote their brands.[27] Fashion theorists Susie Khamis and Alex Munt have noted that, whatever their particular narrative drive, the marketing purposes of fragrance films dictate that the needs of commerce must ultimately overcome "artfulness" and "necessitate the inclusion of the 'money-shot,' when the branded item becomes the necessary and final focal point."[28] In marked contrast, Tom Ford has little need for anything as attention grabbing as a money shot since he appears to operate from a position beyond fashion where commerce and art no longer exist in oppositional tension. In exercising something as outdated as the visionary rights of the classical auteur, Ford spreads his designer style and brand identity across the film in a gesture of unabashed personal publicity that fully expresses what Roland Barthes terms "the economic nature of the Name."[29] Bringing together fictional, biographical, and trademark names, Ford's highly mannered film supports various forms of cinematic and architectural connoisseurship while also meeting the celebrity conditions that underwrite gay authorship in its current popular manifestation.

Although everything in the scene is stylistically marked by his invisible logo, the director of *A Single Man* insists on keeping his own image beyond the film's literal frame. Despite all the other nods to Hitchcock—and the ease with which he puts on display his boyfriend, his dog, his original art, his collectables, his merchandise—Ford stops short of an on-screen cameo as if the diegesis were the one place a flesh-and-blood director must never be seen. Yet, as classically handsome as Hitchcock is not, Ford is still capable of stealing the show. A telling moment in the featurette that accompanies the film in its DVD release is when Colin Firth comments on the strangeness of being on a set where the director is "more glamorous and better put together than those in front of the camera."[30] In having more face or star quality than the talent, Ford and his homosexual to-be-looked-at-ness unsettles the visual hierarchies usually associated with film production. Certainly, in the carefully managed swirl of personality-driven publicity surrounding the film, Ford's image circulated as frequently as Firth's and Moore's. As Firth's comments perhaps acknowledge, in playing the homosexual George Carlyle Falconer he is merely the on-screen stand-in for the gay celebrity director and his brand-name style, a doubling captured in the many paparazzi shots of the two of them standing side by side in matching Tom Ford suits at various red-carpet events. Whether absent or present, seen or unseen, Ford works the relation between celebrity recognition and the creative signature as he has since launching "Tom Ford by Tom Ford."

It almost goes without saying that Christopher Isherwood, like Tom Ford, had a complicated relationship to his own name. If what makes *A Single Man* exceptional in Isherwood's oeuvre is that in it he relinquishes his namesake narrator, the device to which his literary success and innovation is usually credited, that should also remind us that letting go his name was something Isherwood was ambivalent about in life. Although he would legally shorten his surname from Bradshaw-Isherwood to Isherwood on becoming an American citizen in 1946, in *My Guru and His Disciple* he records the violent reaction he had the previous year when, while residing at the Vedanta temple in Los Angeles, it was suggested to him that he was spiritually ready to take a Sanskrit name: "To me 'Christopher Isherwood' was much more than just my name: it was the code word for my identity as a writer, the formula for the essence of my artistic power. So, to force me to take another name would be an act of hostile magic."[31] In this account Isherwood's anxiety is not triggered by the thought of losing his distinctive identity: it is triggered by the thought of losing his writerly code name. He is not concerned with the proper name's identificatory function, its capacity to nominate a unique Christopher Isherwood, but the proper name's authorial function, to use Michel Foucault's term.[32] Isherwood is powerfully attached, that is, to his name's capacity to proliferate effects across an intertextual landscape that knits together fiction and biography, past and present, Vedanta mysticism and homosexuality.

In so often reiterating his own name and its many variants within his writing—Christopher, Christopher Isherwood, Isherwood, Chris, Herr Issyvoo—Isherwood infringes the conventional novelistic contract whereby names act as pegs on which to hang singular identities or characters. "In the novelistic regime," Roland Barthes writes, "'the name' is an instrument of exchange: it allows the substitution of a nominal unit for a collection of characteristics by establishing an equivalent relationship between sign and sum: it is a bookkeeping method in which, the price being equal, condensed merchandise is preferable to voluminous merchandise."[33] In breaking the illusory equivalence that the character name establishes "between sign and sum," Isherwood places himself, and his many novelistic avatars, on the side of "voluminous merchandise." The authorial name, "Christopher Isherwood," does not disappear, but, as a code word sliding sideways across the genres of fiction, diary, and memoir, it is linked to the split enunciation of self, not its seamless actualization. Tom Ford's name, on the other hand, which is never bestowed on a character, functions as an authorial abstraction that exercises naming rights over the "collection of characteristics" or signs that comprise the creative property invested in and radiating out from the film. This is no longer the realist economy Barthes describes in which character names husband textual signs into recognizable sums, but nor is it simply the auteurist economy in which all textual signs are considered the sum of the director's signature style. Rather, in its trademarked manifestations as style, Ford doubles the exchange value of his own name by attaching it to signs of style that circulate both inside and outside the fictional film, or, like the autobiographical elements planted in the story world, undo such obsolete distinctions. While only some of these signs bear the Tom Ford brand name, they all index a denotative celebrity style that extends beyond the homosexual characters it textually connotes.[34]

Whereas Isherwood's ironic deployment of his fictional analogue "Christopher Isherwood" detaches personal and impersonal effects, Ford's celebrity style conflates personal name and public brand in a sentimental approximation of the impersonality that Barthes identifies as the operative code of fiction in which "the person is no more than a collection of semes." Like the characters in fiction, the celebrity name Tom Ford is "an adjective, an attribute, a predicate," but, no longer restrained by the conventions of story or authorship, this "condensed" signifier now extends its personality-based franchise onto "voluminous merchandise" beyond the text.[35] In this name economy in which the authorial function morphs into the gay celebrity brand, "Tom Ford by Tom Ford" denotes neither authorial style nor homosexuality but homosexuality's endless capacity to personify style and the sheer emotionalism that can attach to that.

Far from being an exercise in marketing the celebrity brand name, the gay mood that Ford's film showcases may simply reflect the mood of the times. As David Eng writes of a "current moment" that is not restricted to US jurisdictions, the present is "marked by the merging of an increasingly visible and mass-mediated queer consumer lifestyle with recent judicial protections for gay and lesbian rights to privacy and intimacy."[36] This is the liberal backdrop against which *A Single Man* can make a sentimental case for the legitimacy of same-sex sexual relationships that can be likened to marriage while at the same time contouring the upmarket consumerist ambitions of a new generation of socially aspirant gays and lesbians. In a rare gesture of topicality within an otherwise vintage adaptation, the Ford and Scearce screenplay places the long-term relationship between George and Jim at the melodramatic heart of the film. It is not that this relationship doesn't feature in Isherwood's novel: it does, but as something to be grieved and let go in ways that are mostly beyond George's ken. When the novelistic George forthrightly defends his feelings for Jim, he is scarcely to be trusted. Addressing his straight neighbor, Mrs. Strunk, in terms that will ultimately find their way into Firth's dialogue barely altered, George insists that she is wrong if she thinks "Jim is the substitute I found for a real son, a real kind brother, a real husband, a real wife. Jim wasn't a substitute for anything. And there is no substitute for Jim, if you'll forgive my saying so, anywhere" (17). The film script drops the note of faux apology in favor of a less bitter, more hurt outburst against substitution that George directs at Charley after her insinuation that his and Jim's relationship was not like a marriage. But in the novel this conversation never happens—not with Charley, not even with Mrs. Strunk. It is simply a train of thought—one of many running through George's head as he pleasurably empties his bowels sitting on the toilet reading John Ruskin on taste. Indeed, it would be truer to say that insofar as the novel generates any insight into the nature of long-term relationships, homosexual or otherwise, it tends to press the case for rather than against erotic substitution. The fact that George's melodramatic fantasy of defending his homosexual love for Jim against heterosexual outsiders occurs while his body is anally engaged is the first of many indications that the novel values displacement—upward, outward, bodily, social, aesthetic—as a highly generative process capable of establishing sexual equivalencies across seemingly disparate entities: the anal and the cerebral, the loved and the despised, the beautiful and the flawed, the real and the fantasized.

To take just one example of this adaptive capacity for homosexual substitution, late in Isherwood's novel, George masturbates himself to sleep. Things start well enough until, insufficiently excited by the thought of Kenny and his girlfriend, or Kenny and the dark-haired tennis player seen earlier in the day, George seems about to lose his erection. "Quick," the narration calls out, "we need a substitute," before "George hastily turns Kenny into the big blond boy from the tennis court." Substituting one imagined body for another until the "fierce hot animal play" begins, the now hard George slides efficiently into the pleasurable position afforded by free indirect style, the first principle of which is substitutability: "George hovers above them, watching; then he begins passing in and out of their writhing, panting bodies. He is either. He is both at once" (147). In this fantasy state of embodied impersonality, George comes before fondly resuming his own "slack and sweating body" and wiping his belly dry, a brute action unthinkable on the thousand-thread sheets that Ford's George fusses over while planning his suicide. In the novel, Isherwood's narration proceeds to push his snoring protagonist across the threshold of sleep, a state in which other partially personal, partially impersonal, processes engage: "Just barely awash, the brain inside its skull on the pillow cognizes darkly; not in its daytime manner. It is incapable of decision, now. But, perhaps for this very reason, it can become aware, in this state, of certain decisions apparently not yet made. Decisions that are like codicils which have been secretly signed and witnessed and put away in a most private place, to await the hour of their execution" (148). Introducing an interval between the signatory moment and the execution of will it authorizes, this place of partial cognition enables recognitions that would be questioned in the daytime regime that insists on personal uniqueness and the rational intent with which it is thought to be coterminous: "This is where he found Jim. He believes he will find another Jim here. He doesn't know it, but he has started looking already." Unlike melodramatic feeling that thrives on "condensed singularity" and the irreplaceable, this state of suspended autonomy orients the body on the bed toward metonymic substitution: "Damn the future. Let Kenny and the kids have it. Let Charley keep the Past. George clings only to Now. It is Now that he must find another Jim" (149). Instead of supporting a sexual economy—like the legal state of matrimony—in which there can be only one name, one Jim, the narration calls on its implied reader to secretly witness George's openness to any number of Jims, or Bills, or Dons, and their impersonally personalized substitutes.

Isherwood's novel, like his life, presents a form of domestic relationality that is not easily recuperated to the liberal template of same-sex marriage, if only because it acknowledges the unruly feelings that matrimony is institutionally required to disavow. Exhaustively recorded in the many diaries and memoirs that capture his daily life, Isherwood's sexually open relationship with Bachardy, which generated internal jealousies and resentments about which Isherwood was always honest and ashamed, was also captured by David Hockney in a double portrait from 1968 in which Isherwood glares across their Santa Monica living room at his emotionally remote boyfriend. Exactly how determinedly Isherwood, like many gay men of his generation, would press against the economic and social exclusions endemic to heterosexual

4.11
David Hockney, *Christopher Isherwood and Don Bachardy*, 1968. Acrylic on canvas, 83½ × 119½". © David Hockney. Photo credit: Fabrice Gibert.

privilege is evident in his late-life legal adoption of Bachardy, although it is less certain that he would have lent his name to the cause of gay matrimony.[37] As Kenneth E. Silver has elsewhere discussed, Hockney's domestic portraits of gay men, like Robert Mapplethorpe's images of sadomasochistic couples in their own homes, captures a homosexual domesticity that is not easily reconciled to the established discourse of conjugality.[38] Yet Hockney's double portrait of Isherwood and Bachardy also captures the emergence of the very thing that Ford's film exploits to the hilt: a nascent gay celebrity that, in combination with stylishness and a feeling for marriage, can operate as a point of identification beyond gay and lesbian constituencies.[39]

Laminating together emotionalism and style and carrying with it a credentialing history of social disenfranchisement, the gay mood that so many reviewers detect in Ford's film is all around us, concentrating its political effects in debates around marriage and adoption, topics in which gay communities have historically held little interest. In the Australian context from which I write, gay marriage is no longer a minor pink subset of broader marriage culture: it is the aspirational leader in the field, the brand that best represents the freedom to feel as a hard-won right and the epitome of social legitimation. Well over a decade ago, Lee Edelman famously argued that the child is the perfect carrier for the emotional touchstones and "reproductive futurism" on which US political discourse depends, whereas queerness is the carrier only for death and dead ends.[40] That may still be the case, but Ford's film also suggests that gayness in combination with celebrity style can be retooled as a universal vector for public feelings of aspiration, including the aspiration to feeling itself. Combining affective and consumerist satisfactions in a single aesthetic, Ford extends the appeal of homosexual style beyond its traditional subcultural networks into the impersonal space of the celebrity brand.

This brand of homosexual style does not find favor with everyone, least of all those that have already laid an intellectual claim to the category. In a series of monographs and essays that mark out his distinctive contribution to queer studies, D. A. Miller has demonstrated that whether literary or cinematic, nineteenth- or twentieth-century, homosexuality is first and foremost a property of style.[41] In his book-length discussion of Jane Austen, who is the classically ordained originator of the free indirect style that Isherwood adopts in *A Single Man*, Miller considers Austen's achievement of an absolute, impersonal narrative voice that is unmarked by age, gender, or marital status. Miller argues that Austen's celebrated "genius for detachment" allows the unmarried author to deflect questions about her own sexuality as she goes about skewering her characters, all of whom are caught up in the personalizing discourses of the eighteenth- and nineteenth-century marriage market.[42] From the vantage point afforded her by a sexually unmarked free indirect style, argues Miller, Austen surveys the social terrain of domestic romance and adopts a "way of *saying*" that is "constantly mimicking, and distancing itself from, the character's way of *seeing*," in particular their way of seeing marriage.[43]

What makes Miller's account of Austen's style so compelling—and why I invoke it in the lead-up to my impending discussion of remarriage—is that his book is driven by the impulse to top Austen's way of saying what other people see in marriage by saying something else about it in a similarly impersonal-personal way. In a deft overview of Miller's work occasioned by the publication of *Jane Austen, or the Secret of Style*, Heather Love has drawn attention to the way that Miller uncannily repersonalizes Austen's impersonal style by mimicking it in highly mannered prose that draws simultaneously on his own biography of class displacement and his immersion in twentieth-century gay popular culture, particularly the often-derided aesthetic achievement of musical theater.[44] Acknowledging that "the sociological impulse in Miller's writing is extraordinarily complex" insofar as his ethnographically precise "encounters with the real"—be it the real of a Broadway show or the real of a gay gym—are invariably "marked by irony and ambivalence," Love nonetheless contends that Miller is as interested in gay social history—"the institutions and real social spaces where gay life was made and where it has been sustained"—as he is in style.[45] Put the other way, and as unlikely as it seems, Miller's impulse to the gay demotic, and his long-term interest in gay subcultures that are richly marked by sexual, racial, and class differences, requires a gorgeous and brutal writing style that can be many things at once: funny and sad, butch and queenie, erudite and camp, masterful and abject. Crucially, Love compares Miller's embrace of the broad church of gay life to the contemporary rise of marriage equality which, in comparison, appears to offer gays and lesbians a narrower pathway of social ascension. It is in *Place for Us*, Miller's genre-bending ode to the gay affordances of the Broadway musical, that this ambivalence about social advancement—which Love confesses she shares with Miller to a certain degree—finds its fullest expression as "Miller reflects on the changes wrought by gay liberation and describes his mixed feelings about giving up the 'intense, senseless *joy*' of early 'destitutions.' He writes, 'No gay man could possibly regret the trade, could do anything but be grateful for it.' But as in so many narratives of upward mobility, regret is the name of the game."[46]

Miller's bittersweet account of gay social advancement takes on a different complexion, however, when he turns his attention to the mainstream embrace of marriage equality and the socially bland and sexually neutered version of homosexuality he thinks it emblematizes. Unlike his magisterially detached account of the Austenesque marriage plot, or even the affecting reference to his own former marriage that appears in the preface to *Narrative and Its Discontents*, when it comes to stories of gay marriage things get personal in a blunt way.

Although Miller takes a sophisticated pleasure in casting Austen as perverse maid of honor in relation to the eighteenth- and nineteenth-century marriage plot, he has less tolerance for contemporary writers or directors taking up a similar role in relation to the cause of marriage equality. In his contribution to the *Film Quarterly* roasting of Ang Lee's multi-award-winning *Brokeback Mountain* (2005), a film that explicitly twines the story of homosexuality with the story of marriage, Miller calls out those associated with the film for capturing the homosexual closet for heterosexual use via the self-congratulatory mechanism of liberal sexual tolerance.[47] While Miller finds Lee guilty of filmcraft, the quiet and discrete counterpoint to homosexuality's shameless style, he finds Annie Proulx, the author of the short story that became *Brokeback Mountain*, guilty of a "psychic mix of aggression, paranoia, and identification" that "can hardly be reduced to an innocent reflex of liberal good will." By evidence of her account of how the story came about, Miller credits Proulx with organizing a structure of narrational "sympathy" for the homosexual that maintains a penumbra of heterosexual "*disinterest*" around homosexual characters, as if they were freestanding entities who merely arrive in the fictional world under their own steam. Miller goes on to identify the film's sexually indifferent objectification of gay characters, and the related "self-disengagement" of its female author, as key to understanding the universal "protocol of liberal sympathy" that engaged around *Brokeback Mountain* more generally.[48]

In Miller's account, the Oscar-strength tolerance engaged around the film is not coincidentally lubricated by appeals to the widening gyre of marriage, which he describes as the desexualized cultural "imperium of the Couple and the Child":

> Here is the contradiction under which *Brokeback Mountain* "happens to be" well crafted. On the one hand, homosexuality is only interesting (marketable) if it is the occasion for rehearsing a fantasy of the Homosexual as thrillingly, pointlessly antisocial, a *bête noire* who must die. On the other hand, this fantasy is neither compatible with, nor even tolerable to, the liberal politics of homosexuality as we know them and as *Brokeback Mountain* would espouse them. Thus the film must give us, along with this fantasy, a "progressive" alibi for indulging it; even while trading on the fantasy, it must tame it into appearing to authorize the formation of gay marrieds with children.[49]

According to Miller, this conjugal "domestication" of homosexuality engages two textual strategies that determine the affective style of the film. "The first aims at reducing the sexual excitement" of man-on-man sexual action by making it cinematically tedious, "while the second deals with recycling the sexual waste" thematically. Making the attraction between Jack Twist (Jake Gyllenhaal) and Ennis del Mar (Heath Ledger) appear slow and deep, Lee's visual craft—specifically his cross-cutting of looks and the tying together of Ennis's marriage and his love for Jack—safely ensures that gay sex "signifies the socially redemptive values of 'love' and 'relationship' that alone can give gay sex meaning."[50] In association with the repression of sexual excitement, the technically proficient but boringly understated style of *Brokeback Mountain* renders homosexuality a sign for the universalism of married love, where such a thing is already understood as the dull conduit for socially responsible feeling.

Miller's account of diversity politics getting their deadening grip on homosexuality through an "innocent and ineffable" film style geared to the scenic apprehension of a homoeroticism that is as readily conveyed in landscape scenery as anything else surfaced in a world in which marriage equality was still being debated.[51] Post–marriage equality, however, Miller's continued critique of contemporary cinema and its sexless promulgation of the gay marriage plot has drawn fire from gay admirers of Luca Guadagnino's *Call Me by Your Name* (2017) an adaptation of André Aciman's novel of 2007. Miller considers *Call Me by Your Name* a prime example of the "MGM," or the mainstream gay-themed movie, a category of film that enshrines gay love at the expense of gay sex and stylishly foregrounds itself as "*a thing of beauty*" so "overpowering, or overdone," that it "persuades viewers they are watching a masterpiece, 'gay sex or not.'"[52] In his defense of Guadagnino's film, David Greven describes Miller as one of a generation of Foucauldian-influenced critics who, unlike their gay forbears, no longer champion "beauty, aesthetic sophistication and rigorous craft" but are "unyieldingly adamant arbiters of what counts as appropriate representations not only of gay male sexuality but of sexuality itself."[53] Greven goes on to argue that "a key dimension of this fastidious approach," which he also finds in the work of David Halperin and Michael Warner, "is that anything that smacks of personal investment—emotional ties, personal and mutual—must be evacuated from any depiction of sex and sexuality." This turn against the turn against gay marriage, which Greven associates with an unyielding, theoretically driven style of writing about film, is in keeping with the championing of an open-access gay style—a beautiful, sophisticated, rigorous, and deeply personal aesthetic that could be appreciated by anyone, gay or straight—such as I detect in Tom Ford's film, which puts itself forward as a putative remedy for some of the coarser aspects of straight culture—homophobia, misogyny, racism, and, dare I say it, bad dressing.

Exactly how Ford's gay universalism, to borrow Miller's term, extends its affective and entrepreneurial claim on the world deserves serious attention for what it tells us about contemporaneous changes in film style and the need to develop new reading strategies in response to them. It is worth recalling, for instance, that Ford's film, which begins with the intertitle "Fade to Black," involves the exorbitantly expensive realization of digital color grading, a process that allows the full expression of hue as opposed to celluloid film stock that, as Dyer has pointed out, developed as a technology engineered for the optimal illumination of Caucasian skin.[54] Although many have discussed Ford's thematic use of color, none have linked it to the way in which whiteness is assumed rather than engaged in a film that is otherwise at pains to establish its precise historical moment via reference to the Cuban missile crisis in October 1962, the same month that saw riots generated around the enrollment of the first black student, James Meredith, at the University of Mississippi, an event that seems inexplicable within the placidly nonsegregated student body that mills around on George's Brooks College campus.⁵⁵

In her account of Ford's chromophilia, Kirsten Moana Thompson points out that *A Single Man* combines three different color modalities, all of which derive from different historical moments: first, up-to-the-minute digital color tools applied to analog film in postproduction to produce progressive saturation or desaturation effects; second, a period color design that derives from the 1960s moment when "Technicolor was marked as fantastic" as both "cinema and television shifted from black and white to Eastman color as normative register"; and, third, a contemporaneous pop art aesthetic that is attentive to psychedelic color as seen in the vivid red, yellow, and blue pencil sharpeners that Kenny and George flirt over in the college stationary store.⁵⁶ Seamlessly united, these three different color modalities produce the film's emotional palette or what film color specialist Barbara Flueckiger calls "film's skin," the material membrane that captures both "subjectively infused surface colors in the diegesis" and "their visual representation on the screen." Flueckiger argues that color of this kind—a new amalgamation of analog and digital technologies that are themselves subject to fading in ways we are only beginning to experience—is not merely a means of focalization for expressing a character's inner state of feeing but a powerful instrument "connecting characters' moods and affective states to the audience's bodily reception by directly addressing their sensory and affective responses."⁵⁷ Created through digital animation processes that mimic earlier film processes of dye transfer, Ford's colorist style activates an impersonally personal membrane that appeals to an embodied feeling of history while bleaching out the sexually and racially diverse coordinates of the gay world captured in Isherwood's source text and other early sixties classics such as *Another Country* and *City of Night*.⁵⁸

The coloring of marriage equality is not limited to the racial whitening its critics have observed but bleeds into other domains that are less susceptible to critical castigation. In her astute discussion of *Carol* (2015), Todd Haynes's adaption of Patricia Highsmith's midcentury lesbian romance *The Price of Salt* (1952), Patricia White focuses on the pair of gray-green, kid leather gloves that brings the characters played by Cate Blanchett and Rooney Mara together across the social distance that would otherwise keep separate the middle-class fashion plate and the shopgirl who serves her. White relates the film's aesthetic style to the advent of same-sex marriage with which it seems historically out of step: "There is a sense of belatedness about the whole project—a quiet, period lesbian film released just as marriage equality is guaranteed in the United States."[59] Instead of finding this a flaw in the film, White goes on to argue that the pleasurable surfaces and commodified bourgeois lightness of *Carol* "thwarts those who would read the film as a realistic picture of how hard it was to love your own sex 'back then' before marriage equality."[60] Rather than making melodramatic claims to historical realism on behalf of an imagined constituency of contemporary homosexuals and their straight supporters, everything in Haynes's film, particularly the coolly aggressive feline performance the director draws from Blanchett, is a throwback to the dated pulp trope of the predatory lesbian. Far from being an emotive vehicle for same-sex marriage, writes White, *Carol* is a "retrospective fantasy of a film of the 1950s" that pays allegiance to the all-encompassing state of sexual obsession.[61] Sometimes a glove is a glove, but other times it is a visceral reminder that fetishism thrives in aesthetic realms in ways that defy realist reading practices and the politics we build on them. When we attach to anyone or anything, even something as seemingly stout as the institution of marriage in either its exclusive or inclusive forms, how many of us can say where that attachment comes from or where it might end? For that we need a theory of attachment or, better still, a theory of reattachment such as Stanley Cavell provides in his account of remarriage comedy.

5 Lisa Cholodenko's Attachment Trilogy

If three things resembling each other is enough to found a series, then the three feature-length films Lisa Cholodenko has written and directed since graduating from Columbia film school constitute a trilogy, whether or not she intended them that way. The formal affinities among *High Art* (1998), *Laurel Canyon* (2002), and *The Kids Are All Right* (2010) are so strong that it is barely an exaggeration to say that every Cholodenko film has the same urnarrative: a sexual and emotional ingénue arrives in a tightly circumscribed social world that both resembles and departs from a conventional family. That unconventional world, which is associated strongly with both place and professional activity, has at its heart an established couple whose seemingly secure erotic bond is marked by deep ambivalence. Across the course of the film this dyadic bond will be stretched beyond recognition as it bends to the presence of the sexual outsider, who is first incorporated into, then ejected from the pseudofamilial world, which, having been put through a series of expansions, returns to a semblance of its original form. Although irreparably altered, the established couple survives—may even be strengthened by—the sexual, spatial, and professional infidelity that forms the central plot of the film. No longer disavowed, the ambivalence that has marked the couple's formation from the outset is now understood to be fundamental to their ongoing attachment. The professional-familial world goes on. Allowing for numerous internal doublings and transpositions of the basic formula, this narrative pattern can be found in all three Cholodenko films, whatever their minor differences. Whether the couples and those whom couples counseling prosaically describe as "thirds" are straight, gay, or bisexual; maternal, paternal, or filial; motivated, situational, or opportunistic; whether the worlds they inhabit are those of art photography, popular music, or medicine; whether their compulsions are addictive, obsessive, or narcissistic, the common story is basically the same, as is the lesson that attends it: attachment is always ambivalent, that is part of its satisfaction. End of story. Or, begin again.

But what does it mean for Cholodenko to repeat this particular story? Is her attachment to the story of attachment itself ambivalent, a case of being stuck, or a case of working through? Does the narrative repetition represent an inability to move on or constitute a satisfaction in its own right? Is repetition a consolation for the failure to attach to something new or a form of fidelity to the story of infidelity as couple maintenance? As counterintuitive as it seems, the idea that fidelity is to be found through infidelity is not original to Cholodenko but has been a standard Hollywood trope since the divorce comedies of the 1930s and 1940s, the genre from which Stanley Cavell famously distilled a subgenre of films that he christened the "comedy of remarriage."[1]

To Cavell's way of thinking, the seven Hollywood films that epitomize the subgenre—*The Lady Eve*, *It Happened One Night*, *Bringing Up Baby*, *The Philadelphia Story*, *His Girl Friday*, *Adam's Rib*, and *The Awful Truth*—are alike in advancing, through plots of marital estrangement and reconciliation, a utopian ideal of marriage as perpetual reattachment. For all their apparent difference and tonal range, Cavell insists that all seven films are marital romances in the Shakespearean sense, which is to say that their narratives begin "with a divorce, or some equivalent separation," and end, "not as in classical comedy, with a marriage, but with a remarriage." Crucially, the story of the film or "the adventure of getting the pair not simply together (which had already happened), but together again, back together, is not one of overcoming external obstacles to their union, but one of overcoming internal obstacles."[2] The revivification of marriage that Cavell traces in these films both confirms the Freudian psychoanalytic insight that "the finding of an erotic object is in fact the refinding of it" and imaginatively relegitimates marriage in an era in which divorce has become a socially accepted middle-class phenomenon.[3] Instead of abandoning marriage as a socially tainted form, the notion of remarriage acknowledges the possibility of divorce while keeping the institution relevant to the pursuit of happiness more widely conceived. Since the current era of marriage equality presents a similar quandary insofar as the institution of marriage now includes what it was previously thought to exclude, it should come as no surprise that the trope of remarriage might lend itself to the task of realigning marriage with queer-inflected expectations around intimacy.

For all that Cholodenko's serial retellings of the story of detachment and reattachment are generically alike, they are also generically different from each other. Broadly speaking, the individual films in the series frame their common couple-come-undone story as tragedy (*High Art*), comedy (*Laurel Canyon*), and romance (*The Kids Are All Right*). This particular combination of resemblance and departure—the thing that makes Cholodenko's films so similar to each other while also so different—makes the trilogy an ideal intertext through which to calibrate attachment and detachment to the marriage plot, a story made newly relevant to lesbians and gays across the span of time in which these films appear. Although the third film in Cholodenko's trilogy is the first to center on a married-seeming lesbian couple, considering all three films as reiterations of each other brings to light their shared concern with the ambivalence at the heart of all attachment, whether it takes a socially normative form or not.

The film that inaugurates Cholodenko's attachment trilogy is already a repetition insofar as it borrows much of its setup from Rainer Werner Fassbinder's *The Bitter Tears of Petra von Kant* (1972): "Twenty-five years after *Bitter Tears*, the story of the lesbian ménage repeats: a woman, who shares an apartment with her female lover, remains an impotent observer as an affair unfolds between her girlfriend and another heterosexually identified woman whose motivation remains unclear, doubled as it is between erotic and professional aims."[4] Although this remains an accurate account of *High Art*'s point-to-point relation to Fassbinder's film, other critics downplay the intertextual connection. B. Ruby Rich, for instance, notes the relation to *Bitter Tears* but prefers to concentrate on the freshness of Cholodenko's film by describing it as "a sexy read of a triangulated lesbian relationship such as we'd never seen before on screen," even though the "lesbian infidelity, bisexuality, drug use, social climbing, ambition, and opportunism" that *High Art* catalogues can all be found in Fassbinder's original.[5] Captivated by Cholodenko's "cold-eyed view" of "ambition, greed, emotional blackmail" and all the other behaviors usually left out of lesbian-themed films, Rich issues a call for more films that expose "all the dirty lesbian secrets: the power plays, the naked lust, the sick transference," and other "less savory aspects of our most intimate interactions with those we claim to love."[6] In cinema, as in life, be careful what you wish for. Rich's fantasy of a no-holds-barred account of a lesbian relationship squares remarkably well with the plot of *The Kids Are All Right*, Cholodenko's third film, which reveals the power plays and sick transference between a dysfunctional couple undone by naked lust. Showcasing A-list actors and nominated for multiple awards, *The Kids Are All Right* is in due course cited by Rich as a textbook example of a crossover hit whose mainstream success alienates and divides its minoritarian community audience, which responds viscerally to an implied "interplay between lived behavior and behavior as modeled in movies." Stepping back from some of the more "contrarian" responses to the film and its alleged sexual stereotyping, Rich muses on the difficulty of telling "the difference between a desire that's organic to the self and one that's implanted by the media."[7] In producing this intervention as if it were an external point of analytical leverage, however, Rich misses the fact that this is precisely the question that drives all three of Cholodenko's films: where do attachments come from and what is the difference between their instinctual and mediated forms?

All three films in the trilogy observe the easy making of new attachments and the persistence, often awkward or difficult, of established attachments. That is, as much as they are about infidelity and sexual novelty, Cholodenko's films are also about fidelity and the perseverance of engrained attachments in the face of disavowal or public dishonoring. In a more Cavellian mode, we might say that the problem identified in these films is not the sexual covenant of marriage but its dissolution, or the inability to break bonds that have ostensibly outlasted their sexual and social utility. The persistence of attachment beyond its origins in couple love is most problematic in *High Art*, where both old and new attachments are repeatedly likened to addiction. A homage to the AIDS-ravaged world of 1980s New York and Berlin photographically captured in Nan Goldin's *Ballad of Sexual Dependency*, *High Art* reveals that dependency is everywhere, not just in people's reliance on drugs but in their reliance on each other, whether through love, friendship, illness, professional indebtedness, or plain sucking up.[8] Everything in the film is shared—the drugs in constant use, the apartment that comprises the main setting of the film where multiple people come and go, the artist's book that one woman lends another, even the car that sets the scene for lesbian seduction, and the country house that briefly holds the promise of rehab. Dependency, or the inability to set clear boundaries, also extends to the way in which reality cannot be divided from representation within the film's diegetic world and in the relation of the diegetic art world to extradiegetic models, such as the way that the character of Lucy Berliner (Ally Sheedy) and her art practice seems modeled on Goldin's, or the way her German girlfriend Greta (Patricia Clarkson) seems to share her backstory with Hanna Schygulla, who starred in *Bitter Tears*, or even the way that the editorial brief of the fictional *Frame* magazine recalls *Artforum* in the 1980s when it had the openly lesbian Ingrid Sischy at its helm. Where others have read the narrative recycling and aesthetic "self-referentiality" of *High Art* as consistent with its up-to-the-minute queer challenging of "heteronormativity and identity-based representations of desire," it is hard to ignore the film's dogged insistence on attachment and dependency.[9] While the suturing together of sexual attachment and dependency has strong theoretical credentials insofar as sexual instincts are often thought to have their origins in the state of infantile dependency, Cholodenko seems

5.1
Greta and Lucy: the ballad of sexual dependency
(*High Art*, Lisa Cholodenko, 1998).

more interested in how patterns of wanting find satisfaction at all, let alone in other people on whom we might feel a need to depend.

In *High Art* the question of how to secure or extend satisfaction gets addressed head-on when Lucy, the older, more experienced woman, finally takes Syd (Radha Mitchell), the younger, straight-identified woman, to bed and, in one of many reversals of the standard sex scene formula, lets her establish the sexual tone and pace. Like the overly ambitious intern she is, Syd keeps checking in with Lucy to see if she's doing everything right—"What should I do to you?" "Whatever you want to do to me." "I don't really know what I'm doing." "You're doing fine." "Should I pinch you or bite you or something?" "If you want to"—before the sex scene ends with the declaration of love that would more conventionally launch it. Similarly, Syd's not knowing what she wants but nonetheless knowing how to go about getting it is the key plot driver of the film. When Syd assures her placid boyfriend, James (Gabriel Mann), that she hasn't slept with Lucy, he asks her if she is "working up to it." While James seems to understand that the entrenched familiarities of old attachments can scarcely compete with the adrenaline rush of new attachments, Cholodenko's film reveals that they are not entirely invalidated by them either.

What makes Syd an unreliable proposition in other people's lives is not her bisexuality but her capacity to extract anything she wants from the situation she finds herself in. Lucy, who finds Syd an enlivening antidote to her own inertia, calls this quality her "drive." Others, however, are less beguiled by

5.2
Syd and Lucy: the hit of new attachment
(*High Art*, Lisa Cholodenko, 1998).

Syd's sexual and professional ambition. Greta, who refuses to use Syd's name, keeps coining new monikers to capture her destructive greediness: a "little sycophant," she calls her in her sensual German drawl, a "bootlicker," a "parasite," before nailing her as a "fucking teenager." As played by the twenty-year-old Mitchell, Syd is all this and more, a big-eyed, plump-lipped blond whose flawless skin is often the only source of radiance in darkly lit interiors filled with needle-thin druggies. As the film progresses it becomes clear that Syd is a walking, talking instantiation of D. W. Winnicott's aggressively noncompliant child insofar as she keeps testing the resilience of those who support her without incurring risk to herself. As if she were an actual infant, Syd is frequently seen toileting or in scenes in which her good-enough boyfriend anticipates or responds to her barely articulated needs for food and sex. After Syd takes drugs with Lucy for the first time, for instance, the younger woman returns to the downstairs apartment to find James asleep in their bed. She straddles him without a word and proceeds to fuck him awake in a reversal of type that recalls Winnicott's account of resourceful dependents and their capacity to turn caregivers into objects of scorn in the process of healthy development.[10]

While the second and third films in Cholodenko's attachment trilogy are explicitly concerned with processes of individuation between parents and children, it is startling to realize how much of *High Art*, with its seductive depiction of a queer-inflected art world, is also concerned with dependency

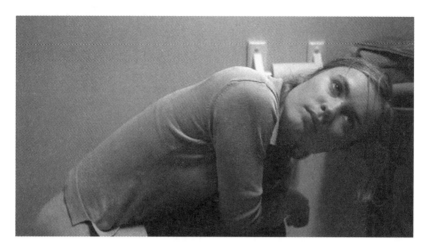

5.3
The toilet of the noncompliant child
(*High Art*, Lisa Cholodenko, 1998).

management protocols first learned in childhood. As sexy as the film is, or perhaps at the root of its sexiness, is the surprising amount of mutual, passive-aggressive, limit setting its characters go in for. When Syd seems bothered by Lucy's proposal that they use their weekend alone together to get high, Lucy turns the tables on her by suggesting she is the one acting like a child: "What is this? Is this some kind of intervention thing? Is that it? What is the point, Syd? Just be an adult. Just say it!" Like a case-study child, Lucy is shown to derive her skills in manipulation and countermanipulation from her relationship with her mother, whose family escaped the Holocaust. In the two scenes we witness between Lucy and her mother, the only love in the room is "mouth love," a greedy fusion of appetite and aggression expressed through the incessant smoking and eating both women engage in as they bicker away.[11] "I didn't give you enough what?" the mother sneeringly asks her daughter, as if there was ever enough of anything to go around, while she kvetches about Lucy's failure to succeed and her decision to take up with a German girlfriend. When Lucy mentions Syd, her mother is momentarily buoyed at hearing a man's name before her daughter confesses her drug problem. "I can't help you with that," she says, before leaving the room, never to return.

Greta, whom Clarkson plays as an alluringly droll narcissist, understands the threat that Syd poses both to her relationship with Lucy and their shared world, a Goldinesque environment that hosts an entourage of friends whose nonthreatening dependencies are calibrated through drugs, liquor, art, and

5.4
Immersive enchantment
(*Laurel Canyon*, Lisa Cholodenko, 2002).

nonsexual play. When Greta comes to on the floor of the bathroom after a drug overdose, she immediately screams for Syd's removal from the apartment as if her life depended on it. Earlier, when Syd first enters Lucy and Greta's apartment in order to fix the bathroom leak that sets the romance plot in motion, Greta introduces herself by saying in heavily accented English, "I'm Greta, I live for Lucy. I mean I live here with Lucy." Purring through her lines like Marlene Dietrich, Greta speaks the tongue-tied language of dependency and so reveals what might otherwise be overlooked within this louche, nonnormative world: there is no independence without dependency.

In *Laurel Canyon*, the second film in Cholodenko's trilogy, the fraught relation between dependency and independence is at issue within a mother-son dyad played by Frances McDormand and the boyishly handsome Christian Bale. For all its bisexual playfulness and scenes that teasingly take characters to the edge of sexual infidelity only to pull them back again, *Laurel Canyon* is primarily concerned with maternal attachment and mother-child differentiation, as well as the ambivalence that persists inside adult relationships that seem destined to repeat infantile patterning. In this mother-dominated world, sexiness attaches to maturity rather than youth. McDormand's long-haired Jane retains a wry sweetness that rubs off on her younger boyfriend Ian, who, as played by the Chris Martin–lookalike Alessandro Nivola, seems oddly innocent despite his rock-star ways. The sexual eclipse of youth by age is most apparent in a nighttime pool scene in which Ian preambles a threesome with Jane and her son Sam's fiancée, Alex (Kate Beckinsale), an uptight New Englander who seems ready to give herself over to Californian ways.

Although the bisexual proposition embedded in the scene comes to nothing, it nonetheless captures the enchanted feel of the Laurel Canyon compound, a Richard Neutra–designed house whose lush garden conceals the sound studio where Jane is producing Ian's new album. This is the upturned world that mother and boyfriend, son and fiancée, temporarily share. It is also the place from which the straight-as-a-die Sam commutes to the Los Angeles hospital where he is completing a psychiatric residency. Unlike the lush green realm of the canyon, Sam's workaday world is defined by the fluorescently lit parking garage in which he lingers with Sara (Natascha McElhone), the medical colleague he has developed a crush on and who, like his fiancée, is long-limbed and long-haired, just like his mother.

Despite his psychiatric specialism, Sam has yet to understand that the precondition of independence is dependence, a recognition Winnicott made after observing the relational matrix that exists between primary caregivers and infants. Instead, Sam has spent his life trying to establish his difference from his mother—a creative spirit in the Joni Mitchell mode—as if this, and the distance between East and West Coasts, were enough to secure his independence from her. That the about-to-be-married adult son is having trouble detaching from his mother, whom he thinks of as sexually immature, is made clear in the opening scene in which the sex Sam is having with Alex is interrupted by a call from Jane that, far from putting a break on things, appears to push his girlfriend to a sexual climax that had seemed out of reach only moments before. As the film's precredit sequence continues, we glimpse the world into which Sam has graduated, a WASP-y habitat filled with Harvard-trained medicos whose professional relationships are bound tightly through intermarriage of the kind he is now committed to with Alex, a biogeneticist completing a dissertation on the mating patterns of fruit flies.

The patriarchal coordinates of the conventional marriage plot quickly give way to the maternal hedonism of the Hollywood foothills as a low helicopter flyover sweeps us up the distinctive turns of Laurel Canyon Boulevard as the first bars of Mercury Rev's "In a Funny Way" burst through on the soundtrack, immediately calling up Phil Spector's opening arrangement for The Ronette's "Be My Baby," a song that fuses infantile demand and sexual need in a scenario in which love is still being measured out, even in conditions of satisfaction: "For every kiss you give me, I'll give you three."[12] In Mercury Rev's alt-pop remix, however, the near-nonsense lyrics rhythmically bolster the seductive fantasy of an erotic energy that knows no bounds or

5.5
The green world of Laurel Canyon
(*Laurel Canyon*, Lisa Cholodenko, 2002).

insufficiencies: "Through the fields and the streams and the lakes and the trees and the grass and the logs run all my dogs, and I am home, home again. In the autumn air, you can see her smile, but in a funny way, she reminds you of a child." While the soundtrack cues in a return to the innocent landscape of childhood, the image track confirms Reyner Banham's pastoral account of the Hollywood Hills as an "unimproved wilderness" that retains an "air of deeply buried privacy."[13] This hidden alt-enclave resembles the enchanted world Cavell considers integral to remarriage comedy, "a place, once removed from the city of confusion and divorce," to which estranged figures repair in order to refind each other.[14]

As if untouched by time, the Laurel Canyon depicted in the film constitutes a creative ecosystem in which the protocols of 1960s counterculture still apply. This ethic is as evident in the intuitive practice that Jane oversees as music producer of Ian's band as in the nonexclusive sexual relationship she appears to have with him. That Jane's relaxed mode of production is also her mode of mothering seems confirmed by the gratuitous flashing of breasts that McDormand spontaneously adds to her scripted performance in one of the many scenes that occur in a music studio filled with professional musicians and sound engineers, nonactors all. Located at the bottom of the garden beyond the swimming pool, the studio—a noncompetitive, inclusive world of uninhibited play and dope smoking, just like the artist's loft in *High Art*—is the place where a plenitude of human impulses is channeled into the indie-rock ballads that define the haplessly sweet and sexually inconsequential tone of the film.[15]

In *Laurel Canyon*—and Cholodenko's trilogy more generally—sexuality is imagined as an immersive or environmental experience rather than an intentional drive toward objects of choice, let alone objects of choice that might become marriage partners. Supported by sound and image, rather than dialogue and character motivation, sexuality seems situational, especially in association with the various uber-LA locations explored in the film: swimming pool, recording studio, underground parking garage, celebrity-haunt hotel. Unlike the oedipal pool in which Dustin Hoffman's Benjamin Braddock sinks under the weight of his father's scuba equipment in Mike Nichols's *The Graduate* (1967), the maternal pool in *Laurel Canyon* is an illuminated space of bisexual play where characters explore the possibilities of connection without enduring consequence.[16] Even the muffled interior of the parked car that Sam and Sara sit in, cautiously arousing each other by talking about the kind of sex they would have with each other if they hadn't decided not to have sex, is a safe space, a Swedish-engineered station wagon that can withstand the impact of a thousand flirtations.

The prototype for this safely experimental space is, according to Winnicott, the relational matrix of mother and infant. Within the film it is clear that Sam thinks this child-centered environment was denied him by the many male and female lovers he knows his mother took throughout his childhood. Although Sam is professionally capable of providing a safe space for his patients, as when he defends the needs of a teenage drug user against the disapproval of the boy's mother, he is the one to breach the film's comic code when he lunges at Ian, whom he mistakenly thinks has slept with his fiancée. As the two men ineffectually wrestle each other around the floor of a suite at the Chateau Marmont, Jane is inadvertently hit in the face, which curbs the faux macho antics and refocuses attention on the unacknowledged aggression and residual hostility at the center of the relationship between mother and son. Embedded within a scene of misrecognition that would not be out of place in Leo McCarey's *The Awful Truth*, a film based on the assumption of infidelity, this accident ultimately permits the recalibration of affective dependencies until the right degree of acknowledgment can enable the right degree of separateness between mother and child. As McDormand and Bale run through the public spaces of the Chateau shouting at each other—"Stop shutting me out!" "Get some therapy!" "You're behaving like a two-year-old!"—the terms are set for their reconciliation the next morning in a poolside scene in which Jane assures Sam that she loves him in the infantile language of rock

5.6–5.7
Detachment and reattachment
(*Laurel Canyon*, Lisa Cholodenko, 2002).

'n' roll: "You're my baby, man." While we have repeatedly seen Bale aggressively take to the water in moments of stress, he is now caught in the early morning glow of a Californian sunrise and seems vulnerable and easy to love, a loose-limbed boyish man, not the sublimation machine we have previously seen doing laps in an attempt to vent sexual and filial frustration.

That the pull of attachment makes children of us all is made patent in the final scene of the film. Standing in the pool, his formerly pale East Coast body now bronzed and fit, Sam takes a phone call from Sara, whose sultry European accent can be heard renewing its erotic claim on him. Before Sam can respond, he sees Ian float past on an inflatable mattress that is attached

122 · Chapter 5

5.8
Suspended in the maternal pool
(*Laurel Canyon*, Lisa Cholodenko, 2002).

by a rope to a miniature speedboat that slowly tugs him across the screen. Driven by a remote-control unit the camera angle places at the young man's groin, this silly mechanical appendage stands in for the impulse to attachment that continues to connect the film's various characters in a mostly benign way, since, although the sexual boundaries between them have repeatedly been tested, they have never yet given way. Sam asks Sara if he can call her back then puts down the phone. Floating in a sensual universe without social prohibition, Sam is suspended between his fraught attachment to his wife-to-be Alex, and his impossible-to-renounce attraction to Sara. He looks across the pool at his mother, who looks directly back at him and shrugs, knowingly, at the way of the world. Secure at last in his mother's love and newly engaged by the ambivalence that attends all satisfaction, the young psychiatrist submerges himself in the swimming pool, and the film's end is the only thing that can save him from having to resolve all the bidden and unbidden attachments that refuse to lessen their claim on him.

Cholodenko's final shot cites *The Graduate*'s famous bottom-of-the-pool shot in which the camera holds on the emotionally sunken son as a sound overlap brings in Anne Bancroft's voice as heard down a crackling phone line.[17] With all the confidence of 1960s misogyny to draw on, Nichols's unambiguous editing establishes that this is the moment in which Benjamin realizes he must escape his overbearing father by commencing an affair with his mother substitute, Mrs. Robinson.[18] Uninterested in heavyweight oedipal scenarios, Cholodenko suspends her male protagonist in a state of liquid self-consciousness that is more consistent with Cavell's claim that comedies of remarriage typically involve inconclusive endings that reveal that "nothing about our lives is more comic than the distance at which we think about them," a quality he associates with the ontology of film and its capacity to change the way we view the world.[19] In *Laurel Canyon*, the observational perspective of remarriage comedy, which is typically aphoristic rather than narratively conclusive, rests on the affective realignment of mother and son, rather than the father-daughter relations Cavell detects at work in the Hollywood originals.

In the director's commentary that accompanies the DVD edition of the film, Cholodenko remarks that, although *Laurel Canyon* is a story about "fidelity" rather than the infidelity it toys with, its "joyfulness" derives from the fact that its five entangled protagonists are "not terribly attached to anything." Indeed, much of the love-play seems serendipitous infatuation whose best token is the AC/DC T-shirt that keeps appearing on different bodies in different scenes as relentlessly beautiful folk keep falling under each other's spell, as if this were a Californian midsummer night's dream. The first premise of this benign world of sexual enchantment is the absence of patriarchal authority, the very thing the third film in Cholodenko's trilogy takes up in a plot built around the appearance of a previously anonymous sperm donor, Paul, played by a sleepily disheveled Mark Ruffalo, in the lives of Nic and Jules, a married lesbian couple played by Annette Bening and Julianne Moore, and their teenage children.

The addition of male DNA to the story of attachment prompts a genre shift from comedy to romance, as Cholodenko's narrative template bends to accommodate a lesbian marriage and the possibility of its revivification. The green world of sexual enthrallment still features, but now it is represented by Paul's organic restaurant, with its roster of nubile female staff who are also his sexual consorts, and the Echo Park landscape project he undertakes with Jules, where Shakespeare's rude mechanicals have become the Hispanic laborers the lead characters disdain.[20] Nothing like the playfully drawn-out seduction scenes that percolate through *High Art* and *Laurel Canyon*, the initial sex scene between the rough-shaven Ruffalo and the palely freckled Moore, a figure film lighting usually makes radiant, seems a clumsy exercise in sexual calisthenics. In contrast to the fledgling threesomes in *Laurel Canyon* in which everyone seems to be cautiously testing boundaries, the sex between consenting adults in *Kids* is either a mad rush of impulse or, in the case of lesbian marital sex, a carefully choreographed script that needs a kick start

5.9–5.10
Man on the land
(*The Kids Are All Right*, Lisa Cholodenko, 2010).

in vintage gay motorcycle porn.[21] Against these sexual alternatives, the teenage children look well balanced if a bit anodyne in the way they negotiate complex relationships with their parents and pseudoparents, friends and pseudofriends. Indeed, they prove themselves capable of both making new attachments and breaking old ones when they cease to serve developmental need, something their two mothers struggle with. Overall, we might say that the film is interested in the relation between satisfaction and dissatisfaction, or the use to which we put other people in order to meet our own needs, whatever they might be. Although all three films in the trilogy play with the idea that grown-ups might refuse the sexual temptations life offers them, together they incline toward the idea that attachments can be neither summoned nor renounced, only experienced in varying degrees of ambivalence.[22]

Within *Kids* this I-love-you-some, I-hate-you-some dynamic finds its anthem in the Joni Mitchell song Bening sings at the dinner table shortly before she realizes she is being cheated on by her wife and the father of her children, a scenario that would seem idiosyncratically lesbian if it were not so Shakespearean, like a queer reboot of the moment in *The Winter's Tale* in which Leontes accuses his pregnant wife of infidelity and, convinced that she bears his male friend's progeny, not his own, orders the infant to be abandoned in the wilderness when born. Both scenarios engage the infantile mechanism Winnicott finds at the heart of all attachment testing, namely our tendency to project our worst fears onto the world in order to have them denied. You have abandoned me. You have returned.[23] From this perspective, Winnicott's theory of attachment is already a theory of reattachment, which finds its generic expression in remarriage comedy as defined by Cavell: if, "in classical comedy people made for one another find one another," he writes, "in remarriage comedy people who *have* found one another find that they *are* made for each other." In order to work its magic on estranged partners, this refinding must be accompanied by "the willingness for remarriage" as "a way of continuing to affirm the happiness of one's initial leap." In Cavell's mind this willingness is not just confirmation of the rightness of the initial falling in love but also confirmation that "the chance of happiness exists only when it seconds itself."[24] In retrospect, and knowing everything we know, we were right to love each other, and now we rightly can again. However, and it is a big however, this willingness of the estranged couple to second each other in remarriage—a willingness *The Philadelphia Story*, probably the most famous of the Hollywood remarriage comedies, tests by having James Stewart's Mike, the man to whom Katharine Hepburn's Tracy has been most romantically responsive through the film, plausibly offer her his hand in marriage before she impulsively commits to remarrying Cary Grant's Dexter—is harder to find in films in which the fact of sexual infidelity is established within the story.

Rather than confirm or deny infidelity, *Laurel Canyon* weaves a tale of misrecognition in which Sam mistakenly thinks his fiancée has betrayed him with his mother's boyfriend just because he sees her sitting on an unmade bed while putting on her brassiere. The comic element lodged in the scene for the audience's delight is the fact that it never crosses Sam's mind that his fiancée might have been thinking of betraying him with his mother as well. The humorous distillation of sexual knowingness in a scene that might otherwise tip toward anger and recrimination recalls those moments in the original

5.11–5.12
I love you some, I hate you some
(*The Kids Are All Right*, Lisa Cholodenko, 2010).

Hollywood comedies of remarriage that play with the remit of the Production Code, such as the scene in Frank Capra's *It Happened One Night* in which the "Blanket of Jericho" strung between two single beds is all that keeps Claudette Colbert safe from Clark Gable's "trumpet." In Cavell's discussion of Capra's film, he puts forward the case that the bond of marriage can be neither mandated nor revoked by any civil code but can only be experienced as a form of "promise" in which "what this pair does together"—including the things that Production Code films can only imply they might do together—"is less important than the fact that they do whatever it is together, that they

Lisa Cholodenko's Attachment Trilogy • 127

know how to spend time together, even that they would rather waste time together than do anything else—except that no time they are together could be wasted." Given time, what the couples in these dialogue-driven Hollywood films chiefly do is talk. Or, as Cavell puts it, the seven comedies of remarriage stage exhilarating conversations in which seemingly broken couples learn "to speak the same language" and thus model for their audience forms of "erotic friendship" that take intensely social forms.[25]

But talk can also be a hindrance in the Hollywood comedies of remarriage. Cavell acknowledges that the problem endemic to the couple form is its inclination to closure, and that the closer it comes to perfect closure, the less sustainable it becomes. This couple paradox—that the sexual couple is inclined to turn its back on the ordinary social world it needs to survive—is, Cavell thinks, represented within the original Hollywood comedies of remarriage in the erotic drive to a language that is shared only by two, like the sublime banter between Cary Grant and Rosalind Russell that rises above the general hilarious babble of the newsroom in Howard Hawks's *His Girl Friday*, number five of Cavell's seven comedies of remarriage. It is this inclination to erotic isolation that the comedies of remarriage must keep in check, since the success of the couple form—its capacity to make a world in which one or, rather, two can do without others—can also be its undoing.

This paradox of the couple, or the fact that its sexual success can also be its social undoing, has queer implications insofar as Cavell's comedies reveal that the tendency to coupled isolation must be mediated by forms of community that are not reducible—perhaps not even compatible—with the claims of family. While much contemporary queer conversation advocates for the social recognition of chosen families and other elective kinship relations, Cavell maintains that it is not by chance that all seven of the classical comedies of marriage present childless couples as the idealized exponents of remarriage.[26] With the exception of Mr. Smith, the dog at the heart of the joint custody story that allows the estranged married couple to get back together in *The Awful Truth*, the swanky couples Hollywood deems remarriageable are alike in having no immediate claims on their affections other than each other. Give or take a fox terrier, it is the married but childless status of these couples that permits them to be standard bearers for the euphoric recalibration of the sexual and social impulses that all couples, straight or gay, need to thrive. Though Cavell relies on political theory to identify why in its classical manifestation remarriage necessarily excludes children, less philosophically trained minds might simply observe that his point seems confirmed by *The Kids Are All Right* in which children function as a social drag on erotic

5.13
Reattachment with child
(*The Kids Are All Right*, Lisa Cholodenko, 2010).

friendship, so much so that when the estranged lesbian couple make it back together the outcome seems almost depressive, certainly so in comparison to any one of the Hollywood comedies of remarriage the endings of which still light up with erotic promise decades after they first screened.

Whatever charms the teenagers played by Mia Wasikowska and Josh Hutcherson in *The Kids Are All Right* might be thought to have, those charms have nothing to do with whatever it was that originally brought their characters' lesbian mothers together. As many have pointed out, it is the kids who invite into the familial world the sexual third that confirms that the lesbian couple are already—possibly irreparably—out of sync with each other erotically, just as the children themselves are associated more with the breaking of attachments than the making of them: Laser breaks off with the best friend he has outgrown, and Joni discovers by kissing her male friend that there is no sexual tension between them. More importantly, the return of the sperm-donor plot makes clear that the making of queer family—and specifically the queer making of children—cannot be confused with the making of community needed to allow erotic friendship to flourish. In the seven films Cavell considers, not just children but their very possibility is banished to the extra-diegetic wilderness, which he interprets as an implicit message that children cannot assist the process of erotic seconding required by remarriage. *The Kids Are All Right* reaffirms this message by making the children initiate the infidelity plot that threatens to drive the couple apart. As it happens, the couple stays together

5.14
Resigned to marriage
(*The Kids Are All Right*, Lisa Cholodenko, 2010).

as a couple and, just as importantly, as a family, but that is not the same as the impulse to reenchantment explored in the earlier remarriage films that end having rekindled erotic friendship. If there is a lesson to be wrung from this observation, it might be that at some level Cholodenko's film suggests that while elective child-making makes for robust queer families, it is perhaps less of a community-oriented activity than elective childlessness, something that gays and lesbians have been very good at, historically speaking.

Acknowledging Cavell's point that in the comedies of remarriage it is community, not family, that enables erotic friendship to thrive, provides a new perspective on the reception of *The Kids Are All Right*, much of which seems to circle around precisely this issue: does family-making support or inhibit the sexual and social happiness of couples? While *New York Times* reviewer A. O. Scott enthusiastically describes the way Cholodenko uses the lesbian conceit to refresh "the ancient and durable wellsprings of comedy" by blending the "anarchic energy of farce—fueled by coincidences and reversals, collisions and misunderstandings—with a novelistic sensitivity to the almost invisible threads that bind and entangle people," most specialist academic commentary seems to miss the elements of Shakespearean romance and take straight the film's vision of domestic "normalcy."[27] In the *Journal of Feminist Family Therapy*, a self-described descendant of "lesbian matriarchs" approaches the film through a "family systems lens." Reading like case notes, the article validates Nic and Jules's capacity to raise "two developmentally normal adolescents" while querying "the role of the phallus in their relationship."[28] An article in *Sexualities* objects to the lackluster sex life *Kids* assigns its lesbian moms, while another in *Lesbian Studies* takes exception to the white homonormativity that gave the film its mainstream appeal at a time when gay activists were agitating against Proposition 8, the Californian state amendment that denied same-sex couples the right to marry.[29] Those articles that engage the bisexual perspective, however, tend to use the film's heterosexual infidelity story line as a stick to beat the unacknowledged gay and lesbian normativity that thrives under cover of queer scholarship.[30] Undaunted, queer-identified scholars took to a range of new media platforms to register their deep ambivalence about the film's representation of the attachment traps that hide in the vicinity of queer family life. In the form of an expanded listicle—part list, part article—Jasbir Puar and Karen Tongson challenge the negative "consensus" around the film's racial and sexual coordinates by insisting that the film be engaged as a "political and social satire about the possibilities and pitfalls of family formations" that "reminds us that the couple form, especially the reproductive couple form, is often not malleable enough to admit these other algebras of affect, attachment and even ambition."[31] Like two Cavellians in millennial mode, Puar and Tongson suggest that, whatever the couple form has going for it, that coupled something is compromised once its internal attachment mechanisms extend to children and make the closed circle of family the first measure of the social rather than other, more open, forms of queer community.

Writing about the film sometime after the critical heat turned down, Jodi Brooks refreshingly encounters *Kids* as the third installment in a series of Cholodenko films that are all concerned with "the spaces between queer and straight, between marriage and not-quite marriage, and between the imagined and the lived."[32] This cinematically complex space, she argues, is the space of disappointment. Noting that Moore has an "impressive history of playing disappointed women in the domestic sphere," Brooks goes on to argue that the film's "ambiguous treatment" of domestic disappointment intersects with "some viewers' disappointments with the film."[33] Thinking about the tonal shift that registers across the trilogy, Brooks points out that *Kids* is unlike *High Art* and *Laurel Canyon* in refusing to provide what they do, namely "worlds that are sexually knowing and visually intoxicating—worlds that turn around female characters who are charismatically indifferent to social expectations." In place of this sexually enchanted, immersive world, *Kids* substitutes a "squarely framed" suburban family home "offered to view with the same frontality as the family home in *The Brady Bunch*."[34] Through an analysis of the use of music in the film, and in particular the scene in which

Bening and Ruffalo perform their "artless" version of "All I Want," Brooks clarifies that disappointment "marks the distance between a then in which a future was imagined and a now in which another is lived."[35] This affective space, which Brooks describes as "an empty present suspended between yesterday's dreams and tomorrow's losses and between yesterday's moribund institutions and tomorrow's dead ends and entrapments," might also be termed remarriage dystopia or, in more Shakespearean terms, the space of disenchantment where the everyday realities of marriage reassert their claim over romantic idealization.[36] The melancholic experience of coupledom gone ordinarily amiss, which Brooks finds at the heart of *Kids*, is the very antithesis of the equally ordinary experience of reenchantment promised to those who marry once, marry twice, but always without children.

While Brooks calls for "something like a lesbian-populated *The Awful Truth*," which she imagines as "a queer comedy of remarriage that would blast apart marriage, transform festival into festivity, and release marriage from itself in favor of a broader spectrum of intimacies and forms of social connection," others have recently declined the offer of remarriage as being too good to be true.[37] Tania Modleski, for one, is not the remarrying kind but prefers to embrace melancholia, something she detects in bromance, a new subgenre that she approaches via the broader category of romantic comedy.[38] Bromance, Modleski argues, "flies in the face of traditional theories of romantic comedy," particularly those "advanced most forcefully by Stanley Cavell, which point to the upbeat utopian aspirations of the genre." In refusing romantic utopianism, Modleski is also explicitly refusing the political perfectionism that Cavell takes the genre to reflect. As if in accordance with the logic of folklore, Cavell sees the seven Hollywood comedies of remarriage as providing seven different perspectives onto the philosophical idea of America. Modleski reserves contempt for Cavell's idealizing enthusiasm for Hollywood perfectionism—a glamorous instantiation of the moral perfectionism for which he is more widely known. "Of course," she writes, "as many critics have noted, it is harder to make a case like Cavell's for many romantic comedies produced after the studio era." To strengthen her historical case against classical remarriage utopia, Modleski points to Woody Allen's *Annie Hall* (1977) as being the "supreme example" of a swatch of "so-called nervous comedies that began to appear in the sixties and seventies, in which couples do not end up together." Modleski thinks that these problem marriage films, with their anxious accounts of failed heterosexual coupledom, should be valued more than those slightly later films—like Rob Reiner's *When Harry Met Sally* (1989) or *Sleepless in Seattle* (1993), a film that explicitly updates the romantic storyline embedded in McCarey's *An Affair to Remember* (1957)—which, even as they frame romance as a film convention, "seem to buy into a belief in the power of romance and its utopian possibilities."[39] In a case of not having your remarriage cake and not eating it too, Modleski critically dismisses marriage comedy both in its generality and in its particular instantiation in specific films. This gesture precisely accords with what Cavell has memorably diagnosed as the "indiscriminate scorn of film study," by which he means both scorn for the study of film and the scorn heaped on the object of study by its practitioners. Cavell considers this scornful gesture, which Modleski repeats, to be a "continuation of America's contempt, or ambivalence, toward its best contributions to world happiness," namely the classical comedies of remarriage and popular Hollywood film more generally.[40]

In Cavell's original account of remarriage comedy, he argues that ambivalence must be acknowledged within the couple and mediated by the community the couple nests inside if ongoing attachment is to be secured. In the first two films in Cholodenko's trilogy, the community in question is the network of queer-friendly creatives that populate the art and music milieu of each film, like diegetic doubles for the independent film industry and post-broadcast television sector in which the director thrives. In *The Kids Are All Right*, however, the ambivalence that necessarily attends coupled attachment is mediated only by family, so that what lies ahead is not the garden of marital reenchantment, or the sublimations and rewards of creative collaboration, but at best the hard graft of conjugal reconciliation and therapy.

In 2004, over twenty years after the publication of *Pursuits of Happiness*, in the context of his second book on the same clutch of films, Cavell explicitly makes the connection between his interest in the Hollywood comedies of remarriage and the worldly expansion of the institution of marriage to include same-sex couples.[41] Although he is no longer around to take up this conversation, Cavell would not, I wager, be surprised to learn that the advent of same-sex marriage has reanimated the trope of remarriage as filmmakers attempt to find a new popular language of erotic promise that can resecure our attachment to each other, to community, and to a social world driven by utopian ambitions. Nor would he be surprised at the critical disparagement generated around this attempt. In the context of Cholodenko's attachment trilogy we might think of the sharpened condescension for popular reworkings of marriage comedy as a continuation of ambivalence about ambivalence, or the mixed feelings that attend attachments of any kind, including general attachments to marriage as they play out in the era of marriage equality.

6 Reattachment Theory

Anyone with the least acquaintance with couples counseling can testify to the strong hold that attachment theory has in the domain of contemporary relationship therapy, where, whatever the circumstance that brings you and your partner into the conversational three-way, somewhere along the line you will be invited to identify as one of three types according to a taxonomy that derives from John Bowlby's classic *Attachment* trilogy: secure, anxious-avoidant, anxious-resistant.[1] Derived from the study of infants and primary caregivers, attachment theory seems key to understanding entrenched problems within the couple form but also flourishes in all manner of critical contexts, from evolutionary anthropology to human-animal studies.[2] In the area of consumption studies, for instance, Elizabeth Chin has recently reframed D. W. Winnicott's notion of the transitional object as "a concept that naturalizes imperatives of capitalist consumer society," specifically the imperative of commodity fetishism, insofar as it "assumes that infants are entitled to private property."[3] While Chin points out that Western cultures are unique in training newborns to accept material objects as substitutes for bodily contact, something that begins in the context of infant sleep regimes but is reinforced in the wider realm of capitalist culture in which things are valued as possessions, many proponents of attachment theory exclude the social from their field of interest and concentrate on tracing difficulties in adult attachment styles back to infantile pathologies that appear innate in their grasp. For the purpose of thinking about the social proposition of gay marriage, something that has only recently come to the historical fore, I propose switching from an attachment to a reattachment analytic, a notion I derive from Stanley Cavell's account of marriage as remarriage, an idea he developed in relation to classical Hollywood comedies of divorce and reparation.[4]

Cavell has been widely criticized for the narrowness with which he initially sets the coordinates of remarriage comedy and the ease with which he then bends them in order to admit certain films.[5] David Shumway, in particular, insists that the elements that identify the remarriage subgenre—sparring repartee between a principal pair and an overall structure that first tests then reaffirms the social bond of marriage—can reliably be found in the wider genre of screwball comedy, which makes the distinction proposed by Cavell moot.[6] More recently, Elizabeth Kraft has engaged in a book-length conversation with Cavell in order to claim that the distinctiveness of remarriage comedy is prefigured in Restoration courtship drama, which likewise centers on couples engaged in battles of wit. Produced in a moment of great social change, the female characters at the center of these Restoration plays, who are for the first time in the history of professional theater played by actual women, speak "on an equal linguistic plane" as their male counterparts and are therefore as innovative as the new apron stages on which they strut. Noting that both Restoration stage drama and classical Hollywood film are products of a repertory system that draws on audience familiarity with the idiosyncratic qualities of specific actors as they resonate across different roles, Kraft argues that "both genres are notable for configuring central couples who possess verbal equality" even as they expose "the sexual imbalance of power or politics in its time."[7] Kraft argues that the Restoration dialogue traded between male and female actors on the Restoration stage, like Hollywood remarriage dialogue, is tuned to what Cavell refers to as the "sound" of a happy marriage, a form of conjugal comedy in which women's voices are heard alongside men's as they wrangle through "the quarrels of romance and the tirades of matrimony." As Cavell argues, and Kraft confirms, conjugal argument of the remarrying kind—a gendered conversation leading to mutual acknowledgment that does not descend into the cynicism that marks divorce comedy—depends on the capacity of certain actors, such as Clark Gable, Cary Grant, Katherine Hepburn, and Spencer Tracy, "to bear up under this assault of words, to give as good as you get, where what is good must always, however strong, maintain its good spirits, a test of intellectual as well as of spiritual stamina, or of what you might call 'ear.'"[8]

Although Kraft is interested in the social proposition of companionate marriage as it is investigated in both Restoration drama and Hollywood remarriage comedy, others sympathetic to the genre have tended to focus on what these films, and their intellectual inheritors, illuminate about the general condition of love and other abstractions, such as memory and time. This philosophical interest in the concept of remarriage coupled with a disinterest in marriage as a social and sexual achievement can be seen most clearly in the response to Charlie Kaufman and Michel Gondry's *Eternal Sunshine of the Spotless Mind* (2002), a film diegetically premised on the conceit that star-crossed lovers might erase their memories of each other. As the philosopher William Day notes, *Eternal Sunshine* was immediately linked with Cavell's account of remarriage comedy in reviews in the popular press, a connection that was pressed further in a second wave of specialist commentary. Day singles out Michael J. Meyer's reading of the film as a misreading of Cavell insofar as it places critical emphasis on the ethical gesture of reconciliation, which Meyer sees repeated throughout *Eternal Sunshine*, as opposed to Cavell's original and abiding concern with how reconciliation can be achieved only via the couple's "ongoing remarriage conversation."[9] By way of correcting Meyer, Day clarifies the philosophical coordinates of the remarriage conversation and, it would seem, its necessarily heterosexual coordinates:

> The characteristic story arc of remarriage comedies is the telling of a couple's journey from estrangement back together, a journey they accomplish through the uniquely human and uniquely philosophical form of intercourse we call conversation. What the remarriage conversation is about, amid the false starts and detours and occasional raised voices, is the nature of men and women: both the differences in their nature (which the couple may feel as the unspecified and unspecifiable but nonetheless palpable obstacle to their finding a way back together) and the nature of their desires, or the nature of human desire itself, which is the quintessentially philosophical wonder.[10]

Given the complacently cross-gendered coordinates of philosophical desire, is it any wonder that the remarriage conversation, which is premised on the natural differences between men and women, might begin to stutter as marriage becomes less exclusively tethered to heterosexual intercourse?

"We think of marriage, or have thought of it," writes Cavell in less gendered terms, "as the entering simultaneously into a new public and a new private connection, the creation at once of new spaces of communality and of exclusiveness, of a new outside and inside to a life, spaces expressible by the private ownership of a house, literally an apartment, a place that is part of and apart within a larger habitation."[11] Looking for a metaphor for marriage, Cavell is drawn to the apartment and its capacity to balance and intermingle the claims of domestic privacy and sociability. Like marriage, the liminal space of the apartment both privately protects and socially acknowledges domestic relationships, which is what made the cinematic apartment plot the preeminent chronotope for telling the story of homosexuality across the late twentieth century, a period in which gays and lesbians were still barred from getting married.[12] Across the opening years of the twenty-first century, however, many of the coordinates by which we plot lesbian and gay stories have changed, the most significant being the legal recognition of same-sex domestic partnerships and the partial absorption of a sexual subculture into the dominant marriage culture from which it had previously derived its outlaw status. Given the social rise of gay marriage, it should be no surprise that the apartment plot has been repointed in its direction, as can be seen to good effect in *Concussion* (Stacie Passon, 2013) and *Weekend* (Andrew Haigh, 2011), two films that derive their timeliness from the contemporary framework of gay marriage and deploy the materiality of apartment space to register the historical passing of an established conception of urban homosexual life. Despite their manifest differences in style and tone and the distinctive metropolitan and provincial imaginaries they engage, these two apartment films can be usefully compared to each other and aligned with a broader cycle of films (and television series) that address gay marriage, either directly or obliquely. As Cavell would say, even if they have no features in common, these two films "*are what they are* in view of one another" and share a reflective relation to the historical conditions that prompted their emergence in the first place.[13]

Indeed, the gay marriage cycle is now so substantive that it is possible to trace patterns and arcs within it that anticipate or respond to the emergence of gay marriage as a recognized structure of feeling prior to its codification in law. Most obviously, the previously dominant thematic emphasis on the social problem of the nonrecognition of same-sex relationships has receded in favor of an emphasis on the problem of discontent generated within same-sex relationships conceived on a continuum with straight marriages. Films that evidence the former include Ang Lee's *Brokeback Mountain* (2005) and Tom Ford's *A Single Man* (2009), both of which use the retrospectively animated framework of historical melodrama to convey a sense of injustice around the denial of long-term gay and lesbian partnerships in the here and now.[14] Films that evidence the latter include Stephen Daldry's *The Hours* (2002) and Lisa Cholodenko's *The Kids Are All Right*, plus the many television series that now incorporate disenchanted same-sex couples among their various configurations of modern families.[15] This is not an absolute shift, nor is it strictly chronological. Rather, the cycle retains its appeal and flexibility in being able to reanimate the theme of gay marriage from different perspectives and to different ends, often within the same text. In this sense, the cycle explores the problem of gay marriage that, like the problem of marriage in general, turns on the primary riddle of sexuality and its expression in attachments of more or less durable form.

As Michael DeAngelis reminds us in his introduction to a recent anthology addressing the rise of the bromance in contemporary film and television, in order to maintain audience interest, films that ostensibly celebrate certain thematic content—in the case of bromance, the possibility of nonsexual intimacy between men; in the case of gay marriage films, sexual intimacy between men or between women—necessarily present that content in the form of a problem either in itself, that is, as something that is attained only with difficulty, or in relation to wider social problems that restrict its articulation, such as heteronormative expectations. Though DeAngelis doesn't stress the relation between bromance and gay marriage, he does link the bromance cycle with the "problem marriage" cycle that emerged in the late 1960s and early 1970s, which he typifies as films that exploit "contemporaneous discourses of sexual liberation" but "generally ended up vilifying the same freedoms that they set out to celebrate."[16] This serves as a reminder that popular film has a long history of catalyzing new cycles that de-idealize—and re-idealize—marriage in response to changes in its social and legal definition as well as changes in the sexual and emotional expectations people bring to it.

According to Cavell, the greatest of those cycles is the Hollywood comedy of remarriage that arose once marriage was secularized by the easy availability and destigmatization of divorce. Emerging in the 1930s and linked to what Cavell describes as the first generation of women who did not have to settle for marriage but might nonetheless choose it, the dialogue-driven comedies of remarriage invariably respond to "the topic of divorce, which raises in a particular form the question of the legitimacy of marriage."[17] Cavell argues that these comedies, which are central to the evolution of the talkie, collectively investigate the terms on which marriage might be ratified anew as both an intimate and a socially utopian form that can meet the contemporary requirements of recognition and reciprocity that radiate out from the heterosexual couple as the first circle of community. Popular attachment to these films, he argues, reflects a complex reattachment to marriage, which in the wake of divorce must necessarily be approached as remarriage, as a revitalized commitment to a form about which no innocence, including sexual innocence, remains. Although the terms of Cavell's engagement with the Hollywood comedy of remarriage are irreducibly idiosyncratic, it is possible to distill from his discussion the simple observation that, at a moment in which the heterosexual assumption assumed cognate with marriage has been dealt a body blow by the social acceptance of same-sex marriage, whether or not that acceptance is canonized in law, we might expect to see a cycle of gay marriage films emerge that interrogate the terms on which marriage might retain its validity as a framework for happiness and social meaning.

If, as Cavell argues, all marriage is remarriage after the social legitimization of divorce, then post–marriage equality, all marriage can be conceived as gay marriage, at least for popular purposes. This renegotiation involves some obvious and some unpredictable critiques of marriage and its simultaneous narrative revitalization. However, since marriage continues to couple both its heterosexual and homosexual exponents with sexual and domestic routine, a notable feature of the gay marriage cycle is the consistency with which it utilizes the apartment plot for its established capacity to plot stories and relationships that speak to wider conceptions of fidelity than those normally associated with conjugality, whether straight or gay. In *Concussion* and *Weekend*, this redeployment of the apartment is key to both the critique of gay marriage and to its revival as an idealized form for the possibilities of sexual and social happiness across the board.

Stacie Passon's independent film *Concussion* is an exemplary instance of how the lesbian apartment plot is reinflected post–gay marriage. A quirky riff on Luis Buñuel's *Belle du Jour* (1967) and numerous other films in which an apartment facilitates sexual encounters outside the family home, *Concussion* tells the story of a sexually frustrated lesbian suburban mom, who, unsettled by a knock on the head, branches into same-sex prostitution from the Manhattan loft she is renovating for capital gain. Although the promotional blurbs that accompany the DVD offer sexual addiction as the framework through which to make sense of this plot, the film is fueled by the more mundane recognition that although marriage is founded in sexual attachment, it cannot guarantee the constancy of mutual attraction or the continued vibrancy of desire in the face of its domestication. At a glance, *Concussion* would seem less interested in engaging the problem of sexual renewal within marriage than imagining a sexual alternative outside it. Beneath the film's awkward occupancy of the codes of prostitution lies the more widespread lesbian wish to claim a symmetry with gay public sex cultures that are thought to assuage the sexual quiescence assumed endemic to long-term relationships in general and to lesbian relationships in particular via the supposed phenomenon of lesbian bed death.[18] Confirmed in both expert and popular discourses as the site for less and less sex across time, long-term lesbian relationships, some of which now take the name marriage, make patent the problem common to all marriage, which is that the institution designed for the social ratification of sexual attachment is also designed to extinguish it. This common problem—that the sexual promise of marriage includes the promise of its disappointment—is also common to common-law marriage, a state defined by habit and repute that many legally single men and women live in whether they want to or not.

Like many straight screen wives before her, *Concussion*'s stay-at-home lesbian wife is trapped in an idyllic New Jersey commuter town, but, unlike them,

6.1
I don't want this. What do I want?
(*Concussion*, Stacie Passon, 2013).

her dilemma has sexual coordinates that cannot be resolved through an appeal to feminism. The film starts crisply with a static title graphic over which a number of female voices can be heard trading the popular piece of advice that after forty a woman has to decide between her ass and her face. When the visuals kick in they reveal a spin class in process, a physical action that places ass and face on the same horizontal plane. The conversation drifts to sex before David Bowie's "Oh You Pretty Things" starts up, its piano-backed vocals perfectly geared to a midlife meditation on the inevitability of aging. As the soundtrack opens into Bowie's chorus, the camera drifts around the uniformly pretty things, row upon row of fit, slim, forty-something women bent to the task of exercise. Among them is Mrs. Abby Abelman (Robin Weigert), who, as this scene makes graphically clear, takes her place inside a matrimonial order in which lesbians are indistinguishable from the straight women who surround them.[19]

The dreamy opening sequence moves between scenes of women holding yoga poses and static shots of suburban houses and autumnal yards before it abruptly terminates with a rushed cut to an exterior scene in which Mrs. and Mrs. Abelman hustle two children toward a late-model SUV. Running beside her wife Kate (Julie Fain Lawrence), Abby clutches at her bleeding forehead, the result of being hit by a softball thrown at her by her son. Once in the car, the injured mother curses the child before declaring, apropos of everything—the car, the child, the pain—"I don't want this." An impulsive reaction that momentarily betrays the faltering of ordinary attachments within the family if not the fundamental ambivalence that drives mother love, Abby's declaration sets up the primary conundrum of the film: what do lesbians want, or, more specifically, what do lesbians want from marriage, now that they can have it?

As I will go on to demonstrate, Abby's declaration—"I don't want this"—might ultimately be read against the declaration that Cavell imagines at the core of *The Philadelphia Story*: "My dream of the story about Philadelphia is a story about people convening for a covenant in or near Philadelphia and debating the nature and the relations of the classes from which they come. It is not certain who will end up as signatories of the covenant, a principal issue being whether the upper class, call it the aristocracy, is to survive and if so what role it may play in a constitution committed to liberty."[20] If, under the intoxicating influence of romantic comedy, Cavell can argue that the covenant of marriage signed in *The Philadelphia Story* philosophically approximates the Declaration of Independence, then I feel obliged to argue more soberly that the conjugal arrangements eventually effected in *Concussion* approximate a Declaration of Dependence. Consistent with this inversion, the shift of the independence story from Philadelphia to New Jersey may also be seen to correspond to the decline of the upper class and the rise of the creative middle class who no longer express their eroticism through luxury items such as the no-lapel jacket famously worn by Grant as C. K. Dexter Haven but, like Abby, adopt a postyouth uniform of black leather pants and rock 'n' roll T-shirts that fly in the face of an imagined establishment. But that is to get ahead myself, philosophically speaking.

Judging by the evidence the film provides (endorsed by official selection at the 2013 Sundance Film Festival), what Abby wants is to abandon her suburban domestic routine—the house and yard chores, the school drop-off and pickup run—and tap back into the urban spaces that constituted lesbian life before it boiled down to being married with children. Principally, however, she wants sex, and it is this want that will stretch the bounds of her lesbian marriage back into apartment territory. The film makes clear that stay-at-home lesbian moms cannot rely on their working wives for sexual satisfaction, a situation efficiently scoped out in a scene in which a restless Abby wakes her partner for sex only to have her fall back to sleep midstroke. Abby's solution is to outsource the sex, in the same way we see her outsource the food she and Kate serve at their dinner parties. Without telling her wife, Abby contacts a low-rent call girl who works from a grungy apartment that brings out numerous inhibitions in her, all of which seem to have as much to do with hygiene or health as sex. Abby doesn't want to share drugs or sex toys. Barely seen, the sex takes place on an unmade bed in a cramped room completely unlike any of the other well-lit designer interiors that feature throughout the rest of the film. Afterward, in a scene in which the camera seems newly capable of movement and magnification, Abby has to check her impulse to clean the call girl's bathroom. She will later recall the whole thing as an off-putting encounter with "this very dirty person," something she would go a long way to avoid repeating.

Like generations of cinematic wives before her, Abby only has to go as far as Manhattan for things to change. The concussion that unsettles her sexually also prompts her to go back to work, a decision her wife encourages. Recognized among her New Jersey friends as a gifted interior designer, Abby's real talent is property speculation, buying up "shit box" apartments in the city and doing them up for quick resale, a project she embarks on with the assistance of a handsome young builder, Justin (Johnathan Tchaikovsky), a semi-intuitive, semi-sleazy guy who subsequently finds economic opportunity in assisting Abby to find sexual partners through his own network of swingers. Although a series of scenes shows Abby and Justin refurbishing an industrial loft, the work of flipping Manhattan real estate is soon superseded by the work of lesbian sex as Abby first orders in a high-end escort and then, reversing her role in the sexual commodity supply chain, starts turning tricks herself in the loft apartment.

None of this is presented as a cynical attack on marriage. At worst, Abby might have led herself to believe that she and Kate had tacitly agreed to her having sex outside the relationship. Like many unspoken understandings between intimates, this one hardly bears scrutiny. Early on in the film we see Abby and Kate eating a family dinner. As soon as the kids are excused from the table, the topic turns adult. Abby tells Kate that one of their friends is breaking up with her husband, and Kate, who is a divorce attorney, tells her to put her in touch and she will handle it for free. As the conversation continues, Kate asks a series of matter-of-fact questions ("So, who cheated? Who gets custody? Who gets the house? Is he paying alimony? What about the dog?"), whereas Abby remains preoccupied with the wife's feelings of emotional distress and panic: "She said she couldn't breathe." "That's code for what?" snaps Kate. "She couldn't breathe," Abby repeats, before Kate responds pragmatically, "So she should go breathe. It's sex. Grow up. Go breathe."

With this line and its implications of negotiated nonmonogamy left hanging in the air, a cut takes the action forward away from the suburban dining room to the newly painted apartment shell, an almost blank space in which Abby sits on the corner of the bed waiting for the call girl Justin has set her up with to arrive. The sex scene that follows leads to a conversation in which the call girl (Kate Rogal) tells Abby that she didn't need to make her come. "I liked that," Abby replies, as much to herself as anyone else, a revelation that speaks to a complicated state of play in which the sexual reciprocity and intimacy considered foundational to the institution of marriage is now satisfied outside it in the institution of prostitution. Central to this reversal is the representation of Abby's wife, Kate—who represents divorce as fully as she represents marriage—as someone who never seems to require anything from anyone, sexually or otherwise. The scene in which Kate goes to the apartment and silently confronts a naked Abby would be almost clinically dissociative if it were not entirely consistent with everything else we have come to expect of someone who makes her living coolly navigating other people's marital smash-ups. As emotionally blunted as Abby is raw, Kate only loosens up when talking to a professional peer about her Myers-Briggs Type Indicator, an exchange that occurs in the context of a party in which the rest of their forty-something friends sit around drunkenly recalling the Manhattan sex clubs they used to visit before they married and moved to Montclair.

It is seeing her wife intensely engaged in conversation with a middle-aged male peer, as much as enjoying giving pleasure to a call girl, that precipitates Abby's switch from sexual client to provider of sexual services. Across a picaresque series of preliminary interviews and subsequent sexual trysts, Abby gets to display many of the same ENTP character traits professionally ascribed to her lawyer wife—extroversion, intuition, thinking, perception—all of which make her an adroit escort insofar as this type, one of sixteen in the Myers Briggs psychological typology, indicates someone who is "Good at reading other people. Bored by routine, will seldom do the same thing the same way, apt to turn to one new interest after another."[21] While each of these encounters is scripted and choreographed to reveal various ostensible truths about female sexuality and its familiar personality types—repressed, masochistic, manipulative—the real story is told by the background detail, the literal walls of the apartment that throw the foregrounded sexual action into visual and thematic relief. Abby insists that she will meet her clients only in the architecturally transforming loft, a large, stripped-down, light-flooded space that accrues more furnishings and collectables as the film progresses. In the sex-free suburban house she shares with Kate and the kids, everything is decked out in gray-tone neutrals, those pattern-free, slightly butch surrounds that say lesbian professionals at nest. In the apartment, however, this mildly androgynous style—not too butch, not too femme—is recoded as edgy by dint of association with Abby's art collection—a poster for a Louise Bourgeois exhibition, pieces by the Guerrilla Girls and other feminist artists name-checked in the credit sequence—as much as by the sex-for-money with which it competes for our visual attention.

6.2–6.3
The beginning and end of lesbian apartment space
(*Concussion*, Stacie Passon, 2013).

Ultimately, the apartment provides the conditions for Abby's sexual undoing in the form of an encounter between her and a client who breaches the code of anonymity that buffers the goings-on in the apartment from the goings-on of married life. By the time the androgynously named Sam (Maggie Siff) turns up in the apartment, it has already been established that not only do the two women share the same New Jersey fitness and parenting routine but that Abby finds her cute. That is not the problem, however. The problem is that as they begin to have sex in the apartment, Sam questions the suitability of the two-by-six tiles Abby has chosen for the kitchen splashback. Abby is so deeply rattled by the suggestion that the tiles would have looked better with a paler grout that, when Sam asks to have her hair pulled, Abby complies despite her no-discipline rule. As soon as Sam leaves the apartment Abby is seen, still in her underwear, crouched on the kitchen bench taking to the tiles with a hammer and chisel.

6.4
Lesbian detachment
(*Concussion*, Stacie Passon, 2013).

From the start Abby has seemed a lesson in insecure attachment, repeatedly displaying ambivalence toward the objects, partners, and children that surround her in the New Jersey home that she compulsively vacuums and cleans, behaviors that are less inclined to manifest in the child-free space of the apartment, an adult play world in which no one eats or shits but every sexual need is met. In an overview of the wider field of object relations, Mary Salter Ainsworth—one of Bowlby's key collaborators—highlights a key shift in Bowlby's thinking about attachment and its mechanisms of control: "Whereas in 1958 he described his as a theory of component instinct responses, in 1969 he describes the new formulation as a control theory of attachment behavior."[22] In this system, three classes of responsive behaviors—orientational, signaling, and executive—flexibly mediate the experience of attachment and ensure that the claims of proximity and reciprocity are constantly corrected inline with a set baseline or goal that is established within the system itself. This sophisticated control system is so finely tuned that "any deviation from the distance specified by the set-goal, whether brought about through the action of the mother, of the child, or of someone else, is likely to activate the systems until the distance specified is restored."[23] Thus control-freak Abby's taking to the tiles after Sam has breached the rules of intimate engagement might be better described not as apartment renovation but distance restoration. Moreover, in Abby's case the distance or set goal that appropriately balances the claims of attachment and detachment is explicitly factored as the distance between Manhattan and Montclair, city and suburb, hence her alarm at the physical-emotional breach enacted by Sam.

Now visually apprehended violently detaching tiles from the apartment wall, Abby's behavioral response brings a classically suburban neurosis to the urban apartment. The catalyst for this transference is Sam, who, unlike Abby, has a marriage setup that appears sexually fulfilling but, like Abby, wants to escape the torpid social world stay-at-home wives inhabit when their spouses (male or female) head to the city to work. In getting involved with Sam against her own better judgment, Abby thwarts her own set goal and muddies the division she has carefully set up between urban and suburban lifestyles so that it is only a matter of time before her wife figures out what is going on. The film's almost depressive outcome sees Abby returned to an exclusively suburban world, her energies once again directed at major and minor home improvements that have none of the transformative impact observed in the loft apartment conversion but seem like microcorrections designed to keep things in a steady state attachment-wise: painting the front door, investing in a sprinkler system, adding a wraparound porch. Seemingly reconciled to her sexually disinterested wife and their joint project of lesbian parenting, Abby's continued regret about forfeiting her lesbian apartment life with its perfect calibration of intimacy and distance is registered in the final scene, a variation on the opening of the film in which a group of women are assembled in a spin class. The same women are seen exercising away, but now the camerawork holds on Abby's face and positions Sam over her shoulder just beyond the point of focus. On the basis of this visual foreshortening of space, and Abby's diegetic intention to take a hot yoga class after the spin class ends, the possibility of an orthodox extramarital affair between the two women hovers on the horizon of closure before Brian Eno's "Some of Them Are Old" ushers in the final credits.

Associated with Abby's postconcussion haze, the apartment briefly functions as a reprieve from lesbian marriage, its frustrations and routine. Unlike earlier lesbian apartment plots that were primarily concerned with visibility and the difficulty of claiming a sexual storyline, the contemporary lesbian apartment plot vents ideological dissatisfaction with suburban marriage in its same-sex iteration. As is made clear in Abby's identification with the divorcing husband to whom she signs over the title deed to the fully renovated apartment, *Concussion* engages the contemporary problem of homosexual conjugality in relation to assumptions about fidelity and infidelity that take their model from straight culture. "Did you leave or did she?" Abby asks him. "It's hard to say," the soon-to-be-ex husband replies, as she nods in agreement. The scene ends there, since the film has nothing to add, no alternative imagining of long-term cohabitation or its dissolution that doesn't finally conflate sexual rights with property rights. Abby's decision to transact sex for

6.5–6.7
The spin of infidelity
(*Concussion*, Stacie Passon, 2013).

money in apartment space is less an alternative to this conjugal logic than its feminist desublimation, a critical action that leaves no space for a satisfactory resolution to the narrative either way. Abby can have sex with Sam, or no sex with Kate, and might even get both in a tacit arrangement of the kind hinted at previously, but it really amounts to the same thing: her emotional

6.8
Married with children
(*Concussion*, Stacie Passon, 2013).

detachment from attachment. Neither in love with Sam nor not in love with Kate, Abby has no generic plot available to her through which to resolve her lesbian dilemma or even scale the alternatives as anything other than the difference between madness and the battened-down normativity proposed in Eno's lyrics:

> Lucy you're my girl, Lucy you're a star.
> Lucy please be still and put your madness in a jar.
> But do beware, it will follow you, it will follow you.[24]

In this respect the end of *Concussion* resembles the end of Cholodenko's *The Kids Are All Right*, which similarly reinstates the lesbian marriage at any cost, presenting it as a sexually and socially exhausted institution through which women bind themselves to the ongoing unhappiness now understood to be at the heart of middle-class family life in its homosexual as well as heterosexual forms. Although both films conclude by restoring the framework of lesbian marriage, they are the very opposite of the Hollywood comedy of remarriage that Cavell celebrates as reimagining marriage as a sexually and socially utopian "undertaking that concerns, whatever else it concerns, change."[25] In the case of *Concussion*, the change-laden world of the apartment, a place of constant renewal in which sexual encounters never shade into routine or incur other responsibilities, is the thing the lesbian wife must give up in order to return to a marital home in which attachment needs are muted by the everyday dependencies of suburban life.[26]

Recalibrating the relation between attachment and dependency is the work of attachment theory and perhaps also the reattachment theory it harbingers. As Ainsworth points out, "Attachment is a synonym of love; dependency is not," before demonstrating the distinction by drawing an example from the attachment system known as marriage: "Does a phobic wife who clings to her husband and constantly seeks his proximity love him more than a woman who is less neurotic and more competent loves *her* husband?" Like the clingy child, the clingy wife is "clearly more dependent" than the healthier wife "even though they do not necessarily love more, and even though they are not more strongly attached." Concluding that "dependency and attachment are by no means identical," Ainsworth also points out that the quantification of either is no accurate measure of love. Indeed, it is the insight of psychoanalysis that measuring stronger or weaker dependencies or attachments is less important than the "qualitative variations among different object relations. How ambivalent is the relationship, what admixture of love and hate, and how well is the ambivalence resolved?"[27] These three questions hang over the ending of *Concussion* like a riddle delivered by a perverse fairy godmother. In Cavell's original account of remarriage comedy, he argues that ambivalence must be both acknowledged within the couple and mediated by the community the couple nests inside if ongoing reattachment is to be secured. In the lesbian marriages that feature in *Concussion* and *The Kids Are All Right*, the ambivalence that necessarily attends coupled attachment is mediated by family, not community, so that what lies ahead is not the sociable chatter of erotic reattachment but an almost wordless conjugal compromise.

Unlike *Concussion*, which presents same-sex marriage as the ideological and narrative counter to a dreamlike apartment space that has few real-world coordinates outside interior design discourses, *Weekend* uses a socially grounded high-rise apartment block to investigate the possibilities of gay marriage from the perspective of those who have yet to, and might never, elect to marry. Initially unsuccessful in his bid to secure funding for the London-based script that became *Weekend*, Haigh reset his film in Nottingham in order to access regionally distributed lottery film funds. As a result, *Weekend* was filmed on location in and around the Lenton Flats, a Nottingham housing estate that has its origins in the postwar slum clearances that transformed the urban fabric of both metropolitan and provincial Britain. Part of a nationwide experiment in social housing, the Lenton Flats are a brutalist corollary to the aspirant middle-class suburban housing estates seen under construction at the end of another Nottingham-based film that *Weekend* clearly references, Karel Reisz's *Saturday Night and Sunday Morning* (1960).[28] In 2011, the year *Weekend* was released, the Lenton Flats were slated for urban redevelopment.

Two years later the five sixteen-story tower blocks were taken down floor by floor in a seven-month demolition process that was aesthetically compressed into a three-minute time-lapse video commissioned by Nottingham City Homes that concludes with artist impressions of the residential streetscape that is their idealized replacement.[29] Situating *Weekend* in the context of innovations in the provision of public housing reminds us that the rise of same-sex marriage might also be contextualized within a longer history of domestic experimentation—and kitchen-sink realism—in which the boundaries between public and private are actively redescribed in socially utopian or dystopian forms.

Already known to audiences as the bleak setting for Shane Meadows's *This Is England* (2006) and Anton Corbijn's *Control* (2007), the Lenton Flats appear in a different light in *Weekend*. Frequently seen in twilight, the potentially monolithic scale of the tower blocks is typically softened by some natural element in the composition of the frame, just as the potentially drab East Midlands landscape on which they stand, a postindustrial nexus of technology parks and dormitory suburbs connected by congested minor roads and traffic roundabouts, lights up beautifully against a darkening night sky. In the pre-title opening sequence, the apartment tower block is entered through a shot that cuts unexpectedly from an exterior view of medium-density sprawl to autumnal vegetation seen through a high-up apartment window. The camera quickly takes in the tight dimensions of an apartment in which a dark-haired young man silently readies himself to go out. Bathing, dressing, smoking a joint—the things the young man does are less important than the claim they make to ordinariness within a diegetic world dictated by the physical constraints of an actual apartment. In this familiar space, the young man's bodily actions seem habitual, like hitting light switches in the dark. As the scene continues, he sits on his bed and takes a pair of pristine sneakers from their original box before putting them away, a change of mind that takes less than the beat it would be given in a film that marked it out as a significant event. Strung between habit and impulse, the young man's unselfconscious actions confirm that he occupies the space of the everyday, a cinematic convention through which homosexuality can appear as an ordinary thing among other ordinary things.[30]

The everyday feel of the film is maintained as the young man leaves the apartment to go to dinner at his friend's house, then takes a tram into town and drops into a nondescript gay bar. The scenes in the dark and noisy gay bar are as flatly routine as the domestic scenes that precede them. The young man's silent attempt to hook up with a handsome stranger he has followed to the urinal is quietly knocked back. He turns his attention to another, shorter man with whom he dances until the club empties out. The scene then cuts forward to the Lenton Flats, seen in morning light before the camera reenters the apartment to show the young man getting up and making coffee for two. He takes the coffee mugs back to the bedroom, where the man who initially rebuffed him lies under the duvet. Insofar as it is represented at all, the gay pickup registers as a makeshift arrangement that has its origins in substitutability, not uniqueness, a point underscored by the difficulty of keeping visually separate the various men who move through the club, including the two leads, who share with each other and most of the gay extras in the film a similar on-trend, bearded, and verging-on-bearish look.

With the initial sexual encounter between the two strangers consigned to a temporal ellipsis, the film goes on to trace the growing intimacy between Russell (Tom Cullen), whose apartment it is, and Glen (Chris New), two men who seem from the start temperamentally at odds though physically at ease with each other in a space in which distance is at a premium. In dramatic terms, the film swivels on the revelation that Glen is due to leave for "the States" on Sunday afternoon to pursue his art studies, but this plot determinant is of little interest except as the basis for the melancholic condition through which the two men, having just found each other, are already stitched into a bittersweet narrative that, for the viewer—and possibly for them—is all the better for being known from the outset.

On first impressions, Russell is as shy and cautious as Glen is brash and cocky, although this difference is less important than the similarly low-key way that they pass back and forth semi-improvised lines that, like every other element in their diegetic world, aspire to realness. As Dennis Lim points out in a brief essay that accompanies the Criterion Collection DVD released in 2012, "Character-driven dramas are not supposed to make a show of backstory, but in the genre of the blossoming romance—focused on two people for whom the rest of the world has fallen away, and who are hungry to know everything about each other—there is nothing more natural than exposition."[31] Yet exposition is raised to an exponential degree in the morning-after scene, when Glen produces a handheld recorder and asks Russell to recount their night together, explaining that it is part of an art project he is working on. A few hours later in story time, as they sit down to lunch in the apartment kitchen, Glen will elaborate the objective behind the art project, but for the film's purposes it is primarily useful as a device for conveying gay sexual history unspectacularly, including the detail that the two men did not have anal sex the night before.

6.9
Gay realism
(*Weekend*, Andrew Haigh, 2011).

Although the two men will be seen, and seen to talk, in various other interior and exterior locations across the course of the weekend, the key setting for the developing relationship is the domestic space provided by the apartment, which is nonetheless not a space for the domestication of sex. Full of comfy used furniture and objects salvaged from the local charity shop, the interior of the apartment provides the backdrop for scenes of personal and sexual disclosure that are as likely to be accompanied by the use of drugs and alcohol as they are the drinking of tea and coffee. Sometime on Saturday afternoon Russell will tell Glen that he has no parents to come out to since he grew up in foster care. This conversation will lead to sex on the couch, followed by the sight of one man assisting the other to wipe semen off his belly as Haigh establishes the council flat as a place for sex, not its exhaustion. As Glen leaves the apartment for the second time, he returns to tell Russell that he is due to leave Nottingham the following day. Transacted in the apartment doorway, this revelation makes clear that the connection between the two men is crucially linked to the apartment's spatial and narrative dimensionalities, which are as naturalistically tight as they are sexually expansive since they include both the sex that is performed as part of the scene and the sexual encounters recounted in dialogue.

As the film proceeds, the wider coordinates of the apartment are revealed in primarily visual terms. The tower block sits inside the larger council estate and its surrounds, a flat spread of grass divided by concrete pathways that appear on the diagonal when seen from above, as they mostly are. Three times between

6.10
Departure in yellow
(*Weekend*, Andrew Haigh, 2011).

Saturday morning and Sunday afternoon, Russell will look out the window of his fourteenth-floor apartment to watch Glen depart on foot, his yellow or red hoodie standing out brightly in an exterior world otherwise bleached of color. Throughout the film red, yellow, and blue accents emotionally punctuate the various scenes in which the two men come together, separate, text each other, and meet up again across the course of a weekend in which it is hard to keep track of time. In the blue-and-white world of the local indoor baths where Russell works as a lifeguard, for instance, there is an oversized clock that marks out not just the hours or minutes in the day but also the racing sweep of seconds, the time to be got through before he can see Glen again.

As the clock suggests, the temporal logic of the film is durational rather than chronological, just as the actions it represents are often framed as repetitions rather than events in the singular and consequential sense of that term. Glen's pseudointellectual art project instantiates this logic but, in also assigning a similar project to the unpretentious Russell, the film perhaps suggests that gay culture in general may have an inclination toward the serial form and its capacity to catch rhythms and intensities missed by more teleological forms, including romantic narratives of the kind that would frame Russell and Glen as star-crossed lovers. Tucked inside the apartment in the early hours of Sunday morning, Russell reveals to Glen that he too records his sexual encounters with other men. The scene cuts forward to the living room, where Russell sits on the floor and reads aloud from his laptop two accounts

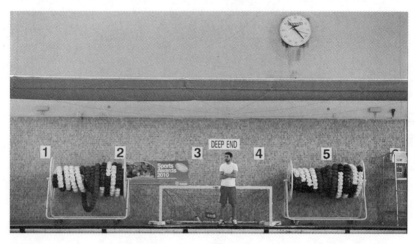

6.11
Marking time
(*Weekend*, Andrew Haigh, 2011).

of casual sex before the task of reading is passed over to Glen. As Glen reads aloud, the camera ratchets focus between his face in the foreground and Russell's face deeper in field, an unusually melodramatic gesture in the context of the rest of the unerringly naturalistic film. The entry recounts Russell's first experience of anal sex with a man who won't exchange numbers with him afterward as he already has a boyfriend, a rejection that makes Russell feel bad about himself. When he has finished reading, Glen closes the laptop, stands, and exits the frame while asking Russell what this guy looked like in order to establish that the man was John, his former boyfriend who lied to him about picking up other men. Though Glen returns to the floor-level shot, the scene abruptly cuts to a close-up of Russell's drugged face in the bathroom mirror as dialogue not synced to the image continues to be heard, another formal innovation out of step with the naturalistic code of the rest of the film.

At the point where the visuals reunite with the sound, the two men are seen sitting on the sofa, but the sense of intimacy between them has dissipated. Pumped up on the lines of cocaine they have taken, they fall into a disinhibited conversation about the pros and cons of gay marriage in which everything one man says arrives as needlessly aggressive to the other. Russell leaves to take a piss, and the image track returns to the close-up on his face in the mirror as it pushes to the brink of tears. A recomposed Russell returns to the living room, where Glen is standing at the open apartment window, and the two men reconcile to the sound of John Grant's "TC and Honeybear,"

6.12–6.14
Gay reconciliation
(*Weekend*, Andrew Haigh, 2011).

6.15
Gay leave-taking
(*Weekend*, Andrew Haigh, 2011).

which plays on the stereo. Back in sync with their apartment surroundings and the untroubled night sky onto which both room and lyrics open, the two men smoke a joint together before a final sexual encounter in which Russell wordlessly invites Glen to fuck him. The most thematically weighted action in the film, this too is a repetition, a serially singular sign of emotional trust that is all the safer for being transacted in the knowledge that the abandonment that will follow is a result of impersonal circumstance rather than personal rejection.

In fucking Russell and then going away to America, Glen therapeutically reenacts his former boyfriend's role, a point underscored in the morning when he pretends to be Russell's father so that Russell, who has known only serial foster parents, can enact coming out to a figure who doesn't exist. While these replayable, pseudopatriarchal dynamics of abandonment and repair are crucial to the emotional satisfactions the film has to offer, they are not all it has to offer. Having established ambivalence and insecurity as the framework within which attachments form, the film releases its gay male protagonists from the apartment into a cinematic ending that can hold them together even as it wrenches them apart. After an interlude that returns everything to a nonreparative present—the tedium of a Sunday morning spent alone in an apartment full of dirty ashtrays and half-empty glasses—the two men meet up in a scene at Nottingham railway station that pays homage to David Lean's *Brief Encounter* (1945), a melodrama that simultaneously de-idealizes and re-idealizes marriage from the perspective of an almost-affair. Amid the

6.16
Reattachment to the world
(*Weekend*, Andrew Haigh, 2011).

station crowd of ordinary folk going about their ordinary days, Glen is visually picked out by his yellow hoodie and red backpack. The two men walk from the station food court to the platform, where the camera positions them at a distance as seen through the wire of a barricade.

They stand talking face-to-face, but the dialogue is drowned out by the sound of the train behind them and an announcement over the station public address system. The camera slowly zooms in through the fence to frame them as a couple, and the dialogue is restored in time for us to hear Glen damn Russell for coming to see him off, before he collapses tearfully into the other man's embrace. The two men kiss openly, and when a catcall breaks through the ambient sound of the station, Russell looks defiantly at the camera, having attained his full height for what seems like the first time in the film. Taller and stronger than before, Russell reassures Glen that he will be great in America. Glen gives Russell a crumpled package, saying he couldn't remember his surname, kisses him a final time, then walks out of shot. Russell trembles on the verge of tears as he turns to look after Glen. A cut shows a train departing before the scene shifts forward in time to resettle Russell in the open window of his apartment at twilight. He takes the package from his jacket, reaches in, takes out Glen's voice recorder, and turns it on. The achingly long take continues over a playback of the morning-after interview between the two men. Russell can be heard to hesitate before Glen instructs him to begin from the start. The image switches to a final exterior vantage point that nestles the gay man in an illuminated window frame, one of several in the darkening hulk of the Lenton Flats, as the opening chords of John Grant's "I Wanna Go to Marz" sear the otherworldly quality of the visuals into the soundtrack. No more than a figural outline suspended in time and light, Russell has become a cipher for our renewed attachment to a world that may not be cut out to meet our needs but remains our best hope for their satisfaction.

But what world is this? In one framing of the story, this world is one in which two men with abandonment issues fall for each other in a relation of growing intimacy, tenderness, and trust that is foreclosed by circumstances and social hostilities beyond their control. But, in another framing of the same story, this world is one in which two men fall for each other in the understanding that their best chance at happiness is supported by spaces outside the apartment that are understood to be continuous with it. Featuring as incidental details in the sexual stories the two men trade between themselves in the process of getting to know each other, these sketchily drawn spaces include bars, saunas, and parks that are the setting for serial encounters with strangers who may or may not become intimates. Always invested with the prospect of gay sex, these spaces—including the space of the apartment itself—are unlike the suburban kitchens, living rooms, pubs, and workplaces featured in the film where straight familiars spend their lives and which, whether gay friendly or potentially hostile, are alike in seeming utterly denuded of cruising possibilities and hence inhospitable to gay life with its practiced sensitivity to strangers.

Throughout the film, the close camera work and careful blocking used inside the apartment are interleaved with distant, zoom-lens shots of an alternative world strongly associated with peripheral noise—the sound of passing traffic or the hubbub of voices and music that drowns out the actors in a pub scene or at the carnival, where the two men go, having abandoned Glen's going-away drinks. In the crowded social scenes outside the apartment, the dialogue, when it is heard, is mostly inconsequential. Glen rants against the heterosexual dominance of popular culture and straight people's disgust for gay sex to anyone that will listen, but in the narrative framework of the film Nottingham appears relatively benign, if provincial. Some youths from the Lenton Estate shout "queer" from the anonymity of off-screen space as Glen leaves the apartment building after his first night with Russell, and a group on the bus makes jokes about camp men, but the homophobia seems rote, the sign of a social backwater rather than pointed aggression. Besides a reference to Glen's former boyfriend being beaten up while cruising in a park, the one genuinely aggressive scene, shocking in its ordinariness, occurs at the pool, where Russell sits apart from his male workmates in the break room, increasingly discomforted as one of them nastily describes fisting his girlfriend in a postporn update of kitchen-sink misogyny. Outside the apartment, Russell seems detached not only from the straight world of work but also from the warmer domestic world of informal dinners and children's parties presented to him by his childhood friend Jamie. Despite being sutured into this family milieu as godfather to Jamie's child, Russell is most at home in the world when moving through it with his new friend Glen at his side or floating above it in his Lenton Flats apartment.

Others have read Russell's return to the apartment as a retreat into the fantasy space of domesticity and marriage. Stephanie Clare, for instance, takes the film to task for its homonormative romanticism, which she defines as "a series of affects and emotions that frame the good life in the form of a couple" before insisting that it is the gay "subject of romance (and not only the subject trying to avoid stigma) that we must query in order to build progressive social imaginaries."[32] Russell bears the brunt of Clare's critique since in her account he is a "homonormative guy" attached to marriage and specifically marriage conceived as an apartment-like structure that "offers the fantasy of happiness because it provides the imaginary of a space that is at once separate from the public sphere and yet not lonely."[33] In a cruel reversal of Cavell's conceptualization of the sexual and social complexity of marriage as "entering simultaneously into a new public and a new private connection, the creation at once of new spaces of communality and of exclusiveness, of a new outside and inside to a life," Clare argues that it is the forces of "heteronormativity and homophobia" that push Russell "into this space of domesticity, the space of his apartment, and it is there that he seeks the good life."[34] According to Clare, it is the romantic fantasy of happiness, and the deferment of its realization to a future utopia, that reconciles Russell to his present state of loneliness and the reality of his social denigration as a gay man.

Open to both the reality of the gay couple and the progressive social imaginaries with which that couple might be compatible, the final frames of the film effortlessly convey Russell's renewed attachment to a socially complex gay world best experienced from the vantage point of apartment space. Framed in the illuminated window of the apartment looking out into the deepening night, Russell might be fantasizing Glen's return, or looking forward to the sexual promise of next weekend, or both. Crucially, these are not presented as exclusive options but framed as mutually supportive ambitions. Neither romantic nor antiromantic, the story's end, like its beginnings in the gay club scene, is geared to affective intensities that may be ephemeral but are also socially sustainable in a community of strangers. Far from presenting the apartment as a space of sexual withdrawal, the film remains resolutely invested in the gay apartment as the place where sexuality and sociality meet. As Cavell points out, traditionally "the joining of the social and the sexual is called marriage," which is why, in the era of marriage equality, a cycle of films might appear in which the notion of marriage can be expanded to include the possibility of continuous and discontinuous attachments, as well as the spaces in which those serial intimacies might be achieved.[35]

More hopeful than *Concussion*, *Weekend* does not settle for marriage or its negation but holds on to the idea of reattachment, which it understands as both a fragile and a resilient thing. Although a lot of the film's improvised talkiness is given over to debating gay marriage, it is more compelling for the quiet testimony it gives to the capacity for intimacy between strangers, even if that intimacy might not stand longer acquaintance. Read together, *Concussion* and *Weekend* reveal that the public-private hybrid form of the apartment remains key to the gay and lesbian narratives of attachment and detachment that circulate in the wake of marriage equality. Equally, though differently, they repurpose the apartment plot as a complex means of working through some of the anxieties that ghost the socially upbeat accounts of same-sex marriage that have surfaced elsewhere in popular culture. Among other things, these films use the materiality of apartment space to register alternative conceptions of urban homosexual life, whether it is the no-strings contractual sex that occurs in the metropolitan lesbian loft or the chance encounter facilitated by a gay bar on an otherwise dull Friday night in a provincial English town. Working through gay marriage and its discontents, these films newly engage the idea of stranger intimacy as the means by which marriage might be expanded beyond the neoliberal version of privatized domesticity that its queer critics often take it to be.

Whether or not this still-unfolding cycle of gay marriage films can reconcile anyone to the idea of the couple as a social answer to the riddle of sexual attachment remains to be seen. As evidence of this uncertainty, I cite nothing less than the look of Haigh's film, which has its origins in his admiration for the work of Manchester-based artists Colin Quinn and Oisín Share, who document their domestic life together under the collaborative name Quinnford + Scout. Captured in high-color photographs going through the motions of daily life, Quinn and Share look like more burly versions of Russell and Glen. Three years after *Weekend* was made, a production Quinn and Share were involved with as set photographers and extras, the two men announced their separation on Flickr.[36] Standing alongside the film it visually conjures, the Quinnford + Scout archive is affective testimony to the lived promise of the gay couple formation come what may.

Another recent departure from the queer critique of the couple can also be found in Maggie Nelson's *The Argonauts*, which interlaces her experience of the bodily transformations attendant on maternity with her partner's experience of gender transitioning plus an account of their rushing to marry in the last hours before Proposition 8 closed the window for same-sex marriage in California. In the final acknowledgment, Nelson thanks her partner for showing her "what a nuptial might be—an infinite conversation, an endless becoming."[37] Although Nelson makes no reference to Cavell among the queer or queer-friendly theorists of attachment that she and I both draw on in what might initially appear as two very different projects—Bersani, Butler, Edelman, Foucault, Phillips, Sedgwick, Winnicott—this phrase recalls Cavell's original conceptualization of the engagement with the comedies of remarriage as a "conversation" through which one learns to check experience, and find authority in it, through the mimesis of film or, perhaps, the mimesis of memoir. I end this chapter by recommending the utility of an open-ended, socially oriented theory of reattachment to queer experience; in the next, I consider a queer framing of heterosexual marriage that explores the consequences of an inability to reattach.

7 The Remarriage Crisis

Perhaps because of the compelling nature of Cavell's engagement with the seven films from which he derives his account of the Hollywood comedy of remarriage, each of which commands a chapter in *Pursuits of Happiness*, it is easy to skip or skim the introduction, "Words for a Conversation," which begins by drawing on the classical distinction between Old and New Comedy as influentially framed by Northrop Frye in "The Argument of Comedy."[1] Although Cavell never questions the heterosexuality of Frye's governing model of romantic comedy—which can be usefully summarized as girl gets boy (Old Comedy) or boy gets girl (New Comedy)—his summary is useful for thinking about the genre of remarriage in the context of gay marriage. According to Cavell, both Old and New Comedy "show a young pair overcoming individual and social obstacles to their happiness" with that happiness "figured as a concluding marriage that achieves individual and social reconciliations." But, whereas New Comedy "stresses the young man's efforts to overcome obstacles posed by an older man (a senex figure) to his winning the young woman of his choice," Old Comedy "puts particular stress on the heroine, who may hold the key to the successful conclusion of the plot, who may be disguised as a boy, and who may undergo something like death and restoration."[2] In Cavell's assessment, Hollywood remarriage comedy can generally be regarded as a form of Old Comedy insofar as it places emphasis on the role played by woman in securing romantic happiness. However, in casting its heroine not as a young girl but as an already married woman, Hollywood remarriage comedy is a significant departure from both New and Old Comedy, just as it departs from both forms in organizing its plot around the necessity "not to get the central pair together, but to get them *back* together, together *again*." What is distinctive about the genre of remarriage comedy—and what makes the form so relevant to the social proposition of gay marriage—is that "the fact of marriage in it is subjected to the fact or threat of divorce."[3] If, as Cavell posits, the rise of divorce results in the inventive skewering of the marriage plot, might we not expect to see an equivalent storied inventiveness when marriage is skewered by the rise of marriage equality?

After making this foundational observation, Cavell asks himself why this particular transformation—the happy rewiring of the marriage plot around the obstacle of divorce—should come about when "classical comedy moves to film?"[4] Roughly speaking, the answers Cavell proposes to this conundrum fall into three different registers of thought. First, there are the relevant social coordinates that might be thought to explain the historical timing of the emergence of the remarriage genre, including changing expectations of sexual compatibility between men and women and the middle-class acceptance of divorce. Second, there is the cinematic context that sharpens the genre for popular wonder and consumption, specifically the ascendency of film technology and its capacity to capture the look and sound of ordinary life, but also the intertextual intensity of the Hollywood studio system at its height and the raft of repertory players it has at its disposal, including Cary Grant, Katherine Hepburn, Claudette Colbert, and Clark Gable. Finally, there is a philosophical framework of established concerns—most of them idiosyncratically indexed to Cavell's name but also linked (most explicitly in *Cities of Words*) to the names of Emerson, Locke, John Stuart Mill, Kant, Rawls, Nietzsche, Freud, Plato, and Aristotle—that look different when seen from the perspective of the talkies: How do we take responsibility for our words and their failure to say what we mean or mean what we say? How do we sidestep skepticism in pursuit of an unambiguous presence in the world now that the world can be captured on film?

As beguiling as Cavell's philosophical propositions are, they engage me less than the problematic of reattachment that remarriage comedy puts on vivid and sophisticated display. While Elisabeth Bronfen has recently revisited Cavell's theory of film as a mode of philosophical thought via a rereading of *The Philadelphia Story*, I consider the origins and afterlife of remarriage comedy in the work of William Shakespeare and Éric Rohmer—two other names that can also be found on high rotation in Cavell's work—from the perspective provided by *45 Years* (2014), Andrew Haigh's hugely successful follow-up to the gay-themed *Weekend*.[5] *45 Years* concerns an aging straight couple approaching their forty-fifth wedding anniversary and has at its center a married woman who is indicatively childless, a state she shares with all the wives in the classical Hollywood remarriage canon. Like those women before her, this wife is also responsible for securing her own romantic happiness, a task that sees her caught between the alternatives of marital tragedy and comedy, death and rebirth, genres and experiences previously understood as universal but, post–marriage equality, perhaps better understood as universally gay.

The final shot in *45 Years* has attracted almost as much attention as the story that it visually resolves. Singled out as one of *Variety*'s Top 10 shots

7.1
Under the disco ball
(*45 Years*, Andrew Haigh, 2014).

of 2015, the steady medium shot shows Charlotte Rampling—one half of a long-married couple—standing in a darkened ballroom with light refracted from an out-of-sight disco ball playing across her face: a middle-class woman caught in a moment of emotional trauma. No ordinary reaction shot, Rampling's performance captures not the slipping of a social veneer that method acting usually delivers but the more difficult-to-watch sight of someone's psychic infrastructure crumpling under the weight of recognitions that are too hard to bear let alone share. Across the crowded dance floor the slow zooming camera keeps a respectful distance from its subject, allowing the viewer to look at, but also look away from, a scene of inner reckoning. All around this isolated figure the social world continues its indifferent spin, making clear that this crisis has no real external coordinates and involves nothing more, but also nothing less, than the recognition that the people closest to us are not adjuncts to our needs but driven by their own, equally obscure, requirements. The culmination of a three-minute long sequence built on the rising emotional pitch of The Platter's "Smoke Gets in Your Eyes"—the song that launched the snowball waltz at her wedding forty-five years ago—the mobile scene ends on a figure who is less still than arrested, a wife who finds herself unable to reconnect with the husband who has just drifted out of frame. Cut to black and the sound of "We've already said goodbye," Denny Laine's legendary opening vocal to the Moody Blues' "Go Now," the emotionally indecisive breakup song that continues to play as the final credits understatedly roll.

Though universally acclaimed as a picture of emotional pain, there is critical disagreement about the precise nature of the crisis registered in Rampling's beautiful face. Writing on the *Film Comment* blog in December 2015, Jonathan Romney describes Haigh's final shot as "an extended, wordless, sublimely choreographed, beautifully painful closing shot that reminds us why the face of Charlotte Rampling is one of the most eloquent signifying surfaces in today's cinema."[6] One month later on the same site, veteran film critic David Thomson countered this account of the final shot with a lengthy discussion of the tough hopelessness he found at the core of Haigh's film and what it was in it that might move "younger critics"—specifically younger critics without experience of the longue durée of marriage—to respond with "reverence."[7] Referring to himself as a man with forty-five years of marriage under his belt—"though I should say that two wives shouldered the burden"—the twice-married Thomson retraces Rampling's film genealogy before stating as graciously as he can that her face is consistently remarkable for its inability to register anything but chill detachment. Coming from someone else this would be a contestable statement, but Thomson's opinion is backed by his encyclopedic knowledge of film biography, a category he all but invented to describe the lives of screen celebrities whose personae seamlessly weld together character and person across careers that can be measured in decades.[8] In his assessment of Haigh's final shot of Rampling as Kate Mercer, a wife whose marriage is rent apart by the revelation that her husband's first girlfriend was pregnant with his child when she died, Thomson suggests that "Charlotte Rampling's face is distressed by a kind of emptiness" that seals the bleakness of the film. As he goes on to reflect,

> We are supposed not to think such things about actors, but how can that be when *45 Years* puts such stress and emotional trust in Rampling's face? She has an unquestioned movie presence, but it is not quite warm or generous. She has always expected the worst, and you can feel that in *The Night Porter*, *The Verdict*, *Stardust Memories*, *Paris by Night* or even *Dexter*. Recast Kate—with Judi Dench, Vanessa Redgrave, or Lindsay Duncan—and I think some pathos or sympathy seeps into the picture so that that final close-up becomes less bleak. Equally, without Rampling some foreboding would be lost.

Confident that "movies deserve and expect to be judged by their casting," Thomson is unrelenting, too, in describing the whiff of death that hangs about the film not only in the misanthropy that has a hold on Tom Courtenay's increasingly angry and mentally befuddled Geoff Mercer—a retired engineer who returns to smoking despite having had a bypass after the heart attack that derailed his and Kate's fortieth anniversary plans—but in the central relationship itself. "There is something else, not just grave but almost dank," he writes, about the marriage between Kate and Geoff. "It is as if Kate has been waiting all along, for 45 years, for something that would confirm the hollowness of her marriage. That is less than kind in her and in the film, and I have to say that it is underlined by the closure that lives in Charlotte Rampling's face." The final shot of the film, he concludes, represents the "futility" of marriage within a "film that has no faith in the institution it is resolved to dismantle."[9] If we accept this account of Haigh's film as pressing a vision of marriage as the engine-house of bad faith—an idea also embedded in the queer critique of marriage—then it would seem that the cinematic proposition engaged by *45 Years* is the very antithesis of remarriage comedy as traced by Cavell in the Hollywood comedy of remarriage, and somewhat closer to the argument he expounds in *Contesting Tears*, which deals with films in which women learn that marriage does not support their flourishing.[10] I prefer to think that *45 Years*, a film directed by a married gay man—a newly minted legal convention that bends established conjugal rules—revisits these counterweighted propositions about marriage as a question of genre: should marriage post–marriage equality be approached as comedy, tragedy, or a version of Shakespearean romance?[11]

In terms of tone, not even the warm auburn highlights in Rampling's casually bobbed hair can disguise the austere brittleness that she brings to the wifely role of Kate, who seems most herself when walking alone through the chill East Anglian countryside in the company of her dog, a shaggy German shepherd. Seen in distantly framed shots of nature, Kate's daily exercise regime serves the purpose of counting down the passage of days leading to the anniversary party that will celebrate the wedding vows she took as a young woman forty-five years earlier. Despite the rude health and energy embodied in Rampling's strikingly upright figure as she strides into frame and moves through the softly misted landscape, there is no disguising the fact that this a tale of winter, and one specifically derived from *The Winter's Tale* (1623), which—like Haigh's film—deals with conjugal jealousy and attachments that persist beyond the grave. But, whereas Shakespeare's late romance centers on a husband deranged by grief and offers marital redemption in the form of a child found and a wife resurrected from the dead, *45 Years* is the story of a wife who, in holding on to one idea of her marriage, is unable to see the possibility of remarriage when it is offered her, as it is by her emotionally floundering husband in the anniversary speech that immediately precedes the dance scene that ends the film.

Despite the obvious Shakespearean coordinates of the story, the publicity material that brokers the film to its international audience makes more of

7.2
Canine attachment
(*45 Years*, Andrew Haigh, 2014).

7.3
A winter's tale
(*45 Years*, Andrew Haigh, 2014).

the fact that it is an adaptation of a short story by David Constantine, "In Another Country," a title that references Christopher Marlowe's *The Jew of Malta*, which famously furnishes the epigraph to T. S. Eliot's "Portrait of a Lady":

> Thou hast committed—
> Fornication: but that was in another country,
> And besides, the wench is dead.

Constantine's short story concerns an aged married couple who first meet during the Second World War but, decades later, have their lives unsettled by the discovery of the frozen body of the husband's former girlfriend, who died in her twenties in a climbing accident.[12] According to Constantine, the story is based on a newspaper report about the actual recovery of the body of a French mountain guide who slipped into a Chamonix glacier in the 1930s. The details are uncanny: frozen in its youthfulness, the young guide's body is returned to his seventy-year-old son, who was conceived but not yet born when his father died. By making the recovered body that of a woman with child, Constantine, a former Oxford academic, shifts the masculinist coordinates of the tale toward the Shakespearean tradition in which the riddle of paternity works its way through a heterosexual framework that is potentially misogynistic if not violently so—"and besides, the wench is dead."

When interviewed about the process of adaptation, Haigh tends to emphasize that he lowered the age of Constantine's married couple from their eighties to their late sixties (she) and early seventies (he) and "shifted the backdrop of their past to the 1960s," the decade that provides most of the music heard within the unscored film. These minor adaptations, however, are less significant than the director's decision to keep the story in the Shakespearean wilderness of sexual jealousy but focalize it through the perspective of the wife, whose childlessness the film tries hard to keep incidental rather that the thematically load-bearing device it threatens to become. Not having children need not be framed as tragedy, or at least that is one of the propositions kept open by the director, who in cutting an intended scene that spoke to the reasons behind the couple's childless state keeps the focus on their present-tense relationship and the question of whether we are watching a marital tragedy unfold or, in keeping with the Shakespearean romance the film replots, a strained version of remarriage comedy. In the DVD commentary he shares with producer and long-term collaborator Tristan Goligher, Haigh can be heard constantly questioning whether the film is a tragedy or a more benign take on the difficulty of finding a language through which a couple might align their independent pasts with their present mutual needs, especially when faced with the sexual and social diminishments of age as they are experienced in the straight middle-class milieu in which Kate and Geoff move, a world in which heterosexual development seems to stop with the advent of marriage, as judged by the couple's taste in popular music and the fact that they seem chiefly to socialize in sex-segregated contexts—she with her female friend, he with his old workmates.

That the film is centered on the persistence of sexual jealousy and doubt, rather than resolvable questions of paternity and maternity, is made clear in the conversation given to Geoff and Kate in which she asks him to recall the events that led up to the catastrophic moment when Katya, his slightly older girlfriend, slipped into an ice crevasse. Delving into the recesses of memory, a place given material dimensionality in the loft above the bedroom that holds his old photographs and journals, Geoff remembers that he and Katya had engaged a guide to help them cross the Alps into Italy. He haltingly recalls that he resented the guide's presence since it broke the charmed existence he and Katya had been leading for weeks on the violet-strewn mountainside, a place in which no obligation rested on either of them except to the other. When Kate suggests that the guide was flirting with Katya and she with him, Geoff acknowledges the jealousy he felt at hearing them talking and laughing together. Prompted by his wife, Geoff remembers that Katya and the guide were out of sight ahead of him when he heard her laugh, then scream, before he rounded a bend in the trail to see the guide staring speechless into a fissure in the ice. Ostensibly occurring in the French Alps, Geoff's dramatic recollection is more obviously set in a land of accident and coincidence in which characters conveniently appear or disappear as required by the greater needs of plot. In *The Winter's Tale* this magic land is called Bohemia, which Antigonus must exit, pursued by a bear, in order that Perdita, King Leontes's infant daughter, might be abandoned to her fate. Raised by shepherds for sixteen years, Perdita becomes the rightful object of princely attention in a complicated plot in which both paternity and conjugality are redeemed in a fantastical ending that involves the revelation of Perdita's true identity—a staple trope of comedy—and, in a borrowing from the emerging genre of court masque, the seeming reanimation of a statue of her mother, Leontes's wife, Hermione, who was thought to have died of grief in the circumstances that broke the royal family apart at the beginning of the play.

Although *The Winter's Tale* manifests as the story of a man's redemption as a husband and father, it has been reimagined cinematically as a woman's story by Éric Rohmer in *Conte d'hiver* (1992), which bears the English title *A Tale of Winter*, a film in which the key protagonist is both mother and daughter in a circuit of maternal attachments that provide the affectionate and nonjudgmental backdrop to the film's romantic action, which reverses the original Shakespearean plot by returning a lost father to his daughter after a lapse of several years. Although Rohmer's film is an obvious cinematic precursor to *45 Years*, this lineage has not been fully acknowledged, perhaps because all the formal elements Haigh's film takes from Rohmer he also takes from himself insofar as they are already on display in *Weekend* (2011). From the decision to shoot in sequence to the emphasis on dialogue to the domestic

7.4
The extraordinary in the ordinary
(*45 Years*, Andrew Haigh, 2014).

ordinariness of the interiors and actions to the role of family celebrations in marking out the course of a life, Haigh's signature as an auteur is indistinguishable from Rohmer's and has been since the start of his career.[13] In particular, Haigh shares Rohmer's sensitivity to local topography, whether urban or rural, and an awareness of the effect it has on human actions as they repeat themselves in the routines of daily life.[14] In *45 Years*, as in *Weekend* but first in Rohmer's *A Tale of Winter*, key scenes—either random encounters or moments of silent reflection—occur on public transport as they often do in provincial or metropolitan life. Above all, *45 Years* recalls *A Tale of Winter* in the scenes filmed in the high streets and pedestrian malls of Norwich that are filled with real people, not extras, going about their day—shopping, pushing children in prams, milling about with friends. Like the scenes shot by Rohmer in which an ash-blond Charlotte Véry, playing a young woman named Félicie, commutes through the streets of Paris or the tiled passages of the Metro, Haigh uses the infrastructure and signage of everyday life to frame the older Rampling as transcendently beautiful in a completely ordinary way, a quality that Cavell associates with the comedies of remarriage and their uncanny capacity to tap into the extraordinary as a felt presence in the world.[15]

For Cavell, this capacity to capture the extraordinary in the everyday is more or less the magic of cinema and, confronted with the sight of a lithe Charlotte Rampling parking a nondescript estate car, locking it, and walking past a row of rubbish skips in a scene from *45 Years*, or another in which she

170 • Chapter 7

rises from bed and silently walks through a creaking house to wave her hand in the audible draft of the attic trapdoor, the claim is very hard to dispute. However, whereas in the comedies of remarriage this extraordinary quality is placed in the service of marital reenchantment, in Haigh's film the possibility of remarriage is deferred beyond formal closure as we observe the married couple become increasingly estranged as they go about their husband-and-wifely routines across the course of several days. "Since marriage," writes Cavell, "is an image of the ordinary of human existence," the way the central couple in remarriage comedy responds to their internal problem or separation crisis will ultimately "transfigure, or resurrect, their vision of their everyday lives." While in other individualist traditions, he continues, this might be called a "transmutation of self," in the cinematic tradition of remarriage this transfiguration or resurrection takes the form of a revisioning or recognition of "the extraordinary in the ordinary, and the ordinary in what we find extraordinary."[16] In the final shot of Haigh's film, something like this recognition is given to the viewer, but not yet to the couple at the film's heart, so that the very genre of the film—and the future of the institution of marriage—hangs in the air, like the unseen disco ball that throws a splintered gay light on the centrally framed straight story. If there is a choice to be made here, it is between straight marriage as duty—as Kate tells Geoff through clenched teeth the night before their anniversary celebrations, "We will go to bed, get up and try and start again"—and a remarriage plot that faintly twinkles in the periphery of this bleak vision. Is the last shot a melodramatic take on the suffering face of a broken ice queen or, somewhere in Charlotte Rampling's straight-backed performance of Kate, can we see a woman capable of bending emotionally in relation to her husband's past and present need, as Katharine Hepburn does under the influence of champagne in George Cukor's *The Philadelphia Story*, another straight marriage film told by a gay man? Call this the paradox of gay remarriage and note, too, that the "inconclusiveness" of this ending is consistent with the "aphoristic ending" that Cavell finds in all of the original comedies of remarriage, a genre that in "depicting people looking to remarry inevitably depicts people thinking about the idea of marriage" as a form of "unfinished business."[17]

As Cavell has made clear, the Hollywood comedy of remarriage is centrally concerned with how people, once joined but now separated, refind one another, which is also the central concern of Shakespeare's late romances. Long before Haigh decided to shine a gay light on remarriage, Rohmer put the Shakespearean romantic conceit through four seasonal variations in what is now known as his masterwork, *Tales of the Four Seasons: A Tale of Springtime*

(1990), *A Summer's Tale* (also known as *Le Rayon vert* or *The Green Ray*) (1996), *An Autumn Tale* (1998), and *A Tale of Winter*. In one of his many discussions of Rohmer's quartet, Cavell identifies the range of motifs that stay remarkably stable across the spring, summer, autumn, and winter expositions of romance: "All concern demands for, and of, specific places, particularly moving between two places; all are about measuring or marking time, or the lapse of time; and about nature or the normal or the trivial; about coincidence, loneliness or separation, chance, and choice; about impressions you cannot put a word to; and all contain a moment of insight that has transformative power, and some fantastic thing that simply and blankly *happens* (a trick of the setting sun, a sudden onset of wind through high trees, an encounter)."[18] In *A Tale of Winter*—the second film made by Rohmer but thematically last in the cycle—this sense of "transcendence entering the everyday" comes about after a performance of Shakespeare's *The Winter's Tale* in which the sight of the statue of Hermione coming alive transforms Félicie's relation to her romantic present and lets her see the possibility of refinding her romantic past in an unknown future.[19]

In the established dramatic tradition of setting a play within a play, Rohmer's film begins with something approximating a dumb show, a near wordless summery seaside prologue in which we see but do not quite hear a mutually besotted twenty-something couple accidentally lose each other when the young woman mistakenly gives the wrong address to the young man before getting on a train. The film proper picks up five years later as we see the still-young Félicie, now raising the child born from her summer romance, trying to decide between two men who are currently courting her, a fleshy hairdresser and a cerebral philosopher, neither of whom she loves as she does the lost young man, a cook who was destined for America. After seeing Hermione come to life, Félicie decides to refuse both suitors in preference for waiting for the father of her child to return, a romantic gamble likened to Pascal's wager about the existence of god. When measured against the return of her former lover, which represents infinite gains, the finite loss of two men, neither of whom she really loves, is as nothing. Having made her choice, the way is clear for coincidence to run its theatrically mandated course. This extraordinary event—the return of the lost lover-cum-father of her child—occurs in the ordinary happenstance of a meeting on a Paris bus, which is followed by a scene in the street in which the young man realizes he is meeting a five-year-old girl who already knows him to be her father, a recognition made possible by the photograph of him as a handsome, curly-headed man in bathing trunks that Félicie keeps by her daughter's bedside. Rohmer's film ends when the newly reunited family returns to Félicie's mother's house with provisions

7.5
Projection
(*45 Years*, Andrew Haigh, 2014).

for a feast. "I have brought you a cook," Félicie gaily tells her mother in full confidence that her wager has paid off royally.

It is this joyous tale that Haigh reimagines as the story of a childless couple who, in rediscovering the infant lost in their deep past, threaten to come undone as husband and wife. Although Thomson's review of *45 Years* doesn't specifically mention either the Shakespearean or Rohmerian antecedents of Haigh's film, it does point out that it "risks being a studious setup: Kate and Katya are giveaway-close as names; and Katya's pregnant tummy counters the childlessness of the Mercer marriage." Like *The Winter's Tale* and *A Tale of Winter*, *45 Years* offers the married couple a second chance by offering to return them to an earlier version of themselves, just as the film brings out a certain childishness in Thomson, who returns to the baby talk of his British childhood when he refers to Katya's visibly pregnant "tummy," a fact confirmed by the projected slide that approximates the showing of a film within a film, which is both a nod to Rohmer, whose *Tale of Winter* stages a play within a screenplay, and a nod to remarriage comedy insofar as the bedsheet on which this image screens recalls the bedsheet used to keep apart, but also bring together, Clark Gable and Claudette Colbert in Frank Capra's *It Happened One Night*.

What is on display in this scene of literal projection is not Kate's childlessness but her inability to be childlike. In the comedies of remarriage, grown-ups

The Remarriage Crisis • 173

7.6
Conjugal dancing
(*45 Years*, Andrew Haigh, 2014).

being childish or retaining the capacity to play with each other is taken very seriously indeed, which is why, according to Cavell, so many remarriage comedies require their separated couples to sing or dance together. Haigh's film twice requires Kate and Geoff to dance. While Geoff is clumsier on the dance floor than his wife, he is the one to initiate dancing. The first time Kate consents to dance with Geoff in the living room, husband and wife reconnect sufficiently to retire to bed early and embark upon sex. The second time they dance together is the formal repetition of their wedding's snowball waltz, a scene in which they are decked out in evening wear and look for all the world like two movie stars playing at being husband and wife. As if to acknowledge the levels of celebrity estrangement that seem to reside in their married imago, whenever Geoff speaks of Katya, whose name is a familiar diminutive of Kate, he adds the possessive—"my Katya"—thereby expressing a fond claim on her that he has more trouble exercising in relation to his wife, who always presents as the more mature and self-possessed half of the couple they make up. The disparity in age between the actors—Courtenay is approaching eighty, Rampling seventy—is reinforced by their embodied performance, particularly in the sex scene in which Geoff is frustrated at his inability to maintain an erection. Against Rampling's poise and stillness, Courtenay's physical agitation reinforces the idea that Geoff is entering his dotage in both senses of the word: enthrallment and decline. In the wake of the news from Switzerland that Katya's body has been discovered, we see Geoff become preoccupied with his memory of her and enter a romantic fugue state, which, for all its sustaining grace, places stress on his ability to navigate the everyday. His skills of ratiocination and recall seem tested by the easiest of tasks. With feelings of anxiety in the ascendant, he resumes smoking and muddles through his days trying to fix the ballcock on the lavatory.

Although dancing, like singing and other forms of fooling around, is part of the repertoire of couple reconciliation as represented in the Hollywood comedies of remarriage, it is clear that Kate and Geoff do not intuitively share a film grammar of movement any more than they share a spoken language of emotional connection. In the repeated scenes in which they lie in bed at night trying to communicate with each other, they struggle to find forms of speech that can acknowledge the disruptive presence of the past in their domestic world. In scene after scene their dialogue, like their dancing, is faltering and distrustful rather than the effortless and effortlessly light language shared by the estranged couples in the Hollywood comedies of remarriage who cannot help but anticipate each other's lines and intentions before they are fully enunciated in the way required by other mortals. Similarly, although husband and wife seem to share a back catalogue of popular song, when Kate turns spontaneously to music it is as form of self-soothing in a scene that, according to Haigh's DVD commentary, was improvised by Rampling to the surprise of everyone on set. With her husband off on an errand of his own, Kate sits down at the piano in an empty room and begins to follow the sheet music before setting it aside and launching into a piece from memory, an isolated woman desperately trying to find pattern and sense in the corridors of creativity alone. Like other aspects of Rampling's performance, this scene seems more appropriate to the melodrama of the unknown woman, the Hollywood subgenre that Cavell opposes to remarriage comedy as centered on women for whom the shared satisfactions of marriage prove impossible.

If there is a moment in Haigh's film that registers the kind of intuitive radar and physical eloquence required for coupled reattachment to marriage, it involves not Kate and Geoff but their friends Lina (Geraldine James) and George (David Sibley), who match them in a double-couple foursome like that around which *The Philadelphia Story* turns. At the Mercers' wedding anniversary celebrations, moments in advance of the formal speech in which Geoff tries to say what his wife means to him before breaking down in tears, we glimpse the Lina and George countercouple at the center of a small huddle of people. George is showing off his ukulele skills, the very thing he

7.7
Love by ukelele
(*45 Years*, Andrew Haigh, 2014).

has previously bored everyone with, including his wry wife, by talking about incessantly. In this scene, however, his beautiful wife sits beside him clapping an accompaniment with a broad smile on her face and eyes for no one but her husband, who rapturously returns her gaze.

In Cavell's account of Leo McCarey's *The Awful Truth*—to him the deepest achievement among the Hollywood comedies of remarriage—he proposes that if, as Frye argues, both Old and New Comedy conclude in a festival—often enough a wedding—then the comedies of remarriage depart from this model insofar as they expect "the pair to find happiness alone, unsponsored, in one another, out of their capacities for improvising a world, beyond ceremony." In compliance with this rule, *The Awful Truth* famously ends by putting the estranged husband and wife unceremoniously to bed in a scene of nocturnal reunion whose only public witness is a cat. If the fraught celebration and speeches at the end of *45 Years* expose the fragility of the Mercer marriage, the fleeting sight of Lina and George's sheer and unassuming happiness confirms their capacity to make coupled life what Cavell describes as "a run of laughs, within life." Like the exemplary scene in *The Awful Truth* when the opera-singing Lucy (Irene Dunne), posing as her husband's sister, does a turn as a burlesque performer in order to stop Jerry (Cary Grant) marrying someone else, the ukulele scene breaks with the stiffness of the formal marriage anniversary ceremony and reveals Lina as someone who laughingly consents to join George in the ongoing comedy of married life. Lina sees in George what Kate seems unable to find in Geoff: someone with whom marriage can become an everyday festive existence, or as Cavell parses it on Lucy's behalf, "He is the one with whom that is possible for me, crazy as he is; that is the awful truth."[20]

For Cavell, the innovation of remarriage comedy, and what makes it stand out as modern against all governing accounts of comedy Old and New, is that it tracks "the comedic to its roots in the everyday" and provides a new answer to the "ancient question concerning whether the comic resides fundamentally in events or in an attitude toward events."[21] Haigh's DVD running commentary on the film seems to echo Cavell on precisely this point when he quizzically remarks that there is nothing in the revelation about Geoff's past that necessarily makes for marital tragedy. Marital tragedy, like remarriage comedy, is rather a question of attitude or genre. If they celebrate anything, remarriage comedies celebrate the human capacity to encounter the hardship of life, and particularly the hardship of married life, "otherwise" in the "achievement" of what Cavell calls, following Montaigne but also anticipating the argument of this book, a "gay and sociable wisdom."[22] That the question of attitude is central to *45 Years* is made clear in the key element that Haigh's film preserves from its Shakespearean, Rohmerian, and Hollywood models, namely that there is no infidelity to be discovered. Finding infidelity is the paranoid work of jealous partners and bedroom dicks, something the original comedies of remarriage deliberately sideline in order to focus not on evidence or fact but on story, or the question of "how a matter"—even a matter as charged as infidelity—"gets *opened* to experience, and how it is *determined* by language or, let us say, by narration."[23] That is the awful truth.

In Thomson's married man's review of the film, the work required to change the narrational attitude to marriage also comes up in startlingly Cavellian terms. "It's even possible," Thomson writes, as if he were an experienced couples counselor and not simply the veteran of two marriages, "that the reawakened past might bring Geoff and Kate closer." This possibility—the possibility of a reawakening—is laid down in the film's diurnal narration, its rhythmic rocking between day and night, something it shares with *The Awful Truth*, which Haigh underscores by laying the names of the days of the week across natural landscapes seen in morning light. Against the backdrop of dailiness, it is significant that Kate sleeps in on Friday and misses her usual walk with the dog, and equally significant that on Saturday morning Geoff joins them for the first time. Cavell persuasively argues that whereas classical comedy promises the redemption of festival as represented in the succession of the seasons, modern remarriage comedy promises the redemption of dailiness and "the acceptance of human relatedness, as the acceptance of repetition" in the everyday. This recasting of comedy, or the pursuit of happiness, in the everyday turns us away from the wedding festival—or even the festival of the affair as celebrated by the many critics of marriage—to "ideas of the diurnal, of weddedness as a mode of intimacy, and of the projection of a metaphysics of repetition."[24] These ideas, which Cavell finds articulated in the cycle of remarriage comedies, he also finds in Søren Kierkegaard's study of the possibility of marriage—titled *Repetition*— and Friedrich Nietzsche's notion of Eternal Return as a "heightening" of time as expressed in "*Hochzeit*," the German term for "marriage." More interesting still, however, is that pursuing this line of thought leads Cavell to recollect a more lesbian source for insight into marriage as remarriage, namely Gertrude Stein's *The Making of Americans*, which he prefers to summon through the dramatic machinery of memory rather than literal citation:

> She speaks, I seem to recall, to the effect that the knowledge of others depends upon an appreciation of their repeatings (which is what we are, which is what we have to offer). This knowing of others as knowing what they are always saying and believing and doing would, naturally, be Stein's description of, or direction for, how her reader is to know her own most famous manner of writing, the hallmark of which is its repeatings. The application of this thought here is the suggestion that marriage is an emblem of the knowledge of others not solely because of its implication of reciprocity but because it implies a devotion in repetition, to dailiness.[25]

Cavell's recollection of Stein's *The Making of Americans* suggests that marriage practiced in this way—as remarriage with no necessary relation to formal celebration or sanctification but every relation to the repetition embedded in the everyday—will be the making of us all, or at least those of us who are predisposed to refind happiness in the repetitive and reciprocal experience of dailiness rather than seeking outbreaks of happiness in what is otherwise experienced as dull routine.

This brings us back to the question of attitude and whether or not we can change the genre through which we experience the happenstance of our life, including the happenstance of our weddedness, whether or not we are married. The revelation of remarriage comedy, Cavell advises, is that, unlike other forms of comedy, the obstacles to happiness are not complications or ignorances of fact that might be sorted out in a conclusive way so as to give closure to the story of married life. Rather, the obstacles reside within the coupled relationship itself. Thus, while the estranged couples of remarriage comedy do "have something to learn," that something "cannot come as news from others," nor will its arrival from within put an end to the story of marriage as perpetual reattachment. If Old and New Comedy, and their schematic derivatives, can rely on a god in the dramatic machinery of plot to deliver the truth about a marriage or an infidelity, the modern comedy of remarriage engages a "redemptive psychology" in which married couples must redeliver themselves to fidelity and happiness "not in a future, a beyond, an ever after, but in a present continuity of before and after" through the "correction not of error but of experience, or of a perspective on experience."[26] Unlike marital comedy, which can deploy the standard dramatic arcs of complication, revelation, and celebration, the narrational challenge faced by remarriage comedy is how to show happiness as an immersive experience of the everyday that can be lost and then regained. Cavell thinks this challenge is exceptionally well met in *The Awful Truth*, in which McCarey chooses not to disrupt the diurnal surface of the film's comedy with a "knock-out scene" but, rather, "empowers the presenting of an unbroken line of comic development, a continuous unfolding of thought and of emotion" sufficient to convey "the courage, the powers, required for happiness" of the coupled kind.[27]

45 Years, it seems to me, similarly puts its central couple to the test of remarriage, a test that is required of all marriages following the social acceptance of divorce and, somewhat differently, the social acceptance of marriage equality. The question posed by the film's final frame might be put in this way: is this wife capable of meeting this husband's repetitions as continuous with their married happiness rather than its irreparable flaw? But perhaps that is too American a question to ask of such deeply British protagonists. Yet the film makes clear, in cinematic if not psychological terms, that in loving Katya, Geoff simply loved a version of Kate before he knew her, a redemptive fiction made available by the visual likeness of the woman photographed as Katya to a young Rampling and the projection of their two faces alongside each other in a scene in the attic in which Kate is pursuing her unhappiness by trying to wring an awful facticity from the past. Happiness lies in the other direction—the direction of Hollywood and Rohmer and Shakespeare—not in the truth of an event but in the possibility of changing one's imaginative relation to event or reading it differently. "The trouble with most marriages," Jerry announces in *The Awful Truth*, "is that people are always imagining things," to which Cavell adds, "It turns out that what is wrong is not with the imagination as such but with the way most people use their imaginations, running it mechanically along ruts of suspicion. This causes, at best, farce, the negation of faith" in others and in oneself.[28] The road to divorce, Cavell concludes, once again quoting Jerry, is "paved with suspicions," but "the discovery of the road back from divorce is explicitly entitled forgiveness" and "the forgoing of revenge."[29] This less-traveled road leads to the recovery of innocence and a kind of forgetfulness, the two elements necessary for the re-idealization of marriage as remarriage. Put another way, the imagination of remarriage—or at least its cinematic imagining as comedy—is "not a matter of the reception of new experience but a matter of a new reception of your own experience, an acceptance of its authority as your own."[30] You know this thing and now you know it differently. Repeat. And repeat again.

No one said this process would be easy, or certainly not as easy as the Hollywood comedies of remarriage can make it look. Indeed, Cavell says the opposite if in a very philosophical way. Finding remarriage in marriage will always be hard, since "there are certain truths to these matters which discover where the concepts come together of time and of childhood and of forgiveness and of overcoming revenge and of an acceptance of the repetitive needs of the body and the soul—of one's motions and one's motives, one's ecstasies and routines, one's sexuality and one's loves—as the truths of oneself. They will, whatever we discover, be awful truths, since otherwise why do truths about ourselves take such pains to find and to say?"[31] When Kate stares at the image of a pregnant Katya, we see her comprehend all these awful truths and not know the way forward. She comes down from the attic and wanders through the empty house. The phone rings and she distractedly picks it up and tersely gets through a conversation with the DJ who has rung to confirm the party playlist. "No Elton John," she tells him, as if to make clear that this celebration will not be a gay affirmation of anything, least of all marriage. The difficulty Kate has in reattaching to her husband is attested to in the remaining scenes between them in which words no longer serve. The conversation that is their marriage becomes increasingly despairing through Thursday and Friday before ending on Saturday in his anniversary speech and her silence.

Although the final scenes of the film are set in the heritage-listed Norwich Assembly Rooms, which are dominated by historical portraits and a thematically significant landscape painting of an alpine scene, the formative backdrop to the Mercer marriage is the flat countryside of East Anglia, specifically the man-made Norfolk Broads. Beautifully captured by Lol Crawley on 35-millimeter film stock, the wintery landscape we see is neither the green world of Shakespearean romance nor the benign setting of Rohmer's *A Tale of Winter*. Despite the strong horizon lines and softly striated natural colors the area around the Mercer house presents to the camera, this seemingly thriving natural environment—like the marriage it visually offsets—is also a broken thing that merely takes the semblance of something organically whole.

7.8
The regeneration of marriage
(*45 Years*, Andrew Haigh, 2014).

Far from being a place of enchantment where the material world magically conforms to the utopian vision we have of it—like the plush world of "Conneckticut" in which many of the original Hollywood comedies of remarriage are set—the Norfolk region that Kate and Geoff inhabit registers the recalcitrance of nature and its refusal to submit to idealization.[32] Part of what was known as the Great Fen of England, this area has been subject to devastating human intervention since the medieval excavation of peat and later schemes designed to drain soggy nature and turn it into arable land for capital gain. As David Alff explains in his recent discussion of the project sensibility at the core of modern discourses of improvement, the Norfolk Broads are the artificial result of centuries of speculative and technocratic endeavor. The putative success of this enterprise reached its apotheosis in the nineteenth-century, when steam engines took over from windmill pumps, resulting in a "self-defeating" landscape of perpetual wastage where the drainage of naturally waterlogged bog produced topsoil that the ever-present wind carried away.[33] Several scenes in *45 Years* place Kate and Geoff within this landscape of continuous self-defeat, which is the very opposite of the self-healing landscape needed for perpetual remarriage.

While many reviewers have noted the incongruous sight of a Mississippi paddle steamer traveling the canals around the ancient town of Horning, none have mentioned the scene where Kate drops Geoff at his old workplace, a factory with massive concrete grain silos that is an industrial-scale monument to the draining of the fens and human indifference to the watery rhythms of the natural environment. Unlike the perpetual reenchantment promised in the Hollywood comedies of remarriage, the environmental sensibility encoded in *45 Years* provides a bleak metaphor for long-term heterosexual marriage. Geoff reads about climate change and the global warming that released his young would-be wife from the glacier but stays detached from the natural world around him.[34] Kate lopes about the countryside but seems stiff in social exchanges and can't persuade the postman she taught as a schoolboy to call her by her first name. The inflexibility in Kate that inhibits her prospects of remarriage also finds a correlative in the Norfolk countryside. Whenever she is seen in her garden or out walking, either alone or with her husband, she is usually framed by beech trees or hedgerows with their distinctive brown winter leaves. Unlike most other deciduous trees that shed their leaves as part of the natural cycle of the seasons, the beech tree holds on to its leaves well into spring. A visual metaphor for an inability to detach rather than the renewal of attachment, the beech leaves also contribute their distinctive rustle to the soundscape of the film, a noise that is amplified by the easterly winds as they blow in from the English Channel across the flat expanse of the fenlands. Rather than whispering, as leaves are poetically said to do, the husk-dry leaves of the beech contribute a deathly rattle that is heard most forcefully in the early scene in which Kate and Geoff sit outside trying to discuss the content of the letter that has just arrived in their Monday morning advising them of Katya's resurrection from the dead.[35] The tension in Haigh's film rests in the difference between the death of marriage and its transfiguration as remarriage, a conundrum made patent by the historical advent of marriage equality, which either spells the end of the institution or its ongoing renewal as a culturally relevant form. The film stops on the cusp of Sunday, the day traditionally given over to celebrating rebirth or resurrection, as if to let us know the achievement of remarriage is still within reach. All it requires is another cinematic dawn.

REACKNOWLEDGMENTS

Rather than launch a new queer manifesto—"What do we want? Remarriage! When do we want it? Now!"—I am happy to acknowledge the others who got there before me. First among them is Stanley Cavell, of course, although he declined to pursue the connection between remarriage and gay marriage. Cavell did, however, belatedly disclose the connection between his thinking about remarriage and the "general sentiments of guilt and failure" that attended the dissolution of his first marriage.[1] In 1994, shortly after he had seen Ingmar Bergman's stage production of Shakespeare's *The Winter's Tale* in Stockholm, Cavell was prompted to recall his first viewing of Bergman's *Smiles of a Summer Night* (1955) in 1960 when he was mired in the difficult process of separating from his wife and child. "I was thirty-four years old," Cavell writes, "precisely half my lifetime ago, evidently lost in the middle of life's journey within the bright parks of Berkeley, where I was completing my fourth year as an assistant professor in the philosophy department."[2] Unable to complete the overdue dissertation that, unless submitted, would mean his position would be terminated the following year, Cavell encounters Bergman's film and "the economy of discredit" it redemptively outlines as a reflection of his own personal and professional dilemma. In this emotionally labile state, he finds himself sharing "elements" with all of the key characters in *Smiles of a Summer Night*, no matter their gender: the "isolated" father, the "unclaimed" wife, the "turbulent" son, and the "skeptical" actress "tending to a child alone."[3] Adopting a retrospectively enlightened autobiographical perspective, Cavell comes to understand that his estrangement from marriage not only coincided with but perhaps brought about his inability to write. Now, with the benefit of intellectual hindsight, Cavell can link both productions—"Bergman's presentation of summer and Shakespeare's of winter and spring"—to his dawning understanding as a young man headed into divorce of the difference between false and true marriage and his appreciation of remarriage comedy as a mechanism to parse that distinction without rancor.[4] On top of this recognition comes the parallel recognition of the ability of film, and particularly the "matter-of-fact" genius of film dialogue, "to redeem academic discourse for human sociability" and the intellectual liberation attendant on that.[5] Needless to say, in the way of comedy all comes out right in the end: the dissertation gets finished, tenure is secured, and eventually the world receives an account of remarriage comedy as popular culture's way of reckoning the difference "between a liberating and a stifling understanding, or between sincerity and cynicism" in the matter of coupled love, a relationship memorably figured as "the civilized violence of one soul's intelligence of another."[6]

Other experts on marriage are less tethered to the idea that a philosophy of remarriage can best be advanced through a philosophy of film. One such person is long-time marriage counselor Esther Perel, the author of the best-selling *Mating in Captivity: Unlocking Erotic Intelligence* and its sequel, *The State of Affairs: Rethinking Infidelity*, the promotional blurb for which flattens the Shakespearean premise of the Hollywood remarriage comedies into contemporary self-help speak: "An affair can even be the doorway to a new marriage—with the same person."[7] With thirty years' experience as a couple counselor under her belt, Perel has recently launched a series of podcasts that are redacted recordings of actual counseling sessions with disenchanted attachers from all points of the erotosphere—straight husbands and wives, gay and lesbian partners, serial philanderers, the polyamorous—in what seems to be an upscaled enterprise version of her hugely successful TEDx talks, "The Secret to Desire in a Long-Term Relationship" (2013, approaching 14 million views) and "Rethinking Infidelity: A Talk for Anyone Who Has Ever Loved" (2015, 12.5 million).

Reviewing Perel's podcasts in the *New Yorker* in May 2017, Alexandra Schwartz refers to the just-breaking internet story, and associated memes, of Melania Trump instinctively batting away her husband's presidential hand as they crossed the tarmac in Tel Aviv to be followed by a similarly chill though more composed public rebuttal of intimacy the following day, as the pair deplaned Air Force One in Paris, a city no longer known for romantic or global accord thanks to the Trumps' visit.[8] As Schwartz points out, these gestures—exemplarily though not exclusively matrimonial—were set against an equally generic attachment scene by Pete Souza, the former president's official photographer, who took the opportunity to post to his Instagram account a photograph of Barack and Michelle Obama in 2015 seated before the Edmund Pettus Bridge in Selma, Alabama, on the fiftieth anniversary of the Bloody Sunday civil rights protest. As Schwartz describes it, Mr. and Mrs. Obama are holding hands in "a gesture that needed no interpretation" but, since *Reattachment Theory* is founded in the drive to interpret, I think

8.1
The state of matrimony
(Official White House photograph, Pete Souza, 2015).

it is worth reflecting on the photograph's semiotic richness, whether that be considered a property of its surface or its depth.

Taken in high sun, the short depth of field of Souza's photograph captures the glint of the gold band on Obama's left hand while visually softening the iconic bridge behind the two evenly balanced figures who fill the foreground in matching black outfits, their profiles crisply aligned in the direction of the commemorative events unfolding outside the frame. The handsome presidential couple are linked by both the arching superstructure of America's racialized history and the diagonal infrastructure of marriage as Mrs. Obama's long, lithe arm reaches across the foreground in an action that perfectly betokens the effortless seaming together of publicity and privacy that is conjugality. Their expressions bear witness to the weight of racial injustice but the sunlight on Michelle Obama's black skin and the block of bright yellow to the right of Barack Obama's head, like the blue sky overhead, imprint the scene with hopefulness. As Schwartz goes on to say, "The difference between the Obamas' obvious intimacy and mutual respect and whatever is going on with the Trumps is enough to make any American despair about the state of modern marriage, along with the state of everything else," in the kind of slick segue from marriage to state that would be familiar to anyone who has read

Stanley Cavell or Lauren Berlant, two names forever joined in my thinking about marital commitment and its funny and unfunny genres.

I began this book by drawing on Katherine Franke's argument that advocates for and against gay marriage have a lot to learn from the historical example of the extension of marriage law to formerly enslaved African Americans. In the time since I first drafted that argument, Ann duCille has edited a collection of essays that address the issue of black marriage from the time of slavery to the time of *Lemonade,* Beyoncé's visual concept album that uses public speculation about her husband's infidelity as the lever through which to explore the sexual legacy of slavery.[9] In his brief contribution to that volume of essays, Kendall Thomas reviews Franke's argument about the whitewashing of the marriage equality movement in order to ask if black marriage is queer. Importantly, his question is not framed as a historical or legal inquiry into the status of black marriage but as a rhetorical gambit. Black experience, Thomas argues, cannot be reduced to the history of enslavement, as if stigma were an indelible and ongoing property of race rather than something that can be reimagined on different terms:

> To be faithful to its aspirations, then, a queer critical theory of black marriage must refuse to restrict its field of vision to what black marriage was in the nineteenth-century past, or even to what it is in our twenty-first-century present; it must also be willing to reflect speculatively on what black marriage might become in a twenty-second-century future. Similarly, in taking up the question of how black intimate alliance and the black intimate imagination can be mobilized to forge new, more democratic forms of sexual and racial citizenship, a critically queer engagement with the politics of black marriage must declare its independence from the ideological terms and institutional terrain of "law and rights-based advocacy."[10]

Setting aside his academic affiliation to legal studies, Thomas finds speculative evidence of these new imaginings of black intimate alliance in narrative films as distinct from each other as Barry Jenkins's Academy Award–winning *Moonlight* (2016) and the Marvel-Disney blockbuster *Black Panther* (2018). Whatever their specific generic affiliations and achievements, Thomas insists that these "cinematic figurations" are alike in that they gesture toward "African American erotic and intimate life *beyond* the binary boundaries of normative whiteness and nonnormative blackness, of white supremacy and black inferiority" and refuse to be limited to the vexed conditions of the present, however well they understand them.[11]

Thomas ends his essay by arguing that the way to shift the "'Americanist' narrative that always and only figures blackness as accreted stain, lack, failure, inferiority, stigma, mark, or curse" is to engage a transnational comparative framework that asks "whether, why, and how bisexual, heterosexual, gay, and lesbian black people around the world experiment with conjugality by crafting spaces *within* marriage that engage and include intimate relational possibilities *outside* it."[12] As someone who writes from outside the United States, it pleases me to close my queer updating of Cavell's account of remarriage by invoking American black marriage as an exemplary instance of matrimonial perfectionism, a form that nurtures utopian imaginings that reverberate transnationally. While others may see this as a universalist extension of the ruse of neoliberalism to black subjects who have nothing to gain from the whitewashed agenda of same-sex marriage equality, I prefer (like Thomas) to regard it as a final reminder that categories of sexuality, like categories of race, have evolved together, not apart, and that in this regard, as in others, the story of marriage has always been more expansive and open to change than we have sometimes thought.

For Cavell, it is the sociable language of the Hollywood comedies of remarriage that allows us to shift our attachment from the imperfectly attained state of marriage to its utopian form. Importantly, the coupled ideal of serial reattachment allows us to recognize our separateness and difference from each other, including those we love most. Unlike queer theoretical skepticism around marriage equality, which likes to imagine itself grounded in the stern stuff of political realism, the work of reattachment is more delicately tethered to the figural and to the notion of repair. Rather than proposing a queer theory of marriage, this book demonstrates my ongoing attachment to close reading as a way of taking a question, or even a deeply personal problem, to a particular film and, through the miracle of writing about it, letting it help you find the answer that you need, perhaps not forever, but for now. That is the awful truth about this book: it originated in something like a marriage crisis.

One of the many insights passed on in Cavell's account of *The Philadelphia Story* is that it takes not a family but a community—perhaps even a community so diverse it can stand for a nation—to hold a couple together. I have found this to be true. The idea for *Reattachment Theory* first came to me in 2015 when my long-term partner and I were on sabbatical in Berlin, the German capital of reunification, although we were working through a lot of stuff pointing in the other direction, the direction of estrangement and separation. The city knew better. In a fourth-floor apartment in the auspiciously named suburb of Wedding, I read *Pursuits of Happiness* for the first time and understood that the book on homosexuality and melodrama that I thought I was writing (although fairer to say I was not writing it) could be reframed as an argument about gay marriage as remarriage that wrested that discussion from its usual moorings.

Across the ellipsis between now and then I have learned that the theory and practice of remarriage is not easy, not for anyone, but it would be impossible without a community of friends in support. Among all those who have contributed to my attachment to reattachment, as both theory and practice, I particularly thank Prudence Black, Anna Breckon, Carolyn Dinshaw, Richard Dyer, Brett Farmer, Melissa Hardie, Chris Healy, Scott Herring, Una Jagose, Mary Kisler, David Kisler, Jenny Keate, Shuchi Kothari, Marget Long, Kate Lilley, Heather Love, Sharon Marcus, Astrida Neimanis, Al Pope, Elspeth Probyn, Susan Potter, Susanna Sachsse, Marc Siegel, Kate Small, Katrina Schlunke, Amy Villarejo, Julie Wallace, Lisa Webb, Patricia White, Robyn Wiegman, Pamela Wojcik, and Nabeel Zuberi.

Most theorists of attachment link it to ambivalence. Lauren Berlant, for instance, suggests that popular genres of attachment, like melodrama, exist to acknowledge ambivalence and make it bearable through an optimistic process of recognition and reflection that approximates a "scene of negotiated sustenance."[13] Raising attachment to the second degree, the popular genre of remarriage comedy is built around the reacknowledgment of ambivalence, which was poorly managed the first time around but is crucial to the fortunate fall back into coupled love. As a student of Leo McCarey, Cavell frames it thus, "It is an awful, an awesome truth that the acknowledgement of the otherness of others, of ineluctable separation, is the condition of human happiness. Indifference is the denial of this condition."[14] In the comedies of remarriage, regaining the knowledge of ambivalence involves a complicated process of seconding that culminates in the rediscovery of a mutual language. To Annamarie Jagose, I tender this book as my half of that promise.

As those familiar with Cavell's account of remarriage will know, reacknowledgment is not enough to secure remarriage, which also requires enchantment and the sense that something miraculous is taking its course. It is a "requirement of the genre," he writes, "that the pair have known each other forever, hence that they are, or have been, something like brother and sister." This "original intimacy," which is based in the kind of sibling resemblance that can also be found between brothers and brothers, sisters and sisters, "must be broken if a different intimacy, that of strangers, or of the exogamous (ultimately, the difficult recognition of the separation, the otherness, of others), is to be achieved."[15] For the satisfaction of this peculiar quirk of the remarriage contract—that familiarity must precede strangeness—I thank Jan Wallace and Anne Jagose, who briefly knew each other as young mothers on the West Coast of New Zealand in the early 1960s before we were born. Three decades later, when Annamarie and I first declared our relationship, our mothers met our newness as a couple—something still strange to us—with recognition, as if our erotic randomness was importantly destined to reunite them in friendship and familiarity. It is this maternal happenstance—the kind of coincidence of fantasy and reality that remarriage comedy is built on—that allows me to stand among all the stars in the remarriage canon and say to the extraordinary stranger whose ordinary company I keep, I loved you all the time. Forever.

NOTES

Chapter 1. Queer Skepticism and Gay Marriage

1. Michael Warner, *The Trouble with Normal: Sex, Politics, and the Ethics of Queer Life* (New York: Free Press, 1999). Though predicted long in advance, many were surprised at the rapid rise of the marriage equality movement and its global reach. Katherine Franke is one of the few to acknowledge in print that the backlash against gay marriage that she, and many others, anticipated never occurred "or at least has been isolated to a few regions of the country. Instead, with speed unimaginable even five years ago, same-sex marriage fever has swept the nation and the predictable foes of marriage equality are revisiting their opposition to including same-sex couples in the domain of legal marriage." Katherine Franke, *Wedlocked: The Perils of Marriage Equality* (New York: New York University Press, 2015), 5.
2. Warner, *Trouble with Normal*, ix.
3. For Warner's expanded account of queer counterpublics—and their various impulses to inclusion and exclusion—as a form of practical social fiction, see Michael Warner, *Publics and Counterpublics* (New York: Zone Books, 2002).
4. Judith Butler, "Is Kinship Always Already Heterosexual?" *differences: A Journal of Feminist Cultural Studies* 15, no. 1 (2002): 14.
5. Butler "Kinship," 15.
6. Louise Richardson-Self, *Justifying Same-Sex Marriage: A Philosophical Investigation* (London: Rowman and Littlefield, 2015), 3.
7. Richardson-Self, *Justifying Same-Sex Marriage*, 6.
8. Richardson-Self, *Justifying Same-Sex Marriage*, 10.
9. Lee Edelman, *No Future: Queer Theory and the Death Drive* (Durham, NC: Duke University Press, 2004), 2. For a linking of Edelman's argument to queer concerns around the rise of gay marriage, see Heather Love, "Wedding Crashers," GLQ: *A Journal of Lesbian and Gay Studies* 13, no. 1 (2007): 125–39.
10. For an agenda-changing account of social science's relation to norms and the idea of sexual deviation, see Heather Love, "Doing Being Deviant: Deviance Studies, Description, and the Queer Ordinary," *differences: A Journal of Feminist Cultural Studies* 26, no. 1 (2015): 74–95.
11. Kimberly D. Richman, *License to Wed: What Legal Marriage Means to Same-Sex Couples* (New York: New York University Press, 2014), 7.

12 Richman, *License to Wed*, xix.
13 Patricia Ewick and Susan S. Silbey, *The Common Place of Law: Stories from Everyday Life* (Chicago, IL: University of Chicago Press, 1998). In their highly influential study, Ewick and Silbey establish three dominant narratives around legal consciousness in everyday life whereby the law is experienced as something magisterial and remote, or a game of rules that can be manipulated to advantage, or an arbitrary power that is resisted, or some combination of the above.
14 Richman, *License to Wed*, 13.
15 Richman, *License to Wed*, 13–14.
16 Richman, *License to Wed*, 18.
17 Lauren Berlant, "Intimacy: A Special Issue," in *Intimacy*, edited by Lauren Berlant (Chicago, IL: University of Chicago Press, 2000), 2.
18 Berlant, "Intimacy," 3–4.
19 Berlant, "Intimacy," 1.
20 Berlant, "Intimacy," 3. The inherent theatricality of marriage as social performance is evident in its exemption from the burden of proof that falls on de facto couples, whether straight or gay, who must establish the legality of their relationship by satisfying interdependency criteria that may shift between different state or national jurisdictions. For further discussion of the legal nonalignment between marriage and de facto couplehood in the context of the Australian nonbinding plebiscite on marriage equality, see Hannah Robert and Fiona Kelly's response to former prime minister Tony Abbott's claim that same-sex couples in committed domestic relationships already have the same rights as couples who are married. Hannah Robert and Fiona Kelly, "Explainer: What Legal Benefits Do Married Couples Have That De Facto Couples Do Not?" https://theconversation.com/explainer-what-legal-benefits-do-married-couples-have-that-de-facto-couples-do-not-83896, accessed September 21, 2017.
21 Berlant, "Intimacy," 5. As I will go on to discuss, melodrama is one aesthetic of the extreme that has given publicity to the affective energies of women and homosexuals in particular. Drawing on Berlant, Jonathan Goldberg has recently contested accounts of melodramatic excess as the means by which minorities are given space in culture. Goldberg argues that the melodramatic remediation of feeling in music and gesture points not to culture or representation but beyond it to a "way beyond words" (167). Jonathan Goldberg, *Melodrama: An Aesthetics of Impossibility* (Durham, NC: Duke University Press, 2016).
22 For discussion of the rights provided and denied same-sex couples under various international legal reforms and their critical import from a variety of queer and feminist positions, see Amy L. Brandzel, "Queering Citizenship? Same-Sex Marriage and the State," *GLQ: A Journal of Lesbian and Gay Studies* 11, no. 2 (2005): 171–204; Butler, "Kinship"; and Ann Ferguson, "Gay Marriage: An American and Feminist Dilemma," *Hypatia* 22, no. 1 (2007): 39–57.
23 Franke, *Wedlocked*, 2–3.
24 Franke, *Wedlocked*, 3.
25 Chandan Reddy, "Race and the Critique of Marriage," *South Atlantic Quarterly* 115, no. 2 (2016): 429.

26 Chandan Reddy, "Time for Rights? *Loving*, Gay Marriage, and the Limits of Legal Justice." *Fordham Law Review* 76, no. 6 (2008): 2849–72.
27 Reddy, "Critique of Marriage," 429.
28 Key texts in this school of thought that specifically address the racialization of sexuality effected by marriage include Roderick A. Ferguson, *Aberrations in Black: Toward a Queer of Color Critique* (Minneapolis: University of Minnesota Press, 2004); Elizabeth A. Povinelli, *Empire of Love: Toward a Theory of Intimacy, Genealogy, and Carnality* (Durham, NC: Duke University Press, 2006); David L. Eng, *The Feeling of Kinship: Queer Liberalism and Racialization of Intimacy* (Durham, NC: Duke University Press, 2010); Nayan Shah, *Stranger Intimacy: Contesting Race, Sexuality, and the Law in the North American West* (Berkeley: University of California Press, 2011); and Amy L. Brandzel, *Against Citizenship: The Violence of the Normative* (Chicago, IL: University of Chicago Press, 2016). In *Cruising Utopia: The Then and There of Queer Futurity* (New York: New York University Press, 2009), José Muñoz provides a slightly different take on the normative impulse at the heart of the gay marriage movement when he describes "being ordinary and being married" as equivalently "antiutopian" wishes (21). Although it does not substantially engage marriage but for a nod to the *Loving* case and a brief citation of Ann duCille's discussion of the African American marriage plot in the early nineties—*The Coupling Convention: Sex, Text, and Tradition in Black Women's Fiction* (Oxford: Oxford University Press, 1993)—Siobhan B. Sommerville's *Queering the Color Line: Race and the Invention of Homosexuality in American Culture* (Durham, NC: Duke University Press, 2000) is an important forerunner to later queer work on the historical intersections of race and sexuality.
29 R. Ferguson, *Aberrations in Black*, 131.
30 Amy Villarejo, "Tarrying with the Normative: Queer Theory and *Black History*," *Social Text* 23, nos. 3–4 (2005): 69–84.
31 Villarejo, "Tarrying with the Normative," 75.
32 Adele M. Morrison, "Same-Sex *Loving*: Subverting White Supremacy through Same-Sex Marriage," *Michigan Journal of Race and Law* 13, no. 1 (2007): 177–225.
33 Morrison, "Same-Sex *Loving*," 177.
34 Morrison, "Same-Sex *Loving*," 208.
35 The connection between Black Lives Matter, queer of color critique, and antimiscegenation rulings as the source of racial foreclosure rather than its remedy is made by Reddy in "Critique of Marriage," 430–31.
36 See, for instance, Sophie Verass, "Illegal Love: Is This N[orthern] T[erritory] Couple Australia's Richard and Mildred Loving?" NITV website, sbs.com.au, August 13, 2017.
37 See Valerie Cooms, "Miscegenation and Intimacy," a review of Fiona Probyn-Rapsey, *Made to Matter: White Fathers, Stolen Generations* (Sydney: Sydney University Press, 2013), *Cultural Studies Review* 21, no. 2 (2015): 291–97.
38 See Lee Wallace, *Sexual Encounters: Pacific Texts, Modern Sexualities* (Ithaca, NY: Cornell University Press, 2003), for an account of how the indigenous sexual behaviors observed in the colonization of the Pacific region contributed

to the emergence of Western sexual categories, particularly the category of homosexuality.

39 Ann Laura Stoler, *Race and the Education of Desire: Foucault's History of Sexuality and the Colonial Order of Things* (Durham, NC: Duke University Press, 1995).
40 Franke, *Wedlocked*, 234.
41 Franke, *Wedlocked*, 211.
42 Franke, *Wedlocked*, 212.
43 Franke, *Wedlocked*, 209.
44 Franke, *Wedlocked*, 8.
45 Brandzel, "Queering Citizenship?" 195.
46 Laura Kipnis, "Adultery," in Berlant, *Intimacy*, 9–47. Laura Kipnis, *Against Love: A Polemic* (New York: Vintage, 2003).
47 Kipnis, "Adultery," 10.
48 David R. Shumway, "Why Same-Sex Marriage Now?" *Discourse* 26, no. 3 (2004): 73–84.
49 Shumway, "Why Same-Sex Marriage Now?" 78.
50 Shumway, "Why Same-Sex Marriage Now?" 75.
51 Shumway, "Why Same-Sex Marriage Now?" 76.
52 Shumway, "Why Same-Sex Marriage Now?" 76.
53 Shumway, "Why Same-Sex Marriage Now?" 76.
54 Kipnis, "Adultery," 11. As Kipnis goes on to argue, "In the Marriage Takes Work regime of normative intimacy, when the work shift ends and the domestic shift begins hardly makes much difference; from surplus labor to surplus monogamy is a short, easy commute. Under conditions of surplus monogamy, adultery—a sphere of purposelessness, outside contracts, not colonized by the logic of production and the performance principle—becomes something beyond a structural possibility. It's a counterlogic to the prevailing system" (18).
55 Shumway, "Why Same-Sex Marriage Now?" 78.
56 Shumway, "Why Same-Sex Marriage Now?" 78.
57 Shumway, "Why Same-Sex Marriage Now?" 79.
58 Candace Vogler, "Sex and Talk," in Berlant, *Intimacy*, 49.
59 Vogler, "Sex and Talk," 51.
60 Vogler, "Sex and Talk," 48–49.
61 Vogler, "Sex and Talk," 64, 72. Although Vogler makes no mention of Stanley Cavell, who likewise draws on Kant to assist his counterintuitive thinking in the realm of marriage, her final conclusions resound deeply with his deliberations on the Hollywood comedies of remarriage and their tonality around marriage, as I will go on to discuss. "Case-study spouses," Vogler writes, "could try for a mode of interested detachment that belongs more to ruefulness than despair and less to romance than irony" (85). See Stanley Cavell, *Pursuits of Happiness: The Hollywood Comedy of Remarriage* (Cambridge, MA: Harvard University Press, 1981) and *Cities of Words: Pedagogical Letters on a Register of the Moral Life* (Cambridge, MA: Harvard University Press, 2004).
62 Shumway, "Why Same-Sex Marriage Now?" 80.
63 Shumway, "Why Same-Sex Marriage Now?" 81.

64 Sedgwick makes this point most succinctly in the coauthored introduction to *Shame and Its Sisters: A Silvan Tomkins Reader*, ed. Eve Kosofsky Sedgwick and Adam Frank (Durham, NC: Duke University Press, 1995), 5. See, also, 24–25n3, which provides a taxonomy of common misunderstandings of Foucault's repressive hypothesis.
65 Michael Cobb, *Single: Arguments for the Uncoupled* (New York: New York University Press, 2012), 174.
66 Cobb, *Single*, 9–14.
67 Cobb, *Single*, 181, 191.
68 Cobb, *Single*, 189.
69 Cobb, *Single*, 192.
70 Cobb, *Single*, 182, 192.
71 Cobb, *Single*, 32.
72 Annamarie Jagose, *Orgasmology* (Durham, NC: Duke University Press, 2013), 66.
73 Jagose, *Orgasmology*, 66–67.
74 Jagose, *Orgasmology*, 83.
75 Jagose, *Orgasmology*, 86.
76 Jagose, *Orgasmology*, 86–67.
77 The first-wave marriage crisis extends from the initial publication of Edward Carpenter's *Love's Coming of Age* in 1896 to its republication in 1930, two years after Ernest Groves's *The Marriage Crisis* appeared. Edward Carpenter, *Love's Coming of Age: A Series of Papers on the Relations of the Sexes* (Manchester, UK: Labour, 1896; repr., London: Allen and Unwin, 1930); Ernest Groves, *The Marriage Crisis* (New York: Longmans, Green, 1928).

Chapter 2. From Gay Marriage to Remarriage

1 Those interested in tracing earlier forms of protogay and lesbian marriage might begin with Alan Bray, *Homosexuality in Renaissance England* (London: Gay Men's Press, 1982), and Lillian Faderman, *Surpassing the Love of Men: Romantic Friendship and Love between Women from the Renaissance to the Present* (New York: William Morrow, 1981).
2 Ian P. Watt, *The Rise of the Novel: Studies in Defoe, Richardson, and Fielding* (Berkeley: University of California Press, 1957).
3 Nancy Armstrong, *Desire and Domestic Fiction: A Political History of the Novel* (Oxford: Oxford University Press, 1987), 9.
4 Armstrong, *Desire and Domestic Fiction*, 7.
5 Armstrong, *Desire and Domestic Fiction*, 51.
6 Armstrong, *Desire and Domestic Fiction*, 7. For Armstrong's discussion of Freud's Dora, see *Desire and Domestic Fiction*, 224–50.
7 Armstrong, *Desire and Domestic Fiction*, 50–51.
8 Lawrence Stone's three-volume, thousand-page history of English marriage is worth citing for its titles alone: *Road to Divorce: England, 1530–1987* (Oxford: Oxford University Press, 1990); *Uncertain Unions: Marriage in England, 1660–*

1753 (Oxford: Oxford University Press, 1992); and *Broken Lives: Separation and Divorce, 1660–1857* (Oxford: Oxford University Press, 1993). With friends like Stone, marriage hardly needs same-sex enemies.

9. Tony Tanner, *Adultery in the Novel: Contract and Transgression* (Baltimore, MD: Johns Hopkins University Press, 1979), 4.
10. Tanner, *Adultery in the Novel*, 15.
11. Tanner, *Adultery in the Novel*, 11.
12. Tanner, *Adultery in the Novel*, 376.
13. Tanner, *Adultery in the Novel*, 374, 375.
14. Tanner, *Adultery in the Novel*, 375. This peculiarly French appreciation of the deep perversity of the marriage contract emerges somewhat differently in Philippe Sollers and Julia Kristeva's jointly written *The Fine Art of Marriage*, translated by Lorna Scott Fox (New York: Columbia University Press, 2015). In interviews about her marriage with Sollers and the terms that underwrite it, Kristeva is always careful to distinguish between the promise of marriage and the promise of fidelity.
15. Tanner, *Adultery in the Novel*, 376. Laura Kipnis's Marxist-inflected dissection of marriage also identifies the disappointment endemic to adultery, which, like marriage, eventually becomes dulled by routine and repetition. This argument comes to the fore in the book-length version of her argument, where the titular focus has shifted away from "Adultery" to a more general takedown of coupled love. Laura Kipnis, *Against Love: A Polemic* (New York: Vintage, 2003).
16. Tanner, *Adultery in the Novel*, 12.
17. Tanner, *Adultery in the Novel*, 15.
18. Tanner, *Adultery in the Novel*, 13.
19. Tanner, *Adultery in the Novel*, 86.
20. Tanner, *Adultery in the Novel*, 17–18.
21. Kimberly A. Freeman, *Love American Style: Divorce and the American Novel, 1811–1976* (London: Routledge, 2003), 17.
22. K. Freeman, *Love American Style*, 140.
23. Tanner, *Adultery in the Novel*, 377.
24. Peter Brooks, *Reading for the Plot: Design and Intention in Narrative* (Cambridge, MA: Harvard University Press, 1983), 35.
25. P. Brooks, *Reading for the Plot*, 34. D. A. Miller's groundbreaking essays on Hitchcock have recently been assembled into the compendium book, *Hidden Hitchcock* (Chicago, IL: University of Chicago Press, 2016), a publishing event that, as Miller acknowledges in his preface, is unable to sustain the heady impact of their first appearance in print, such is the nature of formal perfectionism.
26. D. A. Miller, *Narrative and Its Discontents: Problems of Closure in the Traditional Novel* (Princeton, NJ: Princeton University Press, 1981), xiv.
27. Miller, *Narrative and Its Discontents*, 266.
28. Miller, *Narrative and Its Discontents*, x.
29. Miller's conjugal acknowledgment plays on precisely this point: "To . . . my wife, I owe a debt too extensive to be easily specified. Let it, with the other best things, go without telling." Miller, *Narrative and Its Discontents*, xv.

30 Kelly Hager has recently critiqued Miller's argument for its failure to acknowledge the prevalence of failed-marriage plots in the Victorian novel, particularly the domestically conservative novels of Charles Dickens. It seems that the theory of the marriage plot is now so advanced that those who wish to argue for the cultural centrality of marriage, like Hager, point to its failure, and those that don't, like Miller, point to its success. Kelly Hager, *Dickens and the Rise of Divorce: The Failed-Marriage Plot and the Novel Tradition* (Farnham, UK: Ashgate, 2010).

31 D. A. Miller, *Jane Austen, or The Secret of Style* (Princeton, NJ: Princeton University Press, 2003), 25. For an account of Miller's evolving critical style and its relation to the idea that "sexuality can only be situated in the pleasures and sacrifices of a choice," see Barbara Johnson, "Bringing Out D. A. Miller," *Narrative* 10, no. 1 (2002): 3–8. For Miller's reply, see his homage to Johnson's critical style, "Call for Papers: In Memoriam Barbara Johnson," *GLQ: A Journal of Lesbian and Gay Studies* 17, nos. 2–3 (2011): 365–69.

32 Miller, *Secret of Style*, 18.

33 Joseph Allen Boone, *Tradition Counter Tradition: Love and the Form of Fiction* (Chicago, IL: University of Chicago Press, 1987), 2.

34 Boone, *Tradition Counter Tradition*, 17.

35 Boone, *Tradition Counter Tradition*, 2.

36 Boone, *Tradition Counter Tradition*, 374.

37 Elizabeth Abel, "Foiling the Marriage Plot," review of *Tradition Counter Tradition: Love and the Form of Fiction* by Joseph Allen Boone, *Novel: A Forum on Fiction* 24, no. 1 (1990): 113.

38 Sharon Marcus, *Between Women: Friendship, Desire, and Marriage in Victorian England* (Princeton, NJ: Princeton University Press, 2007), 1.

39 Marcus, *Between Women*, 2. Marcus acknowledges the field-shifting debt owed to Adrienne Rich's "Compulsory Heterosexuality and Lesbian Existence," as well as the work of the literary historiographers of lesbianism who from the late 1980s forward energetically debated the idea of a lesbian continuum that could include nongenital relationships (*Between Women*, 9–12). The Sapphic sorority that Marcus invokes would test the seating plan skills of even the most practiced same-sex wedding organizer: Terry Castle, Lisa Duggan, Lillian Faderman, Diana Fuss, Amber Hollibaugh, Lisa L. Moore, Esther Newton, and Gayle Rubin. It is good to be reminded that in the vicinity of same-sex marriage debates we cannot choose our chosen families. Certainly that is the point Marcus makes when she notes that even sustained engagements with same-sex families and notions of kinship, such as Kath Weston's celebrated *Families We Choose: Lesbians, Gays, Kinship* (New York: Columbia University Press, 1997), start out by unsettling the baseline presumption that lesbians and gay men are opposed to marriage and family but end up insisting on the noncorrespondence between traditional and alternate families: "Studies of same-sex practices of kinship and reproduction have undone the idea that the family must be heterosexual, but continue to detect and in some cases to advocate for a basic conflict between the heterosexual family and its variants. *Between Women* shows, by contrast, that

in Victorian England, female marriage, gender mobility, and women's erotic fantasies about women were at the heart of normative institutions and discourses, even for those who made a religion of the family, marriage, and sexual difference" (*Between Women*, 13).

40 Marcus, *Between Women*, 3.
41 Marcus, *Between Women*, 3.
42 Marcus, *Between Women*, 4.
43 Marcus, *Between Women*, 194. Marcus updates her discussion of the marriage plot and its relation to contemporary expectations around marriage in her review of Jeffrey Eugenides's *The Marriage Plot* (New York: Farrar, Strauss and Giroux, 2011). Sharon Marcus, "The Euphoria of Influence: Jeffrey Eugenides's *The Marriage Plot*," *Public Books*, November 2011, http://www.publicbooks.org/the-euphoria-of-influencejeffrey-eugenidess-the-marriage-plot/.
44 Marcus, *Between Women*, 201. Marcus insists that "changes in heterosexual marriage have made lesbian and gay unions possible, but the influence has not been unilateral. For over a century, same-sex unions have also affected innovations in heterosexual marriage" (193).
45 Marcus, *Between Women*, 225. For a roster of spousal alternates that includes the roommates and motorcycles put forward in the service of expanding the inclusivity of the exclusivity represented by marriage, see Elizabeth Freeman's *The Wedding Complex: Forms of Belonging in Modern American Culture* (Durham, NC: Duke University Press, 2002), x.
46 Marcus, *Between Women*, 206. Celebrated for playing both female and male parts on stage, a talent put down to the full contralto range of her voice, Cushman was informally contracted to Matilda Hays but ten years into that relationship took up with the sculptor Emma Stebbins. In order to stop Hays revealing her prior infidelities, Cushman paid her a sum of money to effectively sever their nonlegal bond. Free to live with Stebbins, with whom she stayed till the end of her life, Cushman quickly embarked on a long-term clandestine affair with the much younger actress Emma Crow, who eventually married Cushman's nephew and adopted son. See Marcus, *Between Women*, 196–203.
47 Marcus, *Between Women*, 206.
48 Although in the previous chapter I drew at length on David Shumway's argument from 2004 about the historical relativization of marriage, I find myself puzzled by his earlier critique of Cavell's *Pursuits of Happiness*, the project of which he takes to be a straightforward reaffirmation of a "romantic view of marriage in the face of the fact of its failure." David Shumway, "Screwball Comedies: Constructing Romance, Mystifying Marriage," *Cinema Journal* 30, no. 4 (1991): 7. I can only put this misunderstanding down to Shumway's approaching marriage in 1991 as an exclusively heterosexual form, even though he will later make a sound historical case against the very presumption.
49 Stanley Cavell, *Cities of Words: Pedagogical Letters on a Register of the Moral Life* (Cambridge, MA: Harvard University Press, 2004), 16.
50 Those familiar with *Pursuits of Happiness* will know that early on in the book Cavell, who is associated with the tradition of ordinary language philosophy,

finds he needs to have a conversation about the form of "conversation" required by the medium of sound film, at least in the era prior to viewer-friendly playback technologies: "I am regarding the necessity of this risk in conversing about film as revelatory of the conversation within film—at any rate, within the kind of film under attention here—that words that on one viewing pass, and are meant to pass, without notice, as unnoticeably trivial, on another resonate and declare their implication in a network of significance. These film words thus declare their mimesis of ordinary words, words in daily conversation. A mastery of film writing and film making accordingly requires, for such films, a mastery of this mode of mimesis" (Cavell, *Pursuits of Happiness*, 11–12).

51 Much of this destigmatization can be traced to the celebrity culture fostered by the Hollywood public relations machinery that could turn divorce into a good story, just as it could a lavender marriage, a conjugal genre that is not limited to the entertainment industry but is a rich and varied practice deserving of its own cultural history.

52 Cavell, *Pursuits of Happiness*, 18–19.

53 The term "romance" was first applied to *Pericles, Prince of Tyre, Cymbeline, The Winter's Tale*, and *The Tempest* by Edward Dowden in *Shakspare: A Critical Study of His Mind and Art* (London: Henry S. King, 1875), which likened these plays to medieval and early modern romances, a narrative genre marked by spatial and temporal expansiveness and actions of mythical proportion.

54 As Stephen Mulhall points out in the exhaustive postscript to his book-length discussion of Cavell's philosophy, Cavell's work, like Freud's, is often condemned as offering a theory of gender rather than a theory of interpretation. This misapprehension can be seen in feminist responses to Cavell's account of the comedies of remarriage as a genre that suppresses the maternal, something he is accused of doing rather than commenting on. Stephen Mulhall, *Stanley Cavell: Philosophy's Recounting of the Ordinary* (Oxford: Oxford University Press, 1999), 314–44.

55 Cavell, *Pursuits of Happiness*, 151–52.

56 Cavell, *Cities of Words*, 10.

57 As Geoffrey Hawthorn has pointed out in a brilliant talkie-inspired review of *Pursuits of Happiness*, most of Cavell's remarriage comedies are set not in Philadelphia but in Connecticut, which in *The Lady Eve* is called "Conneckticut." Extending this word play into literary turf, Hawthorn cleverly responds to Cavell's joyous insistence on "the practical fact of mutual desire and the conceptual puzzle of being one within two" with a new slogan: "Only conneckticut." Geoffrey Hawthorn, "Green Films," *London Review of Books* 4, no. 6, April 1, 1982, 14. Hawthorn's linguistic mash-up of E. M. Forster and Preston Sturges is yet another indication that at some point the story of marriage passes from novel to film in a representational relay that now reaches forward to long-form television. As Forster would be the first to point out, whatever representational platforms they take, marriage plots are always misquested. In a marriage-minded reading of *A Passage to India*, Yonatan Touval has pointed out, "When it comes to marriage," the state Forster's novel advocates "is neither

to get married nor not get married, but rather *to have been married.*" Both "Aziz (who marries once) and Mrs. Moore (who marries twice)" advertise the "benefits" of "widowhood," which "wields the needed authority for legitimating the rebuke of marriage, a rebuke that makes itself a project in all of Forster's novels with the exception of *A Room with a View.*" In the footnote to this passage Touval continues, *A Passage to India* "creates the possibility that Aziz in fact remarries at the end of the novel, but the elusive suggestion seems to raise more questions than it answers, including whether the new attachment is not a bride so much as a mistress." Yonatan Touval, "Colonial Queer Something," in *Queer Forster*, ed. Robert K. Martin and George Piggford (Chicago, IL: University of Chicago Press, 1997), 251 and 254n13. In Touval's citation of the novel, we learn that Aziz "had married again—not exactly a marriage, but he liked to regard it as one," which models the kind of nonliteral approach to conjugality that I am advocating more generally.

58 Cavell, *Pursuits of Happiness*, 159–60. Cavell takes the concept of a "meet conversation" from John Milton's *Doctrine and Discipline of Divorce*, which he describes as "a defense of marriage in the form of a defense of divorce." Considering God's decision to create a "helpmeet" for Adam so that man should not be alone, Milton concludes that "a meet and happy conversation is the chiefest and noblest end of marriage." In Cavell's estimation, the seven Hollywood comedies of remarriage capture the "full weight of the concept of conversation" in the "extravagant expressiveness" and exhilarating verbal compatibility of the central pair, which is "in turn possible only on the basis of our conviction that each of them is capable of, even craves, privacy, the pleasure of their own company." *Pursuits of Happiness*, 87–88.

59 Cavell, *Pursuits of Happiness*, 160.

60 Cavell, *Pursuits of Happiness*, 158–59.

61 Stanley Cavell, *Contesting Tears: The Hollywood Melodrama of the Unknown Woman* (Chicago, IL: University of Chicago Press, 1996).

62 William Rothman, ed. *Cavell on Film* (Albany: State University of New York Press, 2005), xviii.

63 Stanley Cavell, "North by Northwest," cited in Rothman, *Cavell on Film*, xviii–xix.

64 As fans of Grant will know, the actor had already taken up the role of wife ten years earlier in Howard Hawks's *I Was A Male War Bride* (1949).

65 Lauren Berlant, *The Anatomy of National Fantasy: Hawthorne, Utopia, and Everyday Life* (Chicago, IL: University of Chicago Press, 1991) and "Humorlessness (Three Monologues and a Hairpiece)," *Critical Inquiry* 43, no. 2 (2017): 305–40.

66 In order of appearance: Lauren Berlant and Lee Edelman, *Sex, or the Unbearable* (Durham, NC: Duke University Press, 2014), 89–90; Tim Dean, "No Sex Please, We're American," *American Literary History* 27, no. 3 (2015): 614–24; and Lauren Berlant and Lee Edelman, "Reading, Sex, and the Unbearable: A Response to Tim Dean," *American Literary History* 27, no. 3 (2015): 625–29.

67 Berlant and Edelman, "Reading, Sex, and the Unbearable," 628.

68 Berlant and Edelman, *Sex, or the Unbearable*, 13.

69 Berlant and Edelman, *Sex, or the Unbearable*, 89.

70 Lauren Berlant, *The Queen of America Goes to Washington: Essays on Sex and Citizenship* (Durham, NC: Duke University Press, 1997). For a rapid induction into Cavell's obsessions, see Hawthorn's extraordinarily funny contemporary review of *Pursuits of Happiness*, which points out that "despite its sustained extravagance, its few banalities, its intermittent contradictions, its occasional paragraph of pure impenetrability and its soaring vanity, this just must be, in its close readings and its stunning associations, one of the most compelling accounts of its kind. The fact is," Hawthorn ends, "it just is its kind," a statement that, in my opinion, applies to the work of Berlant (*Green Films*, 14).

71 Cavell's discussion of Cukor's film is titled "The Importance of Importance: *The Philadelphia Story*." As Cavell interprets the film, the lesson that Cary Grant's C. K. Dexter Haven has to teach his former wife before they can remarry is that sexuality is founded in mistakes and hence requires the acknowledgment of human imperfection. Cavell, *Pursuits of Happiness*, 148.

72 For someone so interested in the trope of remarriage and its cultural force, Cavell is remarkably discreet about his experience of divorce and remarriage (to his second wife not his first) in the five hundred pages of his autobiography *Little Did I Know: Excerpts from Memory* (Stanford, CA: Stanford University Press, 2010).

73 Lauren Berlant, *The Female Complaint: The Unfinished Business of Sentimentality in American Culture* (Durham, NC: Duke University Press, 2008).

74 Berlant, *Female Complaint*, 307n30.

75 Berlant, *Female Complaint*, 310n11. A final reference to Cavell occurs in the book's epilogue, "Overture/Aperture," which deals with the difficulty of breaking attachments, since acts of breaking "require being optimistic about loss and about the undoing of an affect world, with its promise of reciprocity." By imagining detachment, Berlant writes, each text of female complaint "provides its own scenarios of managing 'the loss of the world' with radical ambivalence" (*Female Complaint*, 267). The attached footnote, which is unusual only in having its reference appear immediately after the quotation as opposed to the end of the sentence, calmly declares that the phrase is taken from Cavell's "The Uncanniness of the Ordinary." The radical ambivalence needs no citation.

76 Lauren Berlant, *Cruel Optimism* (Durham, NC: Duke University Press, 2011), 9.

77 Lauren Berlant, "Humorlessness (Three Monologues and a Hairpiece)," 313n15.

78 In her lengthy review of *Sex, or the Unbearable*, Robyn Wiegman has drawn out the utopian strand in Berlant's account of queer negativity, which she relates to the work of José Muñoz and sets in opposition to the negative negativity of Leo Bersani and Tim Dean. I would add the suggestion that Berlant's negative utopianism is also a queer take on Cavell's ordinary utopianism, a form of thinking and writing that accentuates the positive, eliminates the negative, and latches on to the affirmative in the human drive to attachment and community. Robyn Wiegman, "Sex and Negativity; Or, What Queer Theory Has for You," *Cultural Critique* 95 (2017): 219–43.

79 Barry McCrea, "Heterosexual Horror: *Dracula*, the Closet, and the Marriage-Plot," *Novel: A Forum on Fiction* 43, no. 2 (2010): 253.

80 McCrea, "Heterosexual Horror," 254, 253.
81 McCrea, "Heterosexual Horror," 268. McCrea identifies Talia Schaffer as "the critic most responsible for posthumously outing Stoker" as a homosexual wracked with anxiety by the trials of Oscar Wilde. See Talia Schaffer, "'A Wilde Desire Took Me': The Homoerotic History of *Dracula*," ELH 61, no. 2 (1994): 381–425.
82 For a discussion of how crucial feeling sexually normal has been to the discursive management of the married couple, see Annamarie Jagose, *Orgasmology* (Durham, NC: Duke University Press, 2013), 40–77. For a wider consideration of the role of antinormativity in queer theorizations of the political, see the essays collected in "Queer Theory without Antinormativity," a special issue of *differences: A Journal of Feminist Cultural Studies* 26, no. 1 (2015), particularly Robyn Wiegman and Elizabeth A. Wilson, "Antinormativity's Queer Conventions," 1–25, and Annamarie Jagose, "The Trouble with Antinormativity," 26–47. For an early surfacing of a similar point, see Biddy Martin, "Extraordinary Homosexuals and the Fear of Being Ordinary," *differences: A Journal of Feminist Cultural Studies* 6, nos. 2–3 (1994): 100–125.
83 McCrea, "Heterosexual Horror," 268.

Chapter 3. Dorothy Arzner's *Wife*

1 Talia Schaffer, *Romance's Rival: Familiar Marriage in Victorian Fiction* (Oxford: Oxford University Press, 2016). Schaffer's expansive bibliography indicates the depth and breadth of feminist engagements with the nineteenth-century marriage plot.
2 Wendy Jones, quoted in Schaffer, *Romance's Rival*, 8.
3 Schaffer, *Romance's Rival*, 3.
4 Schaffer, *Romance's Rival*, 9, 15.
5 Schaffer, *Romance's Rival*, 15.
6 Peter Brooks, *Reading for the Plot: Design and Intention in Narrative* (Cambridge, MA: Harvard University Press, 1983), 7.
7 For a discussion of the emergence of this term, see Suzanne Raitt, "Lesbian Modernism?" GLQ: *A Journal of Lesbian and Gay Studies* 10, no. 1 (2003): 111–21, a review of numerous book-length arguments for the coincidence of lesbianism and modernism that appeared circa 2001.
8 Elizabeth Freeman, "Sacra/mentality in Barnes's *Nightwood*," *American Literature* 86, no. 4 (2014): 743.
9 Elizabeth English, *Lesbian Modernism: Censorship, Sexuality, and Genre Fiction* (Edinburgh, UK: Edinburgh University Press, 2015).
10 Julian Carter, "Gay Marriage and Pulp Fiction: Homonormativity, Disidentification, and Affect in Ann Bannon's Lesbian Novels," GLQ: *A Journal of Lesbian and Gay Studies* 15, no. 4 (2009): 584. See also Christopher Nealon's discussion of Bannon's work as the "premier fictional representation of US lesbian life in the fifties and sixties," in "Invert-History: The Ambivalence of Lesbian Pulp Fiction," *New Literary History* 31, no. 4 (2000): 748.

11 As Higashi goes on to point out, former actress Jeanie Macpherson advanced her already successful screenwriting career by repeatedly "embroidering the essential plot of *Old Wives for New* in numerous scenarios about the commodification of marriage throughout the silent era." Sumiko Higashi, *Cecil B. DeMille and American Culture: The Silent Era* (Berkeley: University of California Press, 1992), 146.
12 Higashi, *DeMille and American Culture*, 147.
13 Higashi, *DeMille and American Culture*, 147.
14 For a full account of Haines's onscreen career, see Victoria Sturtevant's suitably titled essay "Stop the Wedding: William Haines and the Comedy of the Closet," in *Hetero: Queering Representations of Straightness*, ed. Sean Griffin (Albany: State University of New York Press, 2009), 19–36.
15 William J. Mann, *Wisecracker: The Life and Times of William Haines, Hollywood's First Openly Gay Star* (New York: Viking Penguin, 1998), 206–8 and 259–69.
16 Mann, *Wisecracker*, 282–83. Formal credit for art direction on the film is given to Stephen Goosson, the original designer.
17 For a richly illustrated account of Haines's influential career as a designer, see Peter Schifando and Jean H. Mathison, *Class Act: William Haines, Legendary Hollywood Decorator* (New York: Pointed Leaf, 1995).
18 Claire Johnston, ed., *The Works of Dorothy Arzner: Towards a Feminist Cinema*, (London: British Film Institute, 1975).
19 The essays anthologized in *Feminism and Film Theory*, ed. Constance Penley (New York: Routledge, 1988) are Claire Johnston, "Dorothy Arzner: Critical Strategies," 36–45; Pam Cook, "Approaching the Work of Dorothy Arzner," 46–56; Jacqueline Suter, "Feminist Discourse in *Christopher Strong*," 89–103; and Janet Bergstrom, "Rereading the Work of Claire Johnston," 80–88.
20 See Judith Mayne, *The Woman at the Keyhole: Feminism and Women's Cinema* (Bloomington: Indiana University Press, 1990), 89–123; "Lesbian Looks: Dorothy Arzner and Female Friendship," in *How Do I Look?*, ed. Bad Object Choices (Seattle, WA: Bay Press, 1991), 103–43; and *Directed by Dorothy Arzner* (Bloomington: Indiana University Press, 1994).
21 Consider, for instance, the many institutional commissions that advanced the architectural career of Arzner's contemporary Julia Morgan. See Sara Holmes Boutelle, *Julia Morgan, Architect* (New York: Abbeville Press, 1995), 83–127. For further discussion of Morgan's career and its place in the spatial history of homosexuality, see Aaron Betsky, *Queer Space: Architecture and Same-Sex Desire* (New York: William Morrow, 1997), 102–4.
22 Elsie de Wolfe began her career by designing stage sets and decorating the interior of the New York home she shared with her partner, Elisabeth Marbury, a theatrical agent and producer. For an account of de Wolfe's career and influence on the field, see Penny Sparke, Mitchell Owens, and Elsie de Wolfe, *Elsie de Wolfe: The Birth of Interior Decoration* (New York: Acanthus Press, 2005). For the queer implications of de Wolfe's style, see Betsky, *Queer Space*, 98–102.
23 Kathleen McHugh, "Housekeeping in Hollywood: The Case of *Craig's Wife*," *Screen* 35, no. 2 (1994): 127. This shift in color scheme was at least partially motivated by the demands of the shift in medium, since white walls allowed

figures to be distinguished in the tonalities of gray registered on black-and-white film stock. For an account of the Hollywood art direction "craze for whites and creams" in late thirties, see Juan Antonio Ramírez, *Architecture for the Screen: A Critical Study of Set Design in Hollywood's Golden Age*, trans. and with foreword by John F. Moffitt (Jefferson, NC: McFarland, 2004), 91.

24 Arzner's reluctance to engage shot/reverse shot sequences, a directorial trait first identified by Suter, is the cornerstone of Beverle Houston's account of *Craig's Wife*. According to Houston, the withholding of the reverse shot in the "last several moments of the film" means the spectator is "denied the primary mechanism of suture and mastery through identification." Beverle Houston, "Missing in Action: Notes on Dorothy Arzner," *Wide Angle* 6, no. 3 (1989): 31.

25 Quoted in Schifando and Mathison, *Class Act*, 60.

26 Somewhat to the side of the first wave of feminist reappropriation of Arzner, Molly Haskell insightfully notes that her directorial input is often concentrated in "costume, set design and editing," through which she "forces a 'high art' motif on material which resists such upgrading." Molly Haskell, "Women in Paris," *Village Voice*, April 28, 1975, 78. In the early nineties, Jane Gaines suggestively placed Arzner's collaborations with costume designers in the context of a gay and lesbian disdain for realism. Jane Gaines, "Dorothy Arzner's Trousers," *Jump Cut* 37 (1992): 88–98.

27 In her account of a 1973 interview with Arzner, Francine Parker recalls Arzner's claim that she deliberately shot *Craig's Wife* "in the right order as though it were a play." Francine Parker, "Approaching the Art of Arzner,'" *Action* 8, no. 4 (1973): 13. The following year, in her heavily cited interview with Gerald Peary and Karyn Kay, Arzner nonetheless delivered a backhanded compliment to her collaborator Robert Milton, whom she considered a "fine stage director" who seemed not to "know the camera's limitations or its expansions." Gerald Peary and Karyn Kay, "Interview with Dorothy Arzner," *Cinema* 34 (1974): 14.

28 Giuliana Bruno, "Fashions of Living," *Quarterly Review of Film and Video* 20, no. 3 (2003): 169–70.

29 As is well known, Arzner's elevation to the status of director was made on the basis of her demonstrated skill as a cutter and editor at Paramount, which culminated in her working with director James Cruze on two historical epics: *The Covered Wagon* (1923) and *Old Ironsides* (1926). Although formal credit for the editing of *Craig's Wife* is given to Viola Lawrence, when interviewed Arzner always maintained she "edited in the camera" as she went along: "I shot the way I thought the mind would wish to progress—from far away to closeup. No medium-range shots and closeups of the whole cast as they do today." Mary Murphy, "Tribute to an Unsung Pioneer," *Los Angeles Times*, January 24, 1975, part 4, 16.

30 In this context, see Lucy Fischer's discussion of the "emphatic (if abstract) sense of sexuality" that imbues the art deco figurines of women frequently seen in Hollywood cinema of the twenties and thirties. Lucy Fischer, *Designing Women: Cinema, Art Deco, and the Female Form* (New York: Columbia University Press, 2003), 6.

31 Commenting on Arzner's film style in general, Richard Henshaw notes that the stage-bound quality of her direction is "invariably uplifted when she takes her camera outside the house and becomes involved with objects, landscape, and movement. In these cases, where cutting is not dependent on lines of dialogue, her strength as an editor surfaces." Richard Henshaw, "Women Directors: 150 Filmographies," *Film Comment* 8, no. 4 (1972): 34.

32 See, for instance, Melissa Sue Kurt, "'Spectacular Spinelessness': The Men in Dorothy Arzner's Films," in *Men by Women*, ed. Janet Todd (New York: Holmes and Meier, 1982), 196–97; Julia Lesage, "The Hegemonic Female Fantasy in *An Unmarried Woman* and *Craig's Wife*," *Film Reader 5: Feminist Film Criticism and Film and Culture Studies* (Evanston, IL: Film Division, Radio-Television-Film Department, Northwestern University, 1982), 90; and McHugh, "Housekeeping in Hollywood," 126–27.

33 Technically layering one recorded scene into another, the illusion of the moving landscape framed by the mocked-up train window prefigures the bizarre death scene in Arzner's *Dance, Girl, Dance* (RKO, 1940), in which the dance teacher Madame Basilova (Maria Ouspenskaya) is mown down by a fake mise-en-scène of Manhattan traffic. Usually attired in a tailored suit and necktie and thus a butch stand-in for the director herself, the dance teacher, according to Mayne, is killed off the moment she puts on a froufrou hat. "Femininity is lethal, at least for Basilova," argues Mayne, although the point might also be that the cinematic contest between those same-sex affiliations represented in the world of dance and the heterosexual relations that otherwise comprise the film's story get played out spatially as well as in terms of costume. Mayne, *Directed by Dorothy Arzner*, 145. Elsewhere Mayne allows that Basilova is killed off "in one of the most absurdly staged death scenes imaginable." Mayne, "Lesbian Looks," 122.

34 For Mayne's lengthy discussion of the train conversation scene, see *Directed by Dorothy Arzner*, 126–29. Bruno also comments on the significance of the scene's composition in "Fashions of Living," 160.

35 See, in particular, Mayne's discussion of women-in-prison films in *Framed: Lesbians, Feminists, and Media Culture* (Minneapolis: University of Minnesota Press, 2000), 115–45.

36 See McHugh's reading of *Craig's Wife* in relation to historical transformations in understandings of marriage and domesticity, namely the shift from contractually based notions of marriage to those that conceive of a companionate relationship between a husband and wife who are considered emotionally and sexually compatible. Formerly dedicated to the rational maintenance of separate spheres, the modern housewife's role is increasingly to provide romantic companionship and emotional training to her husband. In this ideological task, McHugh points out, she is greatly assisted by the developing forms of female melodrama. "In indicting its heroine for not loving, feeling or suffering," McHugh cogently observes, *Craig's Wife* "indicts her for not partaking of a melodramatic sensibility." McHugh, "Housekeeping in Hollywood," 134.

37 Muriel Babcock, review of *Craig's Wife*, *Los Angeles Examiner*, n.d., n.p.; Howard Barnes, review of *Craig's Wife*, *New York Herald Tribune*, October 2, 1936, 17;

Frank S. Nugent, review of *Craig's Wife*, *New York Times*, October 2, 1936; and Robert Garland, "*Craig's Wife* Earns New Glory as Movie; Sincere and Gripping," *New York American*, October 2, 1936, 14.

38 There are numerous readings of the film that, in criticizing Arzner for remaining too loyal to her theatrical source, can thereby highlight her success in wresting the figure of Harriet Craig out of Kelly's misogynist stranglehold and investing her with a conflicted interior that draws an empathetic response from the female spectator. The clearest statement of this impulse can be found in Kurt, "Spectacular Spinelessness," 197–98. For a summary of contemporary responses to the 1925 play, which frequently included charges of misogyny, see William J. Lynch, "*Craig's Wife*," in *Three Plays by George Kelly* (New York: Limelight Editions, 1999), 289.

39 *Modern Screen*, review of *Craig's Wife*, December 1936, 49. Columbia studio boss Harry Cohn, who was already annoyed that the director had engaged bit player Russell for the lead role without consulting him, "threatened to fire Arzner after the expense of [Haines's] redecoration was revealed." Mann, *Wisecracker*, 282.

40 First deployed in *Mäedchen in Uniform* (Leontine Sagan, 1931), the female facial superimposition remains integral to both modernist and postmodernist investigations of the lesbian story, as can be seen in Ingmar Bergman's *Persona* (1966) and David Lynch's *Mulholland Drive* (2001). For anyone who thinks the lesbian superimposition has become a cinematic cliché, I direct you to the final shot of Yorgas Lanthimos's *The Favourite* (2018).

41 Joan Crawford, who was an expert in interior design makeovers and the serial husbands who justify them, saw some connection between herself and Harriet Craig, buying the rights for a 1950 remake, directed by Vincent Sherman, in which she took on the now-title role.

42 Lesage, "Hegemonic Female Fantasy," 90.

43 Mayne, *Directed by Dorothy Arzner*, 123.

44 Mayne, *Directed by Dorothy Arzner*, 124.

45 Mayne, *Directed by Dorothy Arzner*, 130.

46 For an account of how well suited melodrama is to hosting lesbian sentiment in oblique ways, see Patricia White, *Uninvited: Classical Hollywood Cinema and Lesbian Representability* (Bloomington: Indiana University Press, 1999), 94–135.

Chapter 4. Tom Ford and His Kind

1 Patricia White, "Supporting Character: The Queer Career of Agnes Moorehead," in *Out in Culture: Gay, Lesbian, and Queer Essays on Popular Culture*, ed. Corey K. Creekmur and Alexander Doty (Durham, NC: Duke University Press, 1995), 91–114.

2 Stephanie Zacharek, "*A Single Man*: Tom Ford's Shallow but Compelling Debut," *Salon.com*, December 10, 2009, http://www.salon.com/2009/12/10/a_single_man/.

3   Anthony Lane, "The Current Cinema: Free and Uneasy," *New Yorker*, December 21, 2009, 150.
4   Robert Sinnerbrink, "*Stimmung*: Exploring the Aesthetics of Mood," *Screen* 53, no. 2 (2012): 148–63.
5   A parallel phenomenon would be "Same Love" (2012), hip-hop artist Macklemore's rap defense of gay marriage and its accompanying video that, assisted by Mary Lambert's lesbian vocal hook, movingly reveals the life narrative of same-sex interracial love interspersed with archival footage of civil rights demonstrations from the 1960s. But, whereas "Same Love" is explicitly tagged to the issue of marriage equality via the artist's support for Referendum 74, the bill that would legalize same-sex marriage in Washington State, *A Single Man*'s sentimentalizing qualities are both broader and more specific as they apply to the prospect, actuality, or retraction of marriage equality. See, after 200 million others, "Macklemore and Ryan Lewis—Same Love, Featuring Mary Lambert" (2012), http://www.youtube.com/watch?v=hlVBg7_08no. Macklemore recently surfaced in the context of the Australian marriage equality postal survey when he was invited by the National Rugby League Association to perform "Same Love" as the pre-entertainment act to the 2017 Grand Final as a show of the organization's commitment to diversity. For Ryan Lewis's bemused account of being swept into Australian politics and the resulting social media static, see "'Imma Go Harder': Macklemore Responds to NRL Grand Final Controversy," *Sydney Morning Herald*, September 28, 2017, http://www.smh.com.au/entertainment/music/imma-go-harder-macklemore-responds-to-nrl-grand-final-controversy-20170927-gyq6y4.html, accessed October 17, 2017.
6   Richard Dyer, "Homosexuality and Heritage," in *The Culture of Queers* (London: Routledge, 2002), 224.
7   See, for example, "Beginning of the End," Joel Greenberg's review of Christopher Isherwood, *Liberation: Diaries, vol. 3, 1970–1983*, ed. Katherine Bucknell, *Sydney Morning Herald*, September 29–30, 2012, Spectrum, 35.
8   Armistead Maupin, "The First Couple: Don Bachardy and Christopher Isherwood," in *Conversations with Christopher Isherwood*, ed. James J. Berg and Chris Freeman (Jackson: University Press of Mississippi, 2003), 189–96.
9   *Chris and Don: A Love Story*, dir. Guido Santi and Tina Mascara (Los Angeles, CA: Asphalt Stars Productions, 2007), and DVD (New York: Zeitgeist Films, 2009).
10 Dobbin, a stubborn old workhorse, and the more playful Kitty can be found throughout Katherine Bucknell, ed., *The Animals: Love Letters between Christopher Isherwood and Don Bachardy* (New York: Farrar, Straus and Giroux, 2013).
11 For a discussion of Isherwood's use of namesake narrators, see Lisa M. Schwerdt, *Isherwood's Fiction: The Self and Technique* (London: Macmillan, 1989). For a full discussion of Isherwood's contribution to the tradition of twentieth-century gay autobiography, see Paul A. Robinson, *Gay Lives: Homosexual Autobiography from John Addington Symonds to Paul Monette* (Chicago, IL: University of Chicago Press, 1999), 51–64 and 91–112.

12 Christopher Isherwood, *Christopher and His Kind, 1929–39* (New York: Farrar, Straus and Giroux, 1976); Jaime Harker, *Middlebrow Queer: Christopher Isherwood in America* (Minneapolis: University of Minnesota Press, 2013).
13 Harker, *Middlebrow Queer*, xvi.
14 For a discussion of this scene, see Amy Villarejo, "Jewish, Queer-ish, Trans, and Completely Revolutionary," *Film Quarterly* 69, no. 4 (2016): 10–22.
15 Cyril Connolly, *Enemies of Promise and Other Essays* (Garden City, NY: Doubleday, 1960), 82. For a discussion of the relation presumed between a plain or declarative writing style and the supposed straightness of its author, see Scott St. Pierre, "Bent Hemingway: Straightness, Sexuality, Style," *GLQ: A Journal of Lesbian and Gay Studies* 16, no. 3 (2010): 363–87.
16 Isherwood was very attracted to the potential of narrational dubiousness for corroding the cult of personality. Both these tendencies are at work in his autobiographies and other forms of life writing, which, as Rose Kamel identifies, ask us to read Christopher as a "fictional character described by a somewhat unreliable narrator in turn created by an implied omniscient author who can erase and cancel out his narrator at will." Rose Kamel, "'Unraveling One's Personal Myth': Christopher Isherwood's Autobiographical Strategies," *Biography* 5, no. 2 (1982): 163.
17 See, for instance, Alan Wilde, *Christopher Isherwood* (New York: Twayne, 1971), 5. Wilde is not alone in his assessment of Isherwood's ironic consciousness but is the first critic to insist that the author's irony "is almost invariably directed at the narrators and protagonists of the books" (4).
18 Jonathan Raban, *The Technique of Modern Fiction: Essays in Practical Criticism* (South Bend, IN: University of Notre Dame Press, 1969), 30.
19 Christopher Isherwood, *A Single Man* (London: Vintage, 2010), 1, emphasis in original; hereafter cited parenthetically in the text.
20 For a positive account of the suicide plot and its rendering of gay subjectivity as a matter of loving care rather than desire, see Kyle Stevens, "Dying to Love: Gay Identity, Suicide, and Aesthetics in *A Single Man*," *Cinema Journal* 52, no. 4 (2013): 99–120.
21 See, for instance, Wayne M. Bryant's review of the film in which he confidently states, "If George represents Isherwood in this story, then young Kenny Potter is certainly a stand-in for Christopher's lover Don Bachardy." Wayne M. Bryant, review of Tom Ford's *A Single Man*, *Journal of Bisexuality* 10, no. 3 (2010): 351.
22 Armistead Maupin remarks that "anyone who knew them well will tell you how eerie and wonderful it was that a kid from the beaches of Southern California came to adopt the stammer of a well-bred Englishman." Armistead Maupin, foreword to *The Isherwood Century: Essays on the Life and Work of Christopher Isherwood*, ed. James J. Berg and Chris Freeman (Madison: University of Wisconsin Press, 2000), xiv. Bachardy's Isherwoodesque phrasing and stammer can also be heard on *Chris and Don: A Love Story*, where Bachardy refers to himself as "an unconscious impersonator." Rather than think of this as class imposture, it perhaps points to the way gay culture has been historically invested in class and age

stratification, and their sexual remediation, in ways that do not rely on marriage to level the playing field.

23 For a technically exact account of Ford's chromatic method and its diachronic cast, see Kirsten Moana Thompson, "Falling in (to) Color: Chromophilia and Tom Ford's *A Single Man*," *Moving Image* 15, no. 1 (2015): 62–82.

24 Harker, *Middlebrow Queer*, 111. Queer millennials can now access the BBC television adaptation of *Christopher and His Kind*, dir. Geoffrey Sax (London: Mammoth Screen, 2011), via YouTube, where they will hear Isherwood's famous opening—"To Christopher, Berlin meant boys"—bathetically rendered in a first-person voiceover: "To me, Berlin meant boys." Like many camp lines, the opening sentence of Isherwood's memoir has a communicative capacity within gay middlebrow culture that requires no further acquaintance with the book from which it comes. For further discussion of the way in which a gay sensibility is acquired in rituals of cultural instruction that do not rely on book learning alone, see David M. Halperin, *How to Be Gay* (Cambridge, MA: Harvard University Press, 2012).

25 See, further, Lee Wallace, "Fag Men: *Mad Men*, Homosexuality and Televisual Style," *Cultural Studies Review* 18, no. 2 (2012): 207–22.

26 Even those who initially purport to hate it seem to come around to the Tom Ford look. While Nicola Nixon maintains that George spends more time laying out his professorial wardrobe than preparing his lecture on Huxley, she finally acknowledges that at least his clothes set him apart from the "chambray shirt and baggy chinos"–wearing "MIT, Yale and Berkeley" lecturers who populate the video-streamed global classroom. According to Nixon, these "affable, camera-comfortable" representatives of open-access learning uniformly dress from "J Crew, the Gap, and Dockers." The problem, for Nixon, is not simply that these clothes are unfashionable but that these are the labels that "furnish neoliberalism with its dress code." Nicola Nixon, "Smarty Pants," *English Studies in Canada* 35, nos. 2–3 (2009): 26.

27 In his discussion of the fastidiousness of Ford's adaptation of Isherwood, Ben Walters notes that many reviews compared the film to a perfume commercial. Ben Walters, "The Trouble with Perfume," *Film Quarterly* 63, no. 4 (2010): 14–17.

28 Susie Khamis and Alex Munt, "The Three Cs of Fashion: Convergence, Creativity and Control," *Scan: Journal of Media Arts Culture* 7, no. 2 (2010), http://scan.net.au/scan/journal/display.php?journal_id=155.

29 Roland Barthes, *S/Z: An Essay*, trans. Richard Miller (New York: Hill and Wang, 1974), 94–95.

30 Tom Ford, dir., *A Single Man* (Culver City, CA: Sony Pictures Home Entertainment, 2010).

31 Christopher Isherwood, *My Guru and His Disciple* (Harmondsworth, UK: Penguin, 1980), 158.

32 Michel Foucault, "What Is an Author?" *Screen* 20, no. 1 (1979): 13–33.

33 Barthes, *S/Z*, 95.

34 Indeed, this may be Ford's most subtle homage to Alfred Hitchcock, whose own celebrity name denoted suspense or mystery on a range of media products, such as the Random House juvenile detective series *The Three Investigators* (1964–87), in which Hitchcock's name and silhouette imprinted the cover while the authorial name of Robert Arthur Jr. was suppressed. For a discussion of Hitchcock's imbrication in further authorial masquerades, see D. A. Miller, "Hitchcock's Hidden Pictures," *Critical Inquiry* 37, no. 1 (2010): 106–30.

35 Barthes, *S/Z*, 191.

36 David L. Eng, *The Feeling of Kinship: Queer Kinship and the Racialization of Intimacy* (Durham, NC: Duke University Press, 2010), 3.

37 For Bachardy's account of the 1977 adoption, see Niladri R. Chatterjee, "Portrait of the Artist as Companion: Interviews with Don Bachardy," in *The Isherwood Century: Essays on the Life and Work of Christopher Isherwood*, ed. James J. Berg and Chris Freeman (Madison: University of Wisconsin Press, 2000), 105.

38 Kenneth E. Silver, "Master Bedrooms, Master Narratives: Home, Homosexuality and Post-War Art," in *Not at Home: The Suppression of Domesticity in Modern Art and Architecture*, ed. Christopher Reed (London: Thames and Hudson, 1996), 206–22.

39 Even though we may claim not to know Isherwood's work, it is harder to claim that we do not know him. Although he had never met Isherwood, Gore Vidal recalls that in 1948, when he was "famous and unknown (a curious business that Isherwood has dealt with marvelously *vis-à-vis* himself)," he saw Isherwood seated at the Café Flore in Paris: "So famous was he, that we all knew exactly what he looked like." Gore Vidal, introduction to *Where Joy Resides: A Christopher Isherwood Reader*, ed. Don Bachardy and James P. White (New York: Farrar, Straus and Giroux, 1989), xviii. This orientation to public recognition is associated less with systems of enunciation based on writing—an elite system in which Vidal can be both "famous and unknown"—than with the celebrity system spawned by the rise of popular entertainment forms in which being famous—specifically, being recognized on sight—is sufficient if not sole criteria for being known.

40 Lee Edelman, *No Future: Queer Theory and the Death Drive* (Durham, NC: Duke University Press, 2004), 2.

41 In addition to his work on the novel referenced in chapter 2, Miller's engagement with homosexuality and the question of style can be found in D. A. Miller, "Anal Rope," *Representations* 32 (1990): 114–33; *Bringing Out Roland Barthes* (Berkeley: University of California Press, 1992); *Place for Us: Essay on the Broadway Musical* (Cambridge, MA: Harvard University Press, 1998); *8½* (Houndmills, UK: Palgrave Macmillan, BFI Film Classics, 2008); *Hidden Hitchcock* (Chicago, IL: University of Chicago Press, 2016); and the various reviews he has contributed to *Film Quarterly*.

42 D. A. Miller, *Jane Austen, or The Secret of Style* (Princeton, NJ: Princeton University Press, 2003), 2.

43 Miller, *Jane Austen*, 27.

44 Heather Love, "His Way," GLQ: Journal of Lesbian and Gay Studies 17, nos. 2–3 (2011): 371–79.
45 Love, "His Way," 377, 375.
46 Love, "His Way," 377.
47 D. A. Miller, "On the Universality of Brokeback Mountain," Film Quarterly 60, no. 3 (2007): 50–60.
48 Miller, "On the Universality of Brokeback," 53.
49 Miller, "On the Universality of Brokeback," 55.
50 Miller, "On the Universality of Brokeback," 55.
51 Miller, "On the Universality of Brokeback," 58.
52 D. A. Miller, "Elio's Education," Los Angeles Review of Books, February 19, 2018, https://lareviewofbooks.org/article/elios-education/.
53 David Greven, "Unlovely Spectacle: D. A. Miller on Call Me by Your Name," Film International, March 13, 2018, http://filmint.nu/?p=23937.
54 Richard Dyer, White: Essays on Race and Culture (London: Routledge, 1997).
55 For a positive account of Ford's use of color "as a rejoinder to the homophobic rhetoric aimed at gays by organizations like NOM," the US National Organization for Marriage, see Stevens, "Dying to Love," 102.
56 Thompson, "Chromophilia," 64.
57 Barbara Flueckiger, "Color and Subjectivity in Film," Subjectivity across Media: Interdisciplinary and Transmedial Perspectives, ed. Maike Sarah Reineth and Jan-Noël Thon (New York: Routledge, 2016), 158.
58 The relation between cinematic coloring and history effects also comes up in Dana Luciano's discussion of Todd Haynes's Far From Heaven (2002), a film that explicitly links the story of marriage to both the story of homosexuality and the story of race. Luciano concentrates on Haynes's longstanding interest in "suspending repressed, regressive, or infantile protagonists within filmic frameworks built on the aesthetic and narrative conventions of prior historical periods" (250). According to Luciano, in his unironic allegiance to the lush color style of Douglas Sirk's late-Hollywood films, Haynes sidesteps "unabashed nostalgia" and "arch parody," the two critically recognized stances associated with mainstream cinema's relation to its own past, and instead operates in the space of "borrowed time" (249). Although the film narrates its story about a marriage rent apart by the emergence of the husband's repressed homosexuality in forward-tending screen time, the "outmoded feel of its melodramatic pacing and style" unsettles through the "intimate response" it generates in contemporary audiences more familiar with the disruptive sequencing techniques that form a mainstay of new queer cinema. Luciano goes on to explore how the film's formal belatedness, its perverse "play with developmental trajectories, chronology, and periodicity evokes the queer subject's oblique relation to normative modes of synching individual, familial, and historical time" (250). Extravagantly embedded in a recreated fifties world, the story of closeted homosexuality is, in this account, primarily the story of queer spectatorship, which is not something that radiates out from the omniscient perspective of the sexual

present but a mode of attachment subtended by melodrama with its established capacity to fuse sexuality and cinematic style. Characterized by the coexistence of irony and empathy, distance and closeness, and marked by the rejection of narrative in favor of detail, this anachronistic mode of queer attachment renders the spectator "particularly receptive to the ambivalent promise of melodrama's momentum—to feeling, at once, the melancholic force of its emotional foreclosures and the compellingly textured friction that might incorporate affect otherwise" (253). Luciano argues that Haynes's film might be considered a formal experiment in adapting this form of queer retrovision for mainstream use, "not as an actualized truth but as the possible effect of an exploratory process of displacement" (253). Although she is more positive than Miller about the open-ended possibilities of this kind of queer universalism, Luciano's argument about the uncanny ability of melodrama to raise queer affect while displacing other cultural concerns—race, for instance, and class—suggests we should look hard at our ongoing attachment to stories of gay and lesbian attachment, whether considered normative or nonnormative, particularly as they appear on new technical platforms that we are just beginning to critically comprehend. Dana Luciano, "Coming Around Again: The Queer Momentum of *Far From Heaven*," GLQ: *A Journal of Lesbian and Gay Studies* 13, nos. 2–3 (2007). For a sustained engagement with the racialized "media memory" embedded in *Far From Heaven* and its "complex negotiations with television—as cultural institution and domestic technology," see Sharon Willis, *The Poitier Effect: Racial Melodrama and Fantasies of Reconciliation* (Minneapolis: University of Minnesota Press, 2015), 119–60.
59 Patricia White, "Sketchy Lesbians: *Carol* as History and Fantasy," *Film Quarterly* 69, no. 2 (2015): 9.
60 White, "Sketchy Lesbians," 11.
61 White, "Sketchy Lesbians," 17.

Chapter 5. Lisa Cholodenko's Attachment Trilogy

1 Stanley Cavell, *Pursuits of Happiness: The Hollywood Comedy of Remarriage* (Cambridge, MA: Harvard University Press, 1981), 1.
2 Stanley Cavell, *Cities of Words: Pedagogical Letters on a Register of the Moral Life* (Cambridge, MA: Harvard University Press, 2004), 421.
3 As an epigraph, the citation from Freud's *Three Essays on the Theory of Sexuality* (1905) can be found in *Pursuits of Happiness* (43) and refound in *Cities of Words* (x).
4 Lee Wallace, *Lesbianism, Cinema, Space: The Sexual Life of Apartments* (New York: Routledge, 2009), 59.
5 B. Ruby Rich, *New Queer Cinema: The Director's Cut* (Durham, NC: Duke University Press, 2013), 44, 38.
6 Rich, *New Queer Cinema*, 44–45, 38.
7 Rich, *New Queer Cinema*, 265.
8 Nan Goldin, *The Ballad of Sexual Dependency* (New York: Aperture, 1986).

9   See, for instance, Susan Pelle and Catherine Fox who regard the "the drug-induced bodies in Lucy's loft" as productive "desiring machines." "Queering Desire/Querying Consumption: Rereading Visual Images of 'Lesbian' Desire in Lisa Cholodenko's *High Art*," thirdspace: *A Journal of Feminist Theory and Culture* 6, no. 1 (2006), journals.sfu.ca/thirdspace/index.php/journal/article/view/fox-pelle/125.
10 For an overview of D. W. Winnicott's theory of human development as "a radical redescription of erotic possibility," see Adam Phillips, *Winnicott* (London: Penguin, 2007), xi.
11 For an account of "mouth love" as a primitive form of love that is transparent in its coupling together of appetite and aggression, see D. W. Winnicott, "Aggression and Its Roots," in *Deprivation and Delinquency*, ed. Clare Winnicott, Ray Shepherd, and Madeleine Davis (London: Tavistock, 1984), 87–88.
12 In her discussion of Freud's notion of the drive, Avital Ronell notes that even in conditions of satisfaction the ego "becomes insecure and must startup the machinery of testing." Avital Ronell, *The Test Drive* (Champaign: University of Illinois Press, 2005), 70. Ronell also points out that "the extreme experience of attachment easily escalates into a debilitating dependence" (284).
13 The Hollywood foothills are one of the four spatial ecologies that Reyner Banham attributes to Los Angeles in *Los Angeles: The Architecture of Four Ecologies* (New York: Harper and Row, 1971), 99.
14 Cavell, *Pursuits of Happiness*, 19. For a history of Laurel Canyon's symbolic centrality to conceptualizations of the counterculture as disseminated through popular music and the celebrity persona of folk-rock artists, see Michael Walker, *Laurel Canyon: The Inside Story of Rock-and-Roll's Legendary Neighborhood* (New York: Faber and Faber, 2006).
15 The lyrics of Sparklehorse's "Shade and Honey," the song Nivola sings in the studio scene, which also plays over the film's final credits, captures this green world quality.
16 For discussion of how Cholodenko's film reworks *The Graduate*'s mother-marriage plot in order to stage an encounter between second-wave feminism and postfeminism, see Walter Metz, *Engaging Film Criticism: Film History and Contemporary American Cinema* (New York: Peter Lang, 2004), 107–28.
17 For a discussion of this "acoustic flash-forward" and Nichols's general use of telephones and other editing devices to introduce a gap between character and speech, see Kyle Stevens, *Mike Nichols: Sex, Language, and the Reinvention of Psychological Realism* (Oxford: Oxford University Press, 2015), 101.
18 Or, as Nichols puts it, "This boy in this diving suit at the bottom of this pool has been caused by this moment to call Mrs. Robinson." Mike Nichols, quoted in J. W. Whitehead, *Appraising* The Graduate: *The Mike Nichols Classic and Its Impact on Hollywood* (Jefferson, NC: McFarland, 2011), 53.
19 Cavell, *Pursuits of Happiness*, 132. Cavell's account of Hollywood film's capacity to productively reproduce our distance from the world can be found in *The World Viewed* (Cambridge, MA: Harvard University Press, 1979). Elisabeth Bronfen has recently placed Cavell's philosophy of film in the context of his using

popular Hollywood cinema to negotiate his immersion in a culture to which his migrant parents did not belong. Elisabeth Bronfen, "Hurray for Hollywood: Philosophy and Cinema according to Stanley Cavell," *Film as Philosophy*, ed. Bernd Herzogenrath (Minneapolis: University of Minnesota Press, 2017), 180–99.

20 Jill Casid places the garden designed by Jules in a long tradition of lesbian-feminist land experiments that runs from the Ladies of Llangollen to Catherine Opie's football landscapes. Instead of offering utopia, Casid argues that the garden in Cholodenko's film explores "the difficult topography of disappointment and desire at that place where the elastic rubber of the future perfect hits the rough road of reality testing." Jill H. Casid, "Epilogue: Landscape in, around, and under the Performative," *Women and Performance* 21, no. 1 (2011): 107.

21 It is unclear how the motorcycle-riding donor-dad would stack up against Gordon Grant and Paul Storr, the stars of the Colt Studio clip the lesbian couple watch as an on-ramp to marital sex, although several of the film's lesbian daddy reviewers understand that they would come off well in any comparison if someone would just hand them the keys to the Harley.

22 Cholodenko's films are not standard lesbian fare insofar as the director is not really interested in sexual orientation or the story of becoming lesbian so much as the dynamics of established relationships, something she investigates at greater length in the 2014 miniseries *Olive Kitteridge*, which follows a decades-long marriage in which Olive—as played by McDormand—cultivates long-term unhappiness with her husband. The ambivalence that is core to the Kitteridges' marriage plays out in an extraordinary hostage scene in which Olive and her husband, indifferent to the real danger they are in, try to kill each other. Olive would seem to be a woman wedded to her own dissatisfaction who is engaged in a mode of perpetual complaint that might be considered the inverse of remarriage comedy. *Olive Kitteridge* is thus related to Cavell's other famous subgenre, the melodrama of the unknown woman, in which marriage proves impossible for the female protagonist, who ultimately chooses to pursue her individuation alone. See Stanley Cavell, *Contesting Tears: The Hollywood Melodrama of the Unknown Woman* (Chicago, IL: University of Chicago Press, 1996).

23 Unlike Freud, whose account of the fort/da game stresses the child's illusory mastery of the comings and goings of others, Winnicott emphasizes the experience of disillusionment as key to the development of creative play and an independent turn to the world that is based in relationality not separation. See D. W. Winnicott, "Transitional Objects and Transitional Phenomena," in *Playing and Reality*, ed. F. Robert Rodman (New York: Routledge, 2005), 1–34.

24 Cavell, "The Thought of Movies," *Yale Review* 72, no. 2 (1983): 190.

25 Cavell, *Pursuits of Happiness*, 88.

26 Joshua Gamson's *Modern Families: Stories of Extraordinary Journeys to Kinship* (New York: New York University Press, 2015) rounds out this critical and popular conversation with ethnographic depth.

27 As the child of professors and great nephew of the married actors Eli Wallach and Anne Jackson, Scott's genealogy connects him to both the Ivy League and

Hollywood, which no doubt predisposes him to see the Cavellian side of everything. A. O. Scott, "Meet the Sperm Donor: Modern Family Ties," review of Lisa Cholodenko's *The Kids Are All Right* (2010), *New York Times*, July 8, 2010, https://www.nytimes.com/2010/07/09/movies/09kids.html.

28 Margaret M. Reed and Mary S. Green, review of Lisa Cholodenko's *The Kids Are All Right*, *Journal of Feminist Family Therapy* 24, no. 2 (2012): 173.

29 Suzanna Danuta Walters, "The Kids Are All Right but the Lesbians Aren't: Queer Kinship in U.S. Culture," *Sexualities* 15, no. 8 (2012): 17–33; Tammie M. Kennedy, "Sustaining White Homonormativity: *The Kids Are All Right* as Public Pedagogy," *Journal of Lesbian Studies* 18, no. 2 (2014): 118–32.

30 Kristina Gupta, "Picturing Space for Lesbian Nonsexualities: Rethinking Sex-Normative Commitment through *The Kids Are All Right* (2010)," *Journal of Lesbian Studies* 17, no. 1 (2013): 103–18. Maria Pramaggiore, on the other hand, regards *Kids*'s deployment of bisexuality "as a negative" extension of the "compulsory cultural regime that understands the couple as the only type of sexual relationship, as the cornerstone that organizes society, and perhaps, as the very emblem of personhood," which she finds doubly disappointing insofar as *High Art* and *Laurel Canyon* both challenge precisely that logic. Maria Pramaggiore, "Kids, Rock and Couples: Screening the Elusive/Illusive Bisexual," *Journal of Bisexuality* 11, no. 4 (2011): 592. For Pramaggiore's lengthier account of *High Art* as a bisexual film, see "High and Low: Bisexual Women and Aesthetics in *Chasing Amy* and *High Art*," *Journal of Bisexuality* 2, nos. 2–3 (2002): 243–66.

31 Jasbir Puar and Karen Tongson, "The Ugly Truth about Why the Kids Are All Right," *Velvetpark*, January 20, 2012, velvetparkmedia.com/blogs/ugly-truth-about-why-kids-are-all-right.

32 Jodi Brooks, "*The Kids Are All Right*, the Pursuits of Happiness, and the Spaces Between," *Camera Obscura* 85, 29, no. 1 (2014): 114.

33 Brooks, "Spaces Between," 119.

34 Brooks, "Spaces Between," 120.

35 Brooks, "Spaces Between," 124.

36 Brooks, "Spaces Between," 126.

37 Brooks, "Spaces Between," 127.

38 Tania Modleski, "An Affair to Forget: Melancholia in Bromantic Comedy," *Camera Obscura* 86 29, no. 2 (2014): 119–46. Modleski's argument with Cavell dates back to her response to his essay on *Now, Voyager*, which she sees as ignoring prior feminist readings of Irving Rapper's film. See *Critical Inquiry* 17, no. 1 (1990), 237–38, and, for Cavell's lengthy response, 238–44. The following year, Modleski expanded her critique and cast Cavell's wider project on melodrama as an "attempt to contain the threat posed by feminist thought and to reposition the struggle between feminism and the patriarchal traditions as a struggle inhering *in* that tradition" or, in short, a "remystification" of philosophy. Tania Modleski, *Feminism without Women: Culture and Criticism in a "Postfeminist" Age* (London: Routledge, 1991), 8.

39 Modleski, "Affair to Forget," 122.

40 Stanley Cavell, "A Capra Moment," in *Cavell on Film*, ed. William Rothman (Albany: State University of New York Press, 2005), 136.
41 Cavell, *Cities of Words*, 16.

Chapter 6. Reattachment Theory

1 John Bowlby, *Attachment and Loss*, vol. 1, *Attachment* (New York: Basic Books, 1969); John Bowlby, *Attachment and Loss*, vol. 2, *Separation, Anxiety, and Anger* (New York: Basic Books, 1973); and John Bowlby, *Attachment and Loss*, vol. 3, *Loss, Sadness, and Depression* (New York: Basic Books, 1980).
2 See, for example, Hiltrud Otto and Heidi Keller, eds., *Different Faces of Attachment: Cultural Variations on a Universal Human Need* (Cambridge: Cambridge University Press, 2014); and Ben Rockett and Sam Carr, "Animals and Attachment Theory," *Society and Animals* 22, no. 4 (2014): 415–33.
3 Elizabeth Chin, *My Life with Things: The Consumer Diaries* (Durham, NC: Duke University Press, 2016), 43.
4 Stanley Cavell, *Pursuits of Happiness: The Hollywood Comedy of Remarriage* (Cambridge, MA: Harvard University Press, 1981).
5 Cavell has also been criticized for the sexism inherent in his account of remarriage as "the woman's education by the man," which becomes less of a sticking point when the marriages in question are gay or lesbian and the principle of reciprocity assumed to be at the core of erotic friendship less exposed to the torque of gender. Cavell, *Pursuits of Happiness*, 5.
6 David R. Shumway, "Screwball Comedies: Constructing Romance, Mystifying Marriage," *Cinema Journal* 30, no. 4 (1991): 7–23.
7 Elizabeth Kraft, *Restoration Stage Comedies and Hollywood Remarriage Films: In Conversation with Stanley Cavell* (London: Routledge, 2016), 3.
8 Cavell, *Pursuits of Happiness*, 86, quoted in Kraft, *Restoration Stage Comedies*, 2.
9 William Day, "'I Don't Know, Just Wait': Remembering Remarriage in *Eternal Sunshine of the Spotless Mind*," in *The Philosophy of Charlie Kaufman*, ed. Paul LaRocca (Lexington: University Press of Kentucky, 2011), 151n8. See also, Michael J. Meyer, "Reflections on Comic Reconciliations: Ethics, Memory, and Anxious Happy Endings," *Journal of Aesthetics and Art Criticism* 66, no. 1 (2008): 77–87.
10 Day, "Remembering Marriage," 134.
11 Cavell, *Pursuits of Happiness*, 208. For an interesting retake on the issue of female reeducation via marriage, see Áine Mahon, "Marriage and Moral Perfectionism in Siri Hustvedt and Stanley Cavell," *Textual Practice* 29, no. 4 (2015): 631–51.
12 For a longer account of the apartment chronotope and its relation to lesbianism, in particular, see Lee Wallace, *Lesbianism, Cinema, Space: The Sexual Life of Apartments* (New York: Routledge, 2009). For a wider discussion of the usefulness of the urban apartment plot to reconfiguring gender relations, particularly as they intersect with the claims of feminism, see Pamela Robertson Wojcik, *The Apartment Plot: Urban Living in American Film and Popular Culture, 1945–75*

(Durham, NC: Duke University Press, 2010), and the essays gathered in Pamela Robertson Wojcik, ed., *The Apartment Complex: Urban Living and Global Screen Cultures* (Durham, NC: Duke University Press, 2018).

13   Cavell, *Pursuits of Happiness*, 29.
14   In a typically incisive critique of *Brokeback Mountain*, D. A. Miller links the film's success to liberal self-congratulation in the area of marriage equality. D. A. Miller, "On the Universality of *Brokeback Mountain*," *Film Quarterly* 60, no. 3 (2007): 50–60.
15   For discussion of Daldry's film in the context of melodramatic handlings of marriage, see Julianne Pidduck, "The Times of *The Hours*: Queer Melodrama and the Dilemma of Marriage," *Camera Obscura* 82, 28, no. 1 (2013): 36–67. For an account of Cholodenko's film that engages Cavell's notion of remarriage, see Jodi Brooks, "*The Kids Are All Right*, the Pursuits of Happiness, and the Spaces Between," *Camera Obscura* 85, 29, no. 1 (2014): 111–35. As Dana Heller elaborates in a brilliant reading of Showtime's *The L Word* (2004–9) and its unscripted reality spin-off *The Real L Word* (2010–11), the gay marriage cycle has now extended itself into nonfiction franchises. Dana Heller, "Wrecked: Programming Celesbian Reality," in *Reality Gendervision: Sexuality and Gender on Transatlantic Reality Television*, ed. Brenda R. Weber (Durham, NC: Duke University Press, 2014), 123–46.
16   Michael DeAngelis, Introduction to *Reading the Bromance: Homosocial Relationships in Film and Television*, ed. Michael DeAngelis (Detroit, MI: Wayne State University Press, 2014), 15. DeAngelis first explores the marriage-as-problem cycle of films in "Mispronouncing 'Man and Wife': The Fate of Marriage in Hollywood's Sexual Revolution," in *Hetero: Queering Representations of Straightness*, ed. Sean Griffin (Albany: State University of New York Press, 2009), 129–49. Mike Nichols's *Carnal Knowledge* (1971) remains the centerpiece of this cycle. As discussed in the previous chapter, Tania Modleski has recently used bromance as a means of critiquing Cavell's notion of remarriage comedy. See Tania Modleski, "An Affair to Forget: Melancholia in Bromantic Comedy," *Camera Obscura* 86, 29, no. 2 (2014): 119–46.
17   Cavell, *Pursuits of Happiness*, 20.
18   In *American Couples: Money, Work, Sex* (New York: William Morrow, 1983), Philip Blumstein and Pepper Schwartz applied the term "lesbian bed death" to the diminishment of sexual activity reported between women in long-term relationships. Although this research has been contested in the field, lesbian bed death continues to command popular airtime within lesbian-friendly contexts such as Alison Bechdel's syndicated comic strip *Dykes to Watch Out For*, which can be sampled in *The Essential Dykes to Watch Out For* (New York: Houghton Mifflin Harcourt, 2008).
19   Weigert's face is familiar from *Deadwood* (HBO 2004–6), in which she played the haplessly butch Calamity Jane. In her discussion of the show's repurposing of the historical figure of Calamity (Martha Jane Cannary) as a lesbian, Linda Mizejewski links Weigert's performance of female masculinity to the rise of gay marriage in US public consciousness. Mizejewski emphasizes the series finale

in which Calamity and her female lover make their claim to conjugal citizenship by leading a crocodile of schoolchildren down the frontier town's main street, as if marriage equality represented a new high noon for America. Linda Mizejewski, "Calamity Jane and Female Masculinity in *Deadwood*," in *Dirty Words in Deadwood: Literature and the Postwestern*, ed. Melody Graulich and Nicolas S. Witschi (Lincoln: University of Nebraska Press, 2013), 184–207.

20 Cavell, *Pursuits of Happiness*, 153. For Cavell's compelling account of how *The Philadelphia Story* imagines the overcoming of class rather than the crossing of class plotted in other Hollywood genres, see *Pursuits of Happiness*, 153–59. In March 2016, in what can only be described as a Cavellian twist of words, Pennsylvania changed its state motto from "State of Independence" to "Pennsylvania. Pursue Your Happiness."

21 For more information on the Myers-Briggs Type Indicator, see the Myers and Briggs Foundation (http://www.myersbriggs.org). Although her services are never advertised as such, Abby appears to offer her clients two things: sex and talk, or, more correctly, sex or talk, since the sex tends to stop once the talk kicks in. Returning clients, such as the plump women's studies undergraduate in need of alternative mothering or the complicated older woman who seems to identify with Abby as a more successful version of herself, are not shown in sexual clinches but lie around talking, even reading, as if they too had succumbed to lesbian bed death. Once again, this talk is the antithesis of the conversation Cavell finds at the core of the Hollywood remarriage comedies, in which dialogue has to convey the eroticism that the Production Code precludes.

22 Mary D. Salter Ainsworth, "Object Relations, Dependency, and Attachment: A Theoretical Review of the Infant-Mother Relationship," *Child Development* 40, no. 4 (1969): 999.

23 Ainsworth, "Object Relations," 1003.

24 Brian Eno, "Some of Them Are Old," on *Here Come the Warm Jets* (Island Records, 1974), accessed December 29, 2017, https://www.lyrics.com.lyric/821125.

25 Cavell, *Pursuits of Happiness*, 257.

26 The film's dull restoration of married life after infidelity recalls the scenario imagined by Laura Kipnis's account of adultery within a polemic that positions marriage as a training ground for broader forms of social resignation. Laura Kipnis, "Adultery" in *Intimacy*, ed. Lauren Berlant (Chicago, IL: University of Chicago Press), 9–47.

27 Ainsworth, "Object Relations," 1015.

28 In Reisz's film, the philandering factory worker played by Albert Finney finally extracts himself from his serial affairs with terrace-dwelling married women in order to get engaged to a modern young woman who likes to shop and has her sights set on a freestanding family home.

29 The demolition video shows a mechanical crane eating into the building like a crudely animated dinosaur. The effect is beautiful, although Nottingham City Council is keen to dissociate itself from the derelict flat that features in the video, which was the creation of the set design team associated with Anton Corbijn's *Control* and not the result of municipal neglect. See "Total Reclaim Brings

Down Lenton Court in Nottingham, UK," YouTube, February 14, 2017, https://www.youtube.com/watch?v=ZoFyYWX3V9A, accessed November 9, 2017.

30 While many reviewers have noted *Weekend*'s dual affiliation to British social realism and American independent cinema (the latter reflected in its premiering at the sxsw Film Festival), the film also conforms to broader conventions for representing everyday life. For an account of those conventions, see Andrew Klevan, *Disclosure of the Everyday: Undramatic Achievement in Narrative Film* (Trowbridge, UK: Flicks Books, 2000). The US success of *Weekend* led to Haigh directing ten episodes of HBO's gay-themed series *Looking* (2014–15), which leans heavily on a gay marriage plot.

31 Dennis Lim, "*Weekend*: The Space between Two People," Criterion Collection, August 21, 2012, https://www.criterion.com/current/posts/2426-weekend-the-space-between-two-people.

32 Stephanie Deborah Clare, "(Homo)Normativity's Romance: Happiness and Indigestion in Andrew Haigh's *Weekend*," *Continuum: Journal of Media and Cultural Studies* 27, no. 6 (2013): 786. Alternatively, Shannon Weber has used Russell's defense of gay marriage to dispute the queer critique of the same-sex marriage movement as necessarily homonormative and assimilationist. Shannon Weber, "Daring to Marry: Marriage Equality Activism after Proposition 8 as Challenge to the Assimilationist/Radical Binary in Queer Studies," *Journal of Homosexuality* 62, no. 9 (2015): 1147–73. For a sensitive account of how the film uses the parallel traps of assimilationism and queer radicalism to point to the ongoing difficulty of being gay in the "radioactive half-life" of homophobia, see Paul Brunick, "Reach Out and Touch Someone," *Film Comment* 47, no. 3 (2011): 63.

33 Clare, "(Homo)Normativity's Romance," 787 and 788.

34 Clare, "(Homo)Normativity's Romance," 790.

35 Cavell, *Pursuits of Happiness*, 31. For a tonally complex celebration of gay romance and stranger intimacy, see John Grant's official video for "Disappointing," featuring Tracey Thorn, which is filmed in a gym-cum-bathhouse filled with ursine gay men. "John Grant–Disappointing Feat. Tracey Thorn (Official Music Video)," YouTube, September 9, 2015, https://www.youtube.com/watch?v=U2Ig4sMURdc, accessed May 1, 2018.

36 Quinnford and Scout, photostream, https://www.flickr.com/photos/quinnfordandscout/, accessed November 9, 2017.

37 Maggie Nelson, *The Argonauts* (Minneapolis: Graywolf Press, 2015), 180. Cavell, *Pursuits of Happiness*, 11–12.

Chapter 7. The Remarriage Crisis

1 The order of discussion observed in Stanley Cavell's *Pursuits of Happiness: The Hollywood Comedy of Remarriage* (Cambridge, MA: Harvard University Press, 1981) runs: *The Lady Eve* (Preston Sturges, 1941), *It Happened One Night* (Frank Capra, 1934), *Bringing Up Baby* (Howard Hawks, 1938), *The Philadelphia Story* (George Cukor, 1940), *His Girl Friday* (Howard Hawks, 1940), *Adam's Rib* (George Cukor, 1949), and, finally, *The Awful Truth* (Leo McCarey, 1937). This

order is muddled in Stanley Cavell's *Cities of Words: Pedagogical Letters on a Register of the Moral Life* (Cambridge, MA: Harvard University Press, 2004), where *Bringing Up Baby* is also demoted from chapter-length discussion. In the preface to *Cities*, Cavell reflects on the book's origins as lectures in a course on moral perfectionism and invites the reader to skip the retrospectively written introduction and begin reading anywhere. In addition, he hints at his own preference for "post-poning" the reading of introductions, which, although intended to be read first, are often written last, a practice I am here following in returning for the first time to Cavell's preliminary discussion of remarriage as a way of concluding my own. The reader must bear the back-to-front reintroduction of the remarriage discussion as yet another indication that, as Freud writes and Cavell twice seconds in the form of an epigraph, "The finding of an object is in fact the refinding of it" (Cavell, *Pursuits of Happiness*, 43, and *Cities of Words*, xv).

2 Cavell, *Pursuits of Happiness*, 1.
3 Cavell, *Pursuits of Happiness*, 2.
4 Cavell, *Pursuits of Happiness*, 2.
5 Elisabeth Bronfen, "Hurray for Hollywood: Philosophy and Cinema According to Stanley Cavell," in *Film as Philosophy*, ed. Bernd Herzogenrath (Minneapolis: University of Minnesota Press, 2017), 180–99. For Cavell's most sustained account of the connection between these two figures, see Stanley Cavell, "Shakespeare and Rohmer: Two Tales of Winter," in Cavell, *Cities of Words*, 421–43.
6 Jonathan Romney, "Film of the Week: *45 Years*," *Film Comment*, December 17, 2016, https://www.filmcomment.com/blog/film-of-the-week-45-years/, accessed November 29, 2017.
7 David Thomson, "Let Us Go Then: On *45 Years*," *Film Comment*, January 28, 2016, https://www.filmcomment.com/blog/let-us-go-then-on-45-years/, accessed November 29, 2017.
8 In the entry he gives her in his biographical dictionary of film, Thomson is deeply sympathetic to the way Rampling's face determines her characterization and makes her prey to misogyny. "She has not just a chilly edge," he writes, "but the capacity to make us suspect a cold heart. So, she has her share of narrow-faced villains, not always more than baleful gargoyles." David Thomson, *Biographical Dictionary of Film* (New York: Alfred Knopf, 1994), 611. First published in 1975, Thomson's dictionary is now in its sixth edition and over three times the length of the original.
9 Many of the futile elements Thomson finds in Haigh's film have resonance in Rampling's off-screen biography, including the public collapse of her second marriage to Jean-Michel Jarre after she saw him checking into a hotel with a younger woman, and the long-term devastation wrought in her family by her father's decision that she and he must never tell her mother of her sister's suicide but present her death at twenty-three as the result of natural causes. These details about Rampling's life circulated in the promotional press around the release of Laurent Cantet's *Vers le sud* (2005), a film in which she plays an unmarried woman of a certain age who travels to Haiti to find sexual intimacy with local men.

10 Stanley Cavell, *Contesting Tears: The Hollywood Melodrama of the Unknown Woman* (Chicago, IL: University of Chicago Press, 1996).
11 Among these renegotiated rules we might include the decision to allow one's personal life to bleed into one's professional persona, as Haigh, who has two daughters, does, or keep it separate, as Rohmer famously did. For more on Rohmer's strict compartmentalization of his domestic and professional roles, including his role as mentor to the French New Wave, see Antoine de Baecque and Noël Herpe, *Éric Rohmer: A Biography*, trans. Steven Randall and Lisa Neal (New York: Columbia University Press, 2016).
12 Joe Shute, "The True Story (behind the Story) That Inspired *45 Years*," *Telegraph*, August 29, 2015, http://www.telegraph.co.uk/culture/books/11832861/The-true-story-behind-the-story-that-inspired-45-Years.html.
13 For a different account of Haigh's auteurist signature and its imbrication in a contemporary logic of media convergence, see Jack Cortvriend, "Stylistic Convergences between British Film and American Television: Andrew Haigh's *Looking*," *Critical Studies in Television: The International Journal of Television Studies* 13, no. 1 (2018): 96–112.
14 For rural and urban variations on these themes, and Haigh's capacity to observe the ordinariness of sexuality, see *Five Miles Out* (Andrew Haigh, 2009), about a teenage girl sent to a seaside camp while her sister is hospitalized with anorexia, and *Greek Pete* (Andrew Haigh, 2009), a docudrama about a London rent-boy saving to buy a fish-and-chip shop.
15 The following year Véry appears in Krzysztof Kieslowski's *Trois couleurs: Bleu*, a film that also replots the story of paternity around very European coordinates. In *Bleu* a wife, played by Juliette Binoche, grieves the husband and child she lost in a car accident that she survived. Distraught, she steadily withdraws inside herself until she begins to suspect that her late husband had a mistress, a thought put in her head by a television clip of him and another woman attending a recital. The ultimate revelation that this woman, played by Véry, was not only her late husband's mistress but is presently carrying his child, prompts her own emotional revivification and ability to reattach to the world.
16 Stanley Cavell, "Shakespeare and Rohmer: Two Tales of Winter," in Cavell, *Cities of Words*, 422. As philosophically minded readers will recognize, Cavell's defense of marriage is a defense of "the ordinary as what is under attack in philosophy's tendency to skepticism."
17 Cavell, *Pursuits of Happiness*, 132.
18 Stanley Cavell, "On Éric Rohmer's *A Tale of Winter*" (1994), in William Rothman, ed., *Cavell on Film*, (Albany: State University of New York Press, 2005), 288.
19 Cavell, "Éric Rohmer's *A Tale of Winter*," in Rothman, *Cavell on Film*, 288. For Cavell's account of refinding a pathway to happiness through the experience of watching Ingmar Bergman's *Smiles on a Summer Night*, a summery meditation on infidelity and reconciliation, which is linked with his later experience of seeing Bergman's stage production of *The Winter's Tale*, see Stanley Cavell, "Seasons of Love: Bergman's *Smiles of a Summer Night* and *The Winter's Tale*," in Rothman, *Cavell on Film*, 193–203.

20 Cavell, *Pursuits of Happiness*, 239. In the Hollywood original, this recognition about the husband is importantly combined with the wife's discovery of her "difference from herself, or her double nature as socially refined and erotically risky." Cavell, *Cities of Words*, 379.
21 Cavell, *Pursuits of Happiness*, 237–38.
22 Cavell, *Pursuits of Happiness*, 238.
23 Cavell, *Pursuits of Happiness*, 238.
24 Cavell, *Pursuits of Happiness*, 241.
25 Cavell, *Pursuits of Happiness*, 241.
26 Cavell, *Pursuits of Happiness*, 240.
27 Cavell, *Pursuits of Happiness*, 237 and 239.
28 Cavell, *Pursuits of Happiness*, 260.
29 Cavell, *Pursuits of Happiness*, 261.
30 Cavell, *Pursuits of Happiness*, 240.
31 Cavell, *Pursuits of Happiness*, 262.
32 Geoffrey Hawthorn, "Green Films," *London Review of Books* 4, no. 6, April 1, 1984, 14.
33 David Alff, *The Wreckage of Intentions: Projects in British Culture, 1660–1730* (Philadelphia: University of Pennsylvania Press, 2017), 109. Alff points out that this area is now the site of one of the world's largest wetland restoration initiatives.
34 As many reviewers have noted, Geoff also sets about reading Kierkegaard, who, his wife points out, has defeated him before. A bachelor theorist of marriage, Kierkegaard contributes one of the six epigraphs that mark the transition between the introductory chapter and the film case studies that make-up *Pursuits of Happiness*. For more on Kierkegaard's broken engagement and its literary remaking, see Morten Høi Jensen, "A Keeper of Love's Fame: Regine Olsen and Søren Kierkegaard," *Los Angeles Review of Books*, April 9, 2014, https://lareviewofbooks.org/article/keeper-loves-flame-regine-olsen-soren-kierkegaard/#!, accessed February 18, 2019.
35 Like Haigh, though before him, Rohmer is famous for his meteorological sensibility or what Gilbert Adair writing in *The Guardian* has described as his capacity to film air: "Éric Rohmer: Let's Talk about Everything," *Guardian*, January 12, 2010, https://www.theguardian.com/film/2010/jan/12/eric-rohmer-gilbert-adair.

Reacknowledgments

1 Stanley Cavell, "Seasons of Love: Bergman's *Smiles of a Summer Night* and *The Winter's Tale*," in *Cavell on Film*, ed. William Rothman (Albany: State University of New York Press, 2005), 195.
2 Cavell, "Seasons of Love," 194–5.
3 Cavell, "Seasons of Love," 195.
4 Cavell, "Seasons of Love," 203.
5 Cavell, "Seasons of Love," 202.
6 Cavell, "Seasons of Love," 195.

7 Esther Perel, *Mating in Captivity: Unlocking Erotic Intelligence* (New York: Harper Collins, 2006); *The State of Affairs: Rethinking Infidelity* (New York: Harper Collins, 2017).
8 Alexandra Schwartz, "Esther Perel Lets Us in on Couples' Secrets," *The New Yorker*, May 31, 2017, https://www.newyorker.com/culture/cultural-comment/esther-perel-lets-us-listen-in-on-couples-secrets.
9 Ann duCille, ed., "Black Marriage," *differences: Journal of Feminist Cultural Studies* 29, no. 2 (2018).
10 Thomas Kendall, "Is Black Marriage Queer?" *differences: A Journal of Feminist Cultural Studies* 29, no. 2 (2018): 208.
11 Kendall, "Is Black Marriage Queer?," 208.
12 Kendall, "Is Black Marriage Queer?," 211.
13 Lauren Berlant, *Cruel Optimism* (Durham: Duke University Press, 2011), 14. For a lengthy discussion of Berlant's utopian account of "optimism's negativity" and the need to differentiate it from the negative negativity put forward in the work of Leo Bersani and Lee Edelman, see Robyn Wiegman, "Sex and Negativity; Or, What Queer Theory Has for You," *Cultural Critique* 95 (2017): 219–43.
14 Cavell, *Cities of Words*, 381.
15 Cavell, *Cities of Words*, 378–79.

BIBLIOGRAPHY

Abel, Elizabeth. "Foiling the Marriage Plot." Review of *Tradition Counter Tradition: Love and the Form of Fiction* by Joseph Allen Boone. *Novel: A Forum on Fiction* 24, no. 1 (1990): 111–14.

Adair, Gilbert. "Eric Rohmer: Let's Talk about Everything." *Guardian*, January 12, 2010. https://www.theguardian.com/film/2010/jan/12/eric-rohmer-gilbert-adair. Accessed February 15, 2019.

Ainsworth, Mary D. Salter. "Object Relations, Dependency, and Attachment: A Theoretical Review of the Infant-Mother Relationship." *Child Development* 40, no. 4 (1969): 969–1025.

Alff, David. *The Wreckage of Intentions: Projects in British Culture, 1660–1730*. Philadelphia: University of Pennsylvania Press, 2017.

Armstrong, Nancy. *Desire and Domestic Fiction: A Political History of the Novel*. Oxford: Oxford University Press, 1987.

Babcock, Muriel. Review of *Craig's Wife*. *Los Angeles Examiner*, n.d.

Banham, Reyner. *Los Angeles: The Architecture of Four Ecologies*. New York: Harper and Row, 1971.

Barnes, Howard. Review of *Craig's Wife*. *New York Herald Tribune*, October 2, 1936, 17.

Barthes, Roland. *S/Z: An Essay*. Translated by Richard Miller. New York: Hill and Wang, 1974.

Bechdel, Alison. *The Essential Dykes to Watch Out For*. New York: Houghton Mifflin Harcourt, 2008.

Berg, James J., and Chris Freeman, eds. *Conversations with Christopher Isherwood*. Jackson: University Press of Mississippi, 2001.

Berg, James J., and Chris Freeman, eds. *The Isherwood Century: Essays on the Life and Work of Christopher Isherwood*. Madison: University of Wisconsin Press, 2000.

Bergstrom, Janet. "Rereading the Work of Claire Johnston." In *Feminism and Film Theory*, edited by Constance Penley, 80–88. New York: Routledge, 1988.

Berlant, Lauren. *The Anatomy of National Fantasy: Hawthorne, Utopia, and Everyday Life*. Chicago, IL: University Chicago Press, 1991.

Berlant, Lauren. *Cruel Optimism*. Durham, NC: Duke University Press, 2011.

Berlant, Lauren. *The Female Complaint: The Unfinished Business of Sentimentality in American Culture*. Durham, NC: Duke University Press, 2008.

Berlant, Lauren. "Humorlessness (Three Monologues and a Hairpiece)." *Critical Inquiry* 43, no. 2 (2017): 305–40.

Berlant, Lauren, ed. *Intimacy*. Chicago, IL: University of Chicago Press, 2000.
Berlant, Lauren. "Intimacy: A Special Issue." In *Intimacy*, edited by Lauren Berlant, 1–8. Chicago, IL: University of Chicago Press, 2000.
Berlant, Lauren. *The Queen of America Goes to Washington: Essays on Sex and Citizenship*. Durham, NC: Duke University Press, 1997.
Berlant, Lauren, and Lee Edelman. "Reading, Sex, and the Unbearable: A Response to Tim Dean." *American Literary History* 27, no. 3 (2015): 625–29.
Berlant, Lauren, and Lee Edelman. *Sex, or the Unbearable*. Durham, NC: Duke University Press, 2014.
Betsky, Aaron. *Queer Space: Architecture and Same-Sex Desire*. New York: William Morrow, 1997.
Blumstein, Philip, and Pepper Schwartz. *American Couples: Money, Work, Sex*. New York: William Morrow, 1983.
Boone, Joseph Allen. *Tradition Counter Tradition: Love and the Form of Fiction*. Chicago, IL: University of Chicago Press, 1987.
Boutelle, Sara Holmes. *Julia Morgan, Architect*. New York: Abbeville Press, 1988; revised and updated, 1995.
Bowlby, John. *Attachment and Loss*. Vol. 1, *Attachment*. New York: Basic Books, 1969.
Bowlby, John. *Attachment and Loss*. Vol. 2, *Separation, Anxiety, and Anger*. New York: Basic Books, 1973.
Bowlby, John. *Attachment and Loss*. Vol. 3, *Loss, Sadness, and Depression*. New York: Basic Books, 1980.
Brandzel, Amy L. *Against Citizenship: The Violence of the Normative*. Chicago, IL: University of Chicago Press, 2016.
Brandzel, Amy L. "Queering Citizenship? Same-Sex Marriage and the State." *GLQ: A Journal of Lesbian and Gay Studies* 11, no. 2 (2005): 171–204.
Bray, Alan. *Homosexuality in Renaissance England*. London: Gay Men's Press, 1982.
Bronfen, Elisabeth. "Hurray for Hollywood: Philosophy and Cinema according to Stanley Cavell." In *Film as Philosophy*, edited by Bernd Herzogenrath, 180–99. Minneapolis: University of Minnesota Press, 2017.
Brooks, Jodi. "*The Kids Are All Right*, the Pursuits of Happiness, and the Spaces Between." *Camera Obscura 85*, 29, no. 1 (2014): 111–35.
Brooks, Peter. *Reading for the Plot: Design and Intention in Narrative*. Cambridge, MA: Harvard University Press, 1983.
Brunick, Paul. "Reach Out and Touch Someone." *Film Comment* 47, no. 3 (2011): 62–63.
Bruno, Giuliana. "Fashions of Living." *Quarterly Review of Film and Video* 20, no. 3 (2003): 167–76.
Bryant, Wayne M. Review of Tom Ford's *A Single Man*. *Journal of Bisexuality* 10, no. 3 (2010): 350–53.
Bucknell, Katherine, ed. *The Animals: Love Letters between Christopher Isherwood and Don Bachardy*. New York: Farrar, Straus and Giroux, 2013.
Butler, Judith. "Is Kinship Always Already Heterosexual?" *differences: A Journal of Feminist Cultural Studies* 15, no. 1 (2002): 14–44.
Carpenter, Edward. *Love's Coming of Age: A Series of Papers on the Relations of the Sexes*. Manchester, UK: Labour, 1896; repr., London: Allen and Unwin, 1930.

Carter, Julian. "Gay Marriage and Pulp Fiction: Homonormativity, Disidentification, and Affect in Ann Bannon's Lesbian Novels." GLQ: A Journal of Lesbian and Gay Studies 15, no. 4 (2009): 583–609.
Casid, Jill H. "Epilogue: Landscape in, around, and under the Performative." Women and Performance 21, no. 1 (2011): 97–116.
Cavell, Stanley. "A Capra Moment." In Cavell on Film, edited by William Rothman, 135–43. Albany: State University of New York Press, 2005.
Cavell, Stanley. Cities of Words: Pedagogical Letters on a Register of the Moral Life. Cambridge, MA: Harvard University Press, 2004.
Cavell, Stanley. Contesting Tears: The Hollywood Melodrama of the Unknown Woman. Chicago, IL: University of Chicago Press, 1996.
Cavell, Stanley. Little Did I Know: Excerpts from Memory. Stanford, CA: Stanford University Press, 2010.
Cavell, Stanley. "On Eric Rohmer's A Tale of Winter." In Cavell on Film, edited by William Rothman, 287–93. Albany: State University of New York Press, 2005.
Cavell, Stanley. Pursuits of Happiness: The Hollywood Comedy of Remarriage. Cambridge, MA: Harvard University Press, 1981.
Cavell, Stanley. Response to Tania Modleski. Critical Inquiry 17, no. 1 (1990): 238–44.
Cavell, Stanley. "Seasons of Love: Bergman's Smiles of a Summer Night and The Tale of Winter." In Cavell on Film, edited by William Rothman, 193–203. Albany: State University of New York Press, 2005.
Cavell, Stanley. "Shakespeare and Rohmer: Two Tales of Winter." In Cities of Words: Pedagogical Letters on a Register of the Moral Life, 421–43. Cambridge, MA: Harvard University Press, 2004.
Cavell, Stanley. "The Thought of Movies." Yale Review 72, no. 2 (1983): 181–200.
Cavell, Stanley. The World Viewed. Cambridge, MA: Harvard University Press, 1979.
Chatterjee, Niladri R. "Portrait of the Artist as Companion: Interviews with Don Bachardy." In The Isherwood Century: Essays on the Life and Work of Christopher Isherwood, edited by James J. Berg and Chris Freeman, 97–107. Madison: University of Wisconsin Press, 2000.
Chin, Elizabeth. My Life with Things: The Consumer Diaries. Durham, NC: Duke University Press, 2016.
Chris and Don: A Love Story. Directed by Guido Santi and Tina Mascara. New York: Zeitgeist Films, 2007.
Christopher and His Kind. Directed by Geoffrey Sax. London: Mammoth Screen, 2011.
Clare, Stephanie Deborah. "(Homo)Normativity's Romance: Happiness and Indigestion in Andrew Haigh's Weekend." Continuum: Journal of Media and Cultural Studies 27, no. 6 (2013): 785–98.
Cobb, Michael. Single: Arguments for the Uncoupled. New York: New York University Press, 2012.
Connolly, Cyril. Enemies of Promise and Other Essays. Garden City, NY: Doubleday, 1960.
Cook, Pam. "Approaching the Work of Dorothy Arzner." In Feminism and Film Theory, edited by Constance Penley, 46–56. New York: Routledge, 1988.

Cooms, Valerie. "Miscegenation and Intimacy." A review of Fiona Probyn-Rapsey, *Made to Matter: White Fathers, Stolen Generations* (Sydney: Sydney University Press, 2013). *Cultural Studies Review* 21, no. 2 (2015): 291–97.

Cortvriend, Jack. "Stylistic Convergences between British Film and American Television: Andrew Haigh's *Looking*." *Critical Studies in Television: The International Journal of Television Studies* 13, no. 1 (2018): 96–112.

Day, William. "'I Don't Know, Just Wait': Remembering Remarriage in *Eternal Sunshine of the Spotless Mind*." In *The Philosophy of Charlie Kaufman*, edited by Paul LaRocca, 132–54. Lexington: University Press of Kentucky, 2011.

Dean, Tim. "No Sex Please, We're American." *American Literary History* 27, no. 3 (2015): 614–24.

DeAngelis, Michael. Introduction to *Reading the Bromance: Homosocial Relationships in Film and Television*, edited by Michael DeAngelis, 1–26. Detroit, MI: Wayne State University Press, 2014.

DeAngelis, Michael. "Mispronouncing 'Man and Wife': The Fate of Marriage in Hollywood's Sexual Revolution." In *Hetero: Queering Representations of Straightness*, edited by Sean Griffin, 129–49. Albany, NY: State University of New York Press, 2009.

de Baecque, Antoine, and Noël Herpe. *Éric Rohmer: A Biography*. Translated by Steven Randall and Lisa Neal. New York: Columbia University Press, 2016.

Dowden, Edward. *Shakspare: A Critical Study of His Mind and Art*. London: Henry S. King, 1875.

duCille, Ann, ed. "Black Marriage." *differences: Journal of Feminist Cultural Studies* 29, no. 2 (2018): 1–5.

duCille, Ann. *The Coupling Convention: Sex, Text, and Tradition in Black Women's Fiction*. Oxford: Oxford University Press, 1993.

Dyer, Richard. "Homosexuality and Heritage." In *The Culture of Queers*, 204–28. London: Routledge, 2002.

Dyer, Richard. *White: Essays on Race and Culture*. London: Routledge, 1997.

Edelman, Lee. *No Future: Queer Theory and the Death Drive*. Durham, NC: Duke University Press, 2004.

Eng, David L. *The Feeling of Kinship: Queer Kinship and the Racialization of Intimacy*. Durham, NC: Duke University Press, 2010.

English, Elizabeth. *Lesbian Modernism: Censorship, Sexuality, and Genre Fiction*. Edinburgh, UK: Edinburgh University Press, 2015.

Eugenides, Jeffrey. *The Marriage Plot*. New York: Farrar, Straus and Giroux, 2011.

Ewick Patricia, and Susan S. Silbey. *The Common Place of Law: Stories from Everyday Life*. Chicago, IL: University of Chicago Press, 1998.

Faderman, Lillian. *Surpassing the Love of Men: Romantic Friendship and Love between Women from the Renaissance to the Present*. New York: William Morrow, 1981.

Ferguson, Ann. "Gay Marriage: An American and Feminist Dilemma." *Hypatia* 22, no. 1 (2007): 39–57.

Ferguson, Roderick A. *Aberrations in Black: Toward a Queer of Color Critique*. Minneapolis: University of Minnesota Press, 2004.

Fischer, Lucy. *Designing Women: Cinema, Art Deco, and the Female Form.* New York: Columbia University Press, 2003.

Flueckiger, Barbara. "Color and Subjectivity in Film." In *Subjectivity across Media: Interdisciplinary and Transmedial Perspectives,* edited by Maike Sarah Reineth and Jan-Noël Thon, 145–61. New York: Routledge, 2016.

Ford, Tom. *A Single Man.* Culver City, CA: Sony Pictures Home Entertainment, 2010.

Foucault, Michel. "What Is an Author?" *Screen* 20, no. 1 (1979): 13–33.

Franke, Katherine. *Wedlocked: The Perils of Marriage Equality.* New York: New York University Press, 2015.

Freeman, Elizabeth. "Sacra/mentality in Barnes's *Nightwood.*" *American Literature* 86, no. 4 (2014): 737–65.

Freeman, Elizabeth. *The Wedding Complex: Forms of Belonging in Modern American Culture.* Durham, NC: Duke University Press, 2002.

Freeman, Kimberly A. *Love American Style: Divorce and the American Novel, 1811–1976.* London: Routledge, 2003.

Gaines, Jane. "Dorothy Arzner's Trousers." *Jump Cut* 37 (1992): 88–98.

Gamson, Joshua. *Modern Families: Stories of Extraordinary Journeys to Kinship.* New York: New York University Press, 2015.

Garland, Robert. "*Craig's Wife* Earns New Glory as Movie; Sincere and Gripping." *New York American,* October 2, 1936, 14.

Goldberg, Jonathan. *Melodrama: An Aesthetics of Impossibility.* Durham, NC: Duke University Press, 2016.

Goldin, Nan. *The Ballad of Sexual Dependency.* New York: Aperture, 1986.

Greenberg, Joel. "Beginning of the End." Review of Christopher Isherwood, *Liberation: Diaries,* vol. 3, *1970–1983,* edited by Katherine Bucknell. *Sydney Morning Herald,* September 29–30, 2012, Spectrum.

Greven, David. "Unlovely Spectacle: D. A. Miller on *Call Me by Your Name.*" *Film International,* March 13, 2018. http://fimint.nu/?p=23937.

Groves, Ernest. *The Marriage Crisis.* New York: Longmans, Green, 1928.

Gupta, Kristina. "Picturing Space for Lesbian Nonsexualities: Rethinking Sex-Normative Commitment through *The Kids Are All Right* (2010)." *Journal of Lesbian Studies* 17, no. 1 (2013): 103–18.

Hager, Kelly. *Dickens and the Rise of Divorce: The Failed-Marriage Plot and the Novel Tradition.* Farnham, UK: Ashgate, 2010.

Halperin, David M. *How to Be Gay.* Cambridge, MA: Harvard University Press, 2012.

Harker, Jaime. *Middlebrow Queer: Christopher Isherwood in America.* Minneapolis: University of Minnesota Press, 2013.

Haskell, Molly. "Women in Paris." *Village Voice,* April 28, 1975, 78.

Hawthorn, Geoffrey. "Green Films." *London Review of Books* 4, no. 6, April 1, 1982, 14.

Heller, Dana. "Wrecked: Programming Celesbian Reality." In *Reality Gendervision: Sexuality and Gender on Transatlantic Reality Television,* edited by Brenda R. Weber, 123–46. Durham, NC: Duke University Press, 2014.

Henshaw, Richard. "Women Directors: 150 Filmographies." *Film Comment* 8, no. 4 (1972): 33–45.

Higashi, Sumiko. *Cecil B. DeMille and American Culture: The Silent Era.* Berkeley: University of California Press, 1992.

Houston, Beverle. "Missing in Action: Notes on Dorothy Arzner." *Wide Angle* 6, no. 3 (1989): 24–31.

Inside Out Group. "Nottingham City Homes–Lenton Flats Demolition." Filmed May–November 2013. YouTube video, 2:58. Posted January 10, 2014. https://www.youtube.com/watch?v=sMWHfppZf-g.

Isherwood, Christopher. *Christopher and His Kind, 1929–39.* New York: Farrar, Straus and Giroux, 1976.

Isherwood, Christopher. *Liberation: Diaries.* Vol. 3, *1970–1983.* Edited by Katherine Bucknell. London: Chatto and Windus, 2012.

Isherwood, Christopher. *My Guru and His Disciple.* Harmondsworth, UK: Penguin, 1980.

Isherwood, Christopher. *A Single Man.* London: Vintage, 2010.

Jagose, Annamarie. *Orgasmology.* Durham, NC: Duke University Press, 2013.

Jagose, Annamarie. "The Problem with Antinormativity." *differences: A Journal of Feminist Cultural Studies* 26, no. 1 (2015): 26–47.

Johnson, Barbara. "Bringing Out D. A. Miller." *Narrative* 10, no. 1 (2002): 3–8.

Johnston, Claire. "Dorothy Arzner: Critical Strategies." In *Feminism and Film Theory*, edited by Constance Penley, 36–45. New York: Routledge, 1988.

Johnston, Claire, ed. *The Works of Dorothy Arzner: Towards a Feminist Cinema.* London: British Film Institute, 1975.

Kamel, Rose. "'Unraveling One's Personal Myth': Christopher Isherwood's Autobiographical Strategies." *Biography* 5, no. 2 (1982): 161–75.

Kennedy, Tammie M. "Sustaining White Homonormativity: *The Kids Are All Right* as Public Pedagogy." *Journal of Lesbian Studies* 18, no. 2 (2014): 118–32.

Khamis, Susie, and Alex Munt. "The Three Cs of Fashion: Convergence, Creativity and Control." *Scan: Journal of Media Arts Culture* 7, no. 2 (2010). http://scan.net.au/scan/journal/display.php?journal_id=155.

Kipnis, Laura. "Adultery." In *Intimacy*, edited by Lauren Berlant, 9–47. Chicago, IL: University of Chicago Press, 2000.

Kipnis, Laura. *Against Love: A Polemic.* New York: Vintage, 2003.

Klevan, Andrew. *Disclosure of the Everyday: Undramatic Achievement in Narrative Film.* Trowbridge, UK: Flicks Books, 2000.

Kraft, Elizabeth. *Restoration Stage Comedies and Hollywood Remarriage Films: In Conversation with Stanley Cavell.* London: Routledge, 2016.

Kurt, Melissa Sue. "'Spectacular Spinelessness': The Men in Dorothy Arzner's Films." In *Men by Women*, edited by Janet Todd, 189–205. New York: Holmes and Meier, 1982.

Lane, Anthony. "The Current Cinema: Free and Uneasy." *New Yorker*, December 21, 2009, 148–50.

Lesage, Julia. "The Hegemonic Female Fantasy in *An Unmarried Woman* and *Craig's Wife*." In *Film Reader 5: Feminist Film Criticism and Film and Culture Studies*, 83–94. Evanston, IL: Film Division, Radio-Television-Film Department, Northwestern University, 1982.

Lim, Dennis. "*Weekend*: The Space between Two People." The Criterion Collection. Posted on August 21, 2012. https://www.criterion.com/current/posts/2426-weekend-the-space-between-two-people.

Love, Heather. "Doing Being Deviant: Deviance Studies, Description, and the Queer Ordinary." *differences: A Journal of Feminist Cultural Studies* 26, no. 1 (2015): 74–95.

Love, Heather. "His Way." GLQ: *A Journal of Lesbian and Gay Studies* 17, nos. 2–3 (2011): 371–79.

Love, Heather. "Wedding Crashers." GLQ: *A Journal of Lesbian and Gay Studies* 13, no. 1 (2007): 125–39.

Luciano, Dana. "Coming Around Again: The Queer Momentum of *Far From Heaven*." GLQ: *A Journal of Lesbian and Gay Studies* 13, nos. 2–3 (2007): 249–72.

Lynch, William J. "*Craig's Wife*." In *Three Plays by George Kelly*. New York: Limelight Editions, 1999.

Macklemore and Ryan Lewis. "Same Love," featuring Mary Lambert. Official video. Posted on October 2, 2012. http://www.youtube.com/watch?v=hlVBg7_o8no.

Mahon, Áine. "Marriage and Moral Perfectionism in Siri Hustvedt and Stanley Cavell." *Textual Practice* 29, no. 4 (2015): 631–51.

Mann, William J. *Wisecracker: The Life and Times of William Haines, Hollywood's First Openly Gay Star*. New York: Viking Penguin, 1998.

Marcus, Sharon. *Between Women: Friendship, Desire, and Marriage in Victorian England*. Princeton, NJ: Princeton University Press, 2007.

Marcus, Sharon. "The Euphoria of Influence: Jeffrey Eugenides's *The Marriage Plot*." *Public Books*, November 2011. http://www.publicbooks.org/the-euphoria-of-influencejeffrey-eugenidess-the-marriage-plot/.

Martin, Biddy. "Extraordinary Homosexuals and the Fear of Being Ordinary." *differences: A Journal of Feminist Cultural Studies* 6, nos. 2–3 (1994): 100–25.

Maupin, Armistead. "The First Couple: Don Bachardy and Christopher Isherwood." In *Conversations with Christopher Isherwood*, edited by James J. Berg and Chris Freeman, 189–96. Jackson: University Press of Mississippi, 2001.

Maupin, Armistead. "Foreword." In *The Isherwood Century: Essays on the Life and Work of Christopher Isherwood*, edited by James J. Berg and Chris Freeman, xi–xv. Madison: University of Wisconsin Press, 2000.

Mayne, Judith. *Directed by Dorothy Arzner*. Bloomington: Indiana University Press, 1994.

Mayne, Judith. *Framed: Lesbians, Feminists, and Media Culture*. Minneapolis: University of Minnesota Press, 2000.

Mayne, Judith. "Lesbian Looks: Dorothy Arzner and Female Friendship." In *How Do I Look? Queer Film and Video*, edited by Bad Object Choices, 103–43. Seattle, WA: Bay Press, 1991.

Mayne, Judith. *The Woman at the Keyhole: Feminism and Women's Cinema*. Bloomington: Indiana University Press, 1990.

McCrea, Barry. "Heterosexual Horror: *Dracula*, the Closet, and the Marriage-Plot." *Novel: A Forum on Fiction* 43, no. 2 (2010): 251–70.

McHugh, Kathleen. "Housekeeping in Hollywood: The Case of *Craig's Wife*." *Screen* 35, no. 2 (1994): 123–35.

Metz, Walter. *Engaging Film Criticism: Film History and Contemporary American Cinema*. New York: Peter Lang, 2004.
Meyer, Michael J. "Reflections on Comic Reconciliations: Ethics, Memory, and Anxious Happy Endings." *Journal of Aesthetics and Art Criticism* 66, no. 1 (2008): 77–87.
Miller, D. A. "Anal *Rope*." *Representations* 32 (fall 1990): 114–33.
Miller, D. A. *Bringing Out Roland Barthes*. Berkeley: University of California Press, 1992.
Miller, D. A. "Call for Papers: In Memoriam Barbara Johnson." GLQ: *A Journal of Lesbian and Gay Studies* 17, nos. 2–3 (2011): 365–69.
Miller, D. A. *8½*. Houndmills, UK: Palgrave Macmillan, BFI Film Classics, 2008.
Miller, D. A. "Elio's Education." *Los Angeles Review of Books*, February 19, 2018. https://lareviewofbooks.org/article/elios-education/.
Miller, D. A. *Hidden Hitchcock*. Chicago, IL: University of Chicago Press, 2016.
Miller, D. A. "Hitchcock's Hidden Pictures." *Critical Inquiry* 37, no. 1 (2010): 106–30.
Miller, D. A. *Jane Austen, or The Secret of Style*. Princeton, NJ: Princeton University Press, 2003.
Miller, D. A. *Narrative and Its Discontents: Problems of Closure in the Traditional Novel*. Princeton, NJ: Princeton University Press, 1981.
Miller, D. A. "On the Universality of *Brokeback Mountain*." *Film Quarterly* 60, no. 3 (2007): 50–60.
Miller, D. A. *Place for Us: Essay on the Broadway Musical*. Cambridge, MA: Harvard University Press, 1998.
Mizejewski, Linda. "Calamity Jane and Female Masculinity in *Deadwood*." In *Dirty Words in Deadwood: Literature and the Postwestern*, edited by Melody Graulich and Nicolas S. Witschi, 184–207. Lincoln: University of Nebraska Press, 2013.
Modern Screen. Review of *Craig's Wife*. December 1936.
Modleski, Tania. "An Affair to Forget: Melancholia in Bromantic Comedy." *Camera Obscura* 86, 29, no. 2 (2014): 119–46.
Modleski, Tania. *Feminism without Women: Culture and Criticism in a "Postfeminist" Age*. London: Routledge, 1991.
Modleski, Tania. Response to Stanley Cavell. *Critical Inquiry* 17, no. 1 (1990): 237–38.
Morrison, Adele M. "Same-Sex *Loving*: Subverting White Supremacy through Same-Sex Marriage." *Michigan Journal of Race and Law* 13, no. 1 (2007): 177–225.
Mulhall, Stephen. *Stanley Cavell: Philosophy's Recounting of the Ordinary*. Oxford: Oxford University Press, 1999.
Muñoz, José. *Cruising Utopia: The Then and There of Queer Futurity*. New York: New York University Press, 2009.
Murphy, Mary. "Tribute to an Unsung Pioneer." *Los Angeles Times*, January 24, 1975.
Nealon, Christopher. "Invert-History: The Ambivalence of Lesbian Pulp Fiction." *New Literary History* 31, no. 4 (2000): 745–64.
Nelson, Maggie. *The Argonauts*. Minneapolis: Graywolf Press, 2015.
Nixon, Nicola. "Smarty Pants." *English Studies in Canada* 35, nos. 2–3 (2009): 24–27.
Nugent, Frank S. Review of *Craig's Wife*. *New York Times*, October 2, 1936.
Otto, Hiltrud, and Heidi Keller, eds. *Different Faces of Attachment: Cultural Variations on a Universal Human Need*. Cambridge: Cambridge University Press, 2014.

Parker, Francine. "Approaching the Art of Arzner." *Action* 8, no. 4 (1973): 9–14.

Peary, Gerald, and Karyn Kay. "Interview with Dorothy Arzner." *Cinema* 34 (1974): 10–20.

Pelle, Susan, and Catherine Fox. "Queering Desire/Querying Consumption: Rereading Visual Images of 'Lesbian' Desire in Lisa Cholodenko's *High Art*." *thirdspace: A Journal of Feminist Theory and Culture* 6, no. 1 (2006). journals.sfu.ca/thirdspace/index.php/journal/article/view/fox-pelle/125.

Penley, Constance, ed. *Feminism and Film Theory*. New York: Routledge, 1988.

Perel, Esther. *Mating in Captivity: Unlocking Erotic Intelligence*. New York: Harper Collins, 2006.

Perel, Esther. *The State of Affairs: Rethinking Infidelity*. New York: Harper Collins, 2017.

Pidduck, Julianne. "The Times of *The Hours*: Queer Melodrama and the Dilemma of Marriage." *Camera Obscura* 82, 28, no. 1 (2013): 36–67.

Povinelli, Elizabeth A. *Empire of Love: Toward a Theory of Intimacy, Genealogy, and Carnality*. Durham, NC: Duke University Press, 2006.

Pramaggiore, Maria. "High and Low: Bisexual Women and Aesthetics in *Chasing Amy* and *High Art*." *Journal of Bisexuality* 2, nos. 2–3 (2002): 243–66.

Pramaggiore, Maria. "Kids, Rock and Couples: Screening the Elusive/Illusive Bisexual." *Journal of Bisexuality* 11, no. 4 (2011): 587–93.

Phillips, Adam. *Winnicott*. London: Penguin, 2007.

Puar, Jasbir, and Karen Tongson. "The Ugly Truth about Why the Kids Are All Right." *Velvetpark*, January 20, 2012. velvetparkmedia.com/blogs/ugly-truth-about-why-kids-are-all-right.

Raban, Jonathan. *The Technique of Modern Fiction: Essays in Practical Criticism*. South Bend, IN: University of Notre Dame Press, 1969.

Raitt, Suzanne. "Lesbian Modernism?" *GLQ: A Journal of Lesbian and Gay Studies* 10, no. 1 (2003): 111–21.

Ramírez, Juan Antonio. *Architecture for the Screen: A Critical Study of Set Design in Hollywood's Golden Age*. Translated and with a foreword by John F. Moffitt. Jefferson, NC: McFarland, 2004.

Reddy, Chandan. "Race and the Critique of Marriage." *South Atlantic Quarterly* 115, no. 2 (2016): 425–32.

Reddy, Chandan. "Time for Rights? *Loving*, Gay Marriage, and the Limits of Legal Justice." *Fordham Law Review* 76, no. 6 (2008): 2849–72.

Reed, Margaret M., and Mary S. Green. Review of Lisa Cholodenko's *The Kids Are All Right*. *Journal of Feminist Family Therapy* 24, no. 2 (2012): 167–74.

Rich, B. Ruby. *New Queer Cinema: The Director's Cut*. Durham, NC: Duke University Press, 2013.

Richardson-Self, Louise. *Justifying Same-Sex Marriage: A Philosophical Investigation*. London: Rowman and Littlefield, 2015.

Richman, Kimberly D. *License to Wed: What Legal Marriage Means to Same-Sex Couples*. New York: New York University Press, 2014.

Robert, Hannah, and Fiona Kelly. "Explainer: What Legal Benefits Do Married Couples Have That De Facto Couples Do Not?" https://theconversation.com

/explainer-what-legal-benefits-do-married-couples-have-that-de-facto-couples-do-not-83896. Accessed September 21, 2017.

Robinson, Paul A. *Gay Lives: Homosexual Autobiography from John Addington Symonds to Paul Monette*. Chicago, IL: University of Chicago Press, 1999.

Rockett, Ben, and Sam Carr. "Animals and Attachment Theory." *Society and Animals* 22, no. 4 (2014): 415–33.

Romney, Jonathan. "Film of the Week: *45 Years*." *Film Comment*. December 17, 2016. https://www.filmcomment.com/blog/film-of-the-week-45-years/. Accessed November 29, 2017.

Ronell, Avital. *The Test Drive*. Champaign: University of Illinois Press, 2005.

Rothman, William, ed. *Cavell on Film*. Albany: State University of New York Press, 2005.

St. Pierre, Scott. "Bent Hemingway: Straightness, Sexuality, Style." GLQ: *A Journal of Lesbian and Gay Studies* 16, no. 3 (2010): 363–87.

Schaffer, Talia. *Romance's Rival: Familiar Marriage in Victorian Fiction*. Oxford: Oxford University Press, 2016.

Schaffer, Talia. "'A Wilde Desire Took Me': The Homoerotic History of *Dracula*." ELH 61, no. 2 (1994): 381–425.

Schifando, Peter, and Jean H. Mathison. *Class Act: William Haines, Legendary Hollywood Decorator*. New York: Pointed Leaf, 1995.

Schwartz, Alexandra. "Esther Perel Lets Us in on Couples' Secrets." *New Yorker*, May 31, 2017. https://www.newyorker.com/culture/cultural-comment/esther-perel-lets-us-listen-in-on-couples-secrets.

Schwerdt, Lisa M. *Isherwood's Fiction: The Self and Technique*. London: Macmillan, 1989.

Scott, A. O. "Meet the Sperm Donor: Modern Family Ties." Review of Lisa Cholodenko's *The Kids Are All Right* (2010). *New York Times*, July 8, 2010. https://www.nytimes.com/2010/07/09/movies/09kids.html.

Sedgwick, Eve Kosofsky, and Adam Frank. "Shame in the Cybernetic Fold: Reading Silvan Tomkins." *Shame and Its Sisters: A Silvan Tomkins Reader*, edited by Eve Kosofsky Sedgwick and Adam Frank, 1–28. Durham, NC: Duke University Press, 1995.

Shah, Nayan. *Stranger Intimacy: Contesting Race, Sexuality, and the Law in the North American West*. Berkeley: University of California Press, 2011.

Shumway, David R. "Screwball Comedies: Constructing Romance, Mystifying Marriage." *Cinema Journal* 30, no. 4 (1991): 7–23.

Shumway, David R. "Why Same-Sex Marriage Now?" *Discourse* 26, no. 3 (2004): 73–84.

Silver, Kenneth E. "Master Bedrooms, Master Narratives: Home, Homosexuality and Post-War Art." In *Not at Home: The Suppression of Domesticity in Modern Art and Architecture*, edited by Christopher Reed, 206–22. London: Thames and Hudson, 1996.

Sinnerbrink, Robert. "*Stimmung*: Exploring the Aesthetics of Mood." *Screen* 53, no. 2 (2012): 148–63.

Sollers, Philippe, and Julia Kristeva. *The Fine Art of Marriage.* Translated by Lorna Scott Fox. New York: Columbia University Press, 2015.

Sommerville, Siobhan B. *Queering the Color Line: Race and the Invention of Homosexuality in American Culture.* Durham, NC: Duke University Press, 2000.

Sparke, Penny, Mitchell Owens, and Elsie de Wolfe. *Elsie de Wolfe: The Birth of Interior Decoration.* New York: Acanthus Press, 2005.

Stevens, Kyle. "Dying to Love: Gay Identity, Suicide, and Aesthetics in *A Single Man.*" *Cinema Journal* 52, no. 4 (2013): 99–120.

Stevens, Kyle. *Mike Nichols: Sex, Language, and the Reinvention of Psychological Realism.* Oxford: Oxford University Press, 2015.

Stoler, Ann Laura. *Race and the Education of Desire: Foucault's History of Sexuality and the Colonial Order of Things.* Durham, NC: Duke University Press, 1995.

Stone, Lawrence. *Broken Lives: Separation and Divorce, 1660–1857.* Oxford: Oxford University Press, 1993.

Stone, Lawrence. *Road to Divorce: England, 1530–1987.* Oxford: Oxford University Press, 1990.

Stone, Lawrence. *Uncertain Unions: Marriage in England, 1660–1753.* Oxford: Oxford University Press, 1992.

Sturtevant, Victoria. "Stop the Wedding: William Haines and the Comedy of the Closet." In *Hetero: Queering Representations of Straightness*, edited by Sean Griffin, 19–36. Albany, NY: State University of New York Press, 2009.

Suter, Jacqueline. "Feminist Discourse in *Christopher Strong.*" In *Feminism and Film Theory*, edited Constance Penley, 89–103. New York: Routledge, 1988.

Tanner, Tony. *Adultery in the Novel: Contract and Transgression.* Baltimore, MD: Johns Hopkins University Press, 1979.

Thomas, Kendall. "Is Black Marriage Queer?" *differences: Journal of Feminist Cultural Studies* 29, no. 2. (2018): 204–12.

Thompson, Kirsten Moana. "Falling in (to) Color: Chromophilia and Tom Ford's *A Single Man.*" *Moving Image* 15, no. 1 (2015): 62–82.

Thomson, David. *Biographical Dictionary of Film.* New York: Alfred Knopf, 1994.

Thomson, David. "Let Us Go Then: On *45 Years.*" *Film Comment.* January 28, 2016. https://www.filmcomment.com/blog/let-us-go-then-on-45-years/. Accessed November 29, 2017.

Touval, Yonatan. "Colonial Queer Something." In *Queer Forster*, edited Robert K. Martin and George Piggford, 237–54. Chicago, IL: University of Chicago Press, 1997.

Verass, Sophie. "Illegal Love: Is This N[orthern] T[erritory] Couple Australia's Richard and Mildred Loving?" NITV website, sbs.com.au, August 13, 2017.

Vidal, Gore. Introduction to *Where Joy Resides: A Christopher Isherwood Reader*, edited by Don Bachardy and James P. White, ix–xix. New York: Farrar, Straus and Giroux, 1989.

Villarejo, Amy. "Jewish, Queer-ish, Trans, and Completely Revolutionary." *Film Quarterly* 69, no. 4 (2016): 10–22.

Villarejo, Amy. "Tarrying with the Normative: Queer Theory and *Black History.*" *Social Text* 23, nos. 3–4 (2005): 69–84.

Vogler, Candace. "Sex and Talk." In *Intimacy*, edited Lauren Berlant, 48–85. Chicago, IL: University of Chicago Press, 2000.

Walker, Michael. *Laurel Canyon: The Inside Story of Rock-and-Roll's Legendary Neighborhood*. New York: Faber and Faber, 2006.

Wallace, Lee. "Fag Men: *Mad Men*, Homosexuality and Televisual Style." *Cultural Studies Review* 18, no. 2 (2012): 207–22.

Wallace, Lee. *Lesbianism, Cinema, Space: The Sexual Life of Apartments*. New York: Routledge, 2009.

Wallace, Lee. *Sexual Encounters: Pacific Texts, Modern Sexualities*. Ithaca, NY: Cornell University Press, 2003.

Walters, Ben. "The Trouble with Perfume." *Film Quarterly* 63, no. 4 (2010): 14–17.

Walters, Suzanna Danuta. "The Kids Are All Right but the Lesbians Aren't: Queer Kinship in U.S. Culture." *Sexualities* 15, no. 8 (2012): 17–33.

Warner, Michael. *Publics and Counterpublics*. New York: Zone Books, 2002.

Warner, Michael. *The Trouble with Normal: Sex, Politics, and the Ethics of Queer Life*. New York: Free Press, 1999.

Watt, Ian. *The Rise of the Novel: Studies in Defoe, Richardson and Fielding*. Berkeley: University of California Press, 1957.

Weber, Shannon. "Daring to Marry: Marriage Equality Activism after Proposition 8 as Challenge to the Assimilationist/Radical Binary in Queer Studies." *Journal of Homosexuality* 62, no. 9 (2015): 1147–73.

Weston, Kath. *Families We Choose: Lesbians, Gays, Kinship*. New York: Columbia University Press, 1997.

White, Patricia. "Sketchy Lesbians: *Carol* as History and Fantasy." *Film Quarterly* 69, no. 2 (2015): 8–18.

White, Patricia. "Supporting Character: The Queer Career of Agnes Moorehead." In *Out in Culture: Gay, Lesbian, and Queer Essays on Popular Culture*, edited by Corey K. Creekmur and Alexander Doty, 91–114. Durham, NC: Duke University Press, 1995.

White, Patricia. *Uninvited: Classical Hollywood Cinema and Lesbian Representability*. Bloomington: Indiana University Press, 1999.

Wiegman, Robyn. "Sex and Negativity; Or, What Queer Theory Has for You." *Cultural Critique* 95 (2017): 219–43.

Wiegman, Robyn, and Elizabeth A. Wilson. "Introduction: Antinormativity's Queer Conventions." *differences: A Journal of Feminist Cultural Studies* 26, no. 1 (2015): 1–25.

Wilde, Alan. *Christopher Isherwood*. New York: Twayne, 1971.

Willis, Sharon. *The Poitier Effect: Racial Melodrama and Fantasies of Reconciliation*. Minneapolis: University of Minnesota Press, 2015.

Winnicott, Donald W. "Aggression and Its Roots." In *Deprivation and Delinquency*, edited by Clare Winnicott, Ray Shepherd, and Madeleine Davis, 84–99. London: Tavistock, 1984.

Winnicott, Donald W. "Transitional Objects and Transitional Phenomena." In *Playing and Reality*, edited by F. Robert Rodman, 1–34. New York: Routledge, 2005.

Wojcik, Pamela Roberston, ed. *The Apartment Complex: Urban Living and Global Screen Cultures*. Durham, NC: Duke University Press, 2018.

Wojcik, Pamela Robertson. *The Apartment Plot: Urban Living in American Film and Popular Culture, 1945–75*. Durham, NC: Duke University Press, 2010.

Zacharek, Stephanie. "*A Single Man*: Tom Ford's Shallow but Compelling Debut." Salon.com. December 10, 2009. http://www.salon.com/2009/12/10/a_single_man/.

INDEX

Abel, Elizabeth, 38
Aberrations in Black (Ferguson), 9
Aciman, André, 108
Adam's Rib (film), 1, 112
adultery: in film, 70–71, 218n27; in novels, 31–32, 196n15; in same-sex marriage, 14–15, 22–23, 194n54
affective intimacy, 27–28, 30–31
African Americans: pathologization of culture of, 9; post-slavery marriage rights of, 7–8, 11
Against Love (Kipnis), 14
Agamben, Giorgio, 50
Ainsworth, Mary Salter, 145, 149
Alff, David, 181, 222n33
Allen, Robert, 71
Allen, Woody, 16, 132
"Americanist narrative," racism and, 187
American Literary History, 48
An Affair to Remember (film), 133
Annie Hall (film), 16, 132
Another Country (Baldwin), 95, 109
Anthony, Lon, 65, 71
antimiscegenation laws, 8–10
apartment plot, 136–37; in *Concussion* (film), 139–49; in *Weekend* (film), 149–61
The Argonauts (Nelson), 161
"The Argument of Comedy" (Frye), 162
Aristotle, 163
Armstrong, Nancy, 29–31
Arzner, Dorothy, 23–24, 58–81, 204n27, 204n29, 205n31
As You Like It (Shakespeare), 43
attachment: Cholodenko's trilogy of, 112–33; in *Concussion* (film), 139–49; marriage in English novel and, 31–43; in queer theory, 24–25; same sex marriage and, 6–7; Winnicott's theory of, 116, 119, 126. *See also* reattachment
Attachment (Bowlby), 134
Auden, W. H., 84
Austen, Jane, 30–31, 35–36, 52, 105
Australia, antimiscegenation laws in, 10–11
Australian Marriage Law Postal Survey, 2, 192n20
The Awful Truth (film), 1, 112, 121, 128, 132, 176–79

Bachardy, Don, 24, 84–85, 88–90, 103–4, 208n22
Baldwin, James, 95
Bale, Christian, 118, 121
Ballad of Sexual Dependency (Goldin), 114
Bancroft, Anne, 123–24
Bannon, Ann, 56
Barnes, Djuna, 55
Barnes, Harold, 74
Barry, Phillip, 43
Barthes, Roland, 32, 99–101
Bataille, Georges, 32
Beckinsdale, Kate, 119
Belle du Jour (film), 139
"Be My Baby" (song), 119
Benham, Reyner, 120
Bening, Annette, 124, 126, 131–32
Bergman, Ingmar, 183, 221n19
Bergstrom, Janet, 59
Berlant, Lauren, 6–7, 47–51, 186, 201n75, 201n78

Bersani, Leo, 17, 33, 201n78
bisexuality, in Cholodenko's films, 119–22, 215n30
Bishop, Dan, 96
The Bitter Tears of Petra von Kant (film), 113–14
Black Panther (film), 186
Blanchett, Cate, 109
Blonde Venus (film), 46
Blueboy: The National Magazine about Men, 95
Blumstein, Philip, 217n18
Boles, John, 61
Boone, Joseph Allen, 37–38
Boorman, John, 85
Boston marriages, 27, 38, 55
Bowlby, John, 134, 145
Brief Encounter (film), 156–57
Bringing Up Baby (film), 1, 112, 219n1
Brokeback Mountain (film), 106–8, 137
bromance films, 132, 137–38, 217n16
Bronfen, Elisabeth, 163
Brooks, Jodi, 131
Brooks, Peter, 34–36, 55
Bruno, Giuliana, 66–67
Buckley, Richard, 89–90
Buñuel, Luis, 139
Burke, Billie, 75
Burke, Kathleen, 70
Butler, Judith, on gay marriage, 2–3

Call Me by Your Name (film), 108
Cantet, Laurent, 220n9
capitalism, rise of marriage and, 15
Capra, Frank, 1
Carol (film), 109–10
Carter, Julian, 56
Caskey, William (Bill), 85
Cavell, Stanley: attachment and reattachment in film theory of, 1, 23, 112, 126, 134–37, 160–61, 199n54; on *The Awful Truth*, 176–80; on community vs. family, 130; *Contesting Tears* by, 46, 48–49, 166; criticism of, 216n5; on divorce, 161–63, 179–80, 183–84, 221n19; on extraordinary in the everyday, 170–71; films

discussed by, 41–42, 198n48, 198n50, 199n57, 200n58, 201nn70–72, 219n1; on *It Happened One Night*, 127–28; on lesbianism and marriage, 178–79; on melodrama, 46, 49–50, 136–37, 215n38; on Old and New Comedy, 162, 177–82; on remarriage, 25–26, 43–45, 112–13, 128–33, 138–39, 177–83, 186–89; on Rohmer's film quartet, 172; on singing and dancing in film, 174
celebrity culture, divorce and, 199n51
Chin, Elizabeth, 134
Cholodenko, Lisa, 1, 24–25. *See also* specific films
Chris and Don: A Love Story (documentary), 85, 89–90
Christopher and His Kind (Isherwood), 86, 95, 209n24
Cities of Words: Pedagogical Letters on a Register of the Moral Life (Cavell), 42, 219n1
City of Night (Rechy), 95, 109
Clare, Stephanie, 159
Clarkson, Patricia, 114, 117–18
class conflict: sexuality and, 29–30. *See also* middle class
climate change, in film, 181–82
Coate, Roland E., 62
Cobb, Michael, 19–21
Cohn, Harry, 206n39
Colbert, Claudette, 42, 127, 163, 173
colonialism, interracial intimacy and, 10–13, 193n38
common law, straight and gay marriages and, 29
companionate marriage: in film, 82; in literature, 29–30. *See also* marriage plot
concubinage, colonialism and, 11
Concussion (film), 25, 137, 139–49, 160–61
conjugal relations: homosexuality and, 146–49; in media images, 184–86
Connolly, Cyril, 86
Constantine, David, 167–68
Conte d'hiver (*A Tale of Winter*) (film), 169–73, 180–82

Contesting Tears: The Hollywood Melodrama of the Unknown Woman (Cavell), 46, 48–49, 166
contractual relationships, marriage and, 32
Control (film), 150
Cook, Pam, 59–60
Corbijn, Anton, 150
The Country of the Pointed Firs (Jewett), 38
couplehood: gay and lesbian experiments in, 28; heteronormative concepts of, 27–28; homosexuality and, 27; remarriage comedies and, 128
Courtney, Tom, 165–66
Coward, Noel, 42
Cowie, Elizabeth, 50
Craig's Wife (film), 23–24, 58–59, 61–81
Crawford, Joan, 64, 206n41
Crawley, Lol, 180
critical legal studies, same-sex marriage in, 7
Cruel Optimism (Berlant), 50
Cukor, George, 43–44, 62–63, 171
Cullen, Tom, 151
Cushman, Charlotte, 198n46

Daldry, Stephen, 137
Dance, Girl, Dance (film), 60, 205n33
Darwell, Jane, 70, 82
Day, William, 135–36
Deadwood (HBO series), 217n19
De Angelis, Michael, 137–38, 217n16
Dean, Tim, 47–48, 201n78
de facto law, same-sex marriage and, 28–29
de Lauretis, Teresa, 50
DeMille, Cecil B., 56–57
dependency: in *Concussion* (film), 141–49; in *High Art* (film), 114–15
de Wolfe, Elsie, 61, 203n22
Dickens, Charles, 39, 197n30
divorce: adultery and, 32–34; in American novel, 34; Cavell on, 161–63, 179–80; celebrity culture and, 199n51; cross-class acceptance of, 28; in remarriage comedy films, 41–52, 138–39; same-sex marriage and, 11–13, 22–23, 41; Victorian marriage and, 39

Divorce and Matrimonial Causes Act of 1857, 39
Doctrine and Discipline of Divorce (Milton), 200n58
Dolena, James E., 62
domesticity, in novels, 29–30
Don't Change Your Husband (film), 56
Dracula (Stoker), 51–52
duCille, Ann, 186
Dunne, Irene, 42, 176
Dyer, Richard, 85, 108

Edelman, Lee, 4–5, 33, 47–48, 50, 104–5
Edgerton, Joel, 10
Eliot, George, 35–36
Eliot, T. S., 167
Emerson, Ralph Waldo, 163
Emma (Austen), 36
Eng, David, 101–2
English, Elizabeth, 55–56
English novel, love and marriage in, 29–43
erotic reciprocity, 27–28
Eternal Sunshine of the Spotless Mind (film), 135–36
Ewick, Patricia, 5, 192n13

family, in *The Kids Are All Right*, 129–30
Far From Heaven (film), 211n58
Fassbinder, Rainer Werner, 113
feeling, gendered discourse of, 31–43
The Female Complaint: The Unfinished Business of Sentimentality in American Culture (Berlant), 49–50, 201n75
feminism: criticism of marriage in, 27–28; film theory and, 59–61
Feminism and Film Theory (Penley), 59
Ferguson, Roderick, 9
fidelity: in Cholodenko's films, 114, 124; in *Concussion* (film), 146–49; in film, 70, 139; Kristeva on, 196n14; marriage and, 31–33, 179. *See also* infidelity
film: brand name style in, 97, 100–101; cinematic *vs.* literary perspectives and, 87–91, 94–99, 101–3; fragrance films, 99; homosexuality in, 83–84, 93–94,

Index · 241

film (*continued*)
  99–100, 105–10, 207n5; intertextuality of, 163; remarriage comedies, 23, 25–26, 41–52, 112, 199n57; singing and dancing in, 91–93, 174. *See also* specific films; specific directors
Film Comment (blog), 165
Film Quarterly, 35, 106
The Fine Art of Marriage (Sollers and Kristeva), 196n14
Finney, Albert, 218n29
Firth, Colin, 83, 88, 90–95, 99–100
Five Miles Out (film), 221n14
Fonda, Henry, 42
Ford, Tom, 24, 83–84, 88–110, 137, 209nn26–27
Forster, E. M., 199n57
45 Years (film), 25, 173–82, 222n34; critical analysis of, 165–66; literary influences in, 166–68; marriage plot in, 163–64; Shakespearean influences in, 166, 169
Foucault, Michel, 19; authorial function of, 100; on disciplinary power, 29; on sexual acts and identities, 32–33
Franke, Katherine, 7–8, 11–13, 186, 191n1
Freeman, Cathy, 10
Freeman, Elizabeth, 55
Freeman, Kimberly, 33–34
French novels, marriage and adultery in, 32, 196n14
Freud, Sigmund, 163, 213n12
Frye, Northrop, 162

Gable, Clark, 42, 127, 135, 163, 173
Garland, Robert, 74
Gaslight (film), 46
gay marriage: in Cavell's film theory, 138–39; in film, 106–8; Ford's *A Single Man* and, 104–5; kinship and, 9; in melodrama, 217n15; Old and New Comedy and, 162; prehistory of, 27–28, 38–40; reattachment and, 135–38
gender: adultery and, 31–33; power discourses and, 29–30; same-sex marriage and role of, 7; separatist alternatives to marriage and, 37–38

Giddens, Anthony, 18
Goldberg, Jonathan, 192n21
The Golden Bowl (James), 33
Goldin, Nan, 114
Goligher, Tristan, 168
Gondry, Michel, 135
"Go Now" (song), 164
Goode, Matthew, 89–91
The Graduate (film), 121, 123
Grant, Cary, 42, 44–46, 51, 126, 128, 135, 163, 176
Grant, John, 154, 158, 219n36
Great Expectations (Dickens), 39
Greek Pete (film), 221n15
Greven, David, 108
Guadagnino, Luca, 108
Gyllenhaal, Jake, 107

Haigh, Andrew, 1, 25, 149, 163, 165–82, 221n11, 221n14. *See also* specific films
Haines Foster Incorporated, 58
Haines, William, 58–59, 61–64, 78
Hall, Radclyffe, 55–56
Halperin, David, 108
Harker, Jaime, 86, 95
Haskell, Molly, 204n26
Hawks, Howard, 1, 128
Hawthorne, Nathaniel, 47
Hawthorn, Geoffrey, 199n57, 201n70
Haynes, Todd, 109, 211n58
Hemingway, Ernest, 86
Hepburn, Katharine, 42, 44, 51, 126, 135, 163, 171
heterosexuality: Frye's model of comedy and, 162; marriage and, 167–82; in novels, 34–37
Higashi, Sumiko, 57
High Art (film), 24–25, 111–17, 131
Highsmith, Patricia, 109
His Forgotten Wife (film), 56
His Girl Friday (film), 1, 112, 128
Hitchcock, Alfred, 35, 46, 95, 99–100, 210n34
Hockney, David, 103–4
Hoffman, Dustin, 121

homophobia, same-sex marriage and persistence of, 4
homosexuality: conjugal relations and, 146–49; couple formation and, 27–28; diversity politics and, 107–8; in film, 83–110; in Hollywood, 58; marriage and, 1, 17–23; style and, 97–98, 101–2, 105–6
Hoult, Nicholas, 91
The Hours (film), 137
Houston, Beverle, 204n24
Howell, William Dean, 34
How to Educate a Wife (film), 56
Hussey, Ruth, 44
Hutcherson, Josh, 129

"In a Funny Way" (song), 119–20
"In Another Country" (Constantine), 167
indigenous sexuality, colonization and, 10–11, 193n38
infidelity: in Cholodenko's films, 114, 124; in *Concussion* (film), 146–49; in film, 70, 139; marriage and, 31–33, 179. See also fidelity
interracial intimacy, colonialism and, 10–13, 193n38
intimacy discourse: orgasm in, 21–22; same-sex marriage and, 14–18
Isherwood, Christopher, 24, 83–110, 208nn16–17
It Happened One Night (film), 1, 112, 127, 173
"I Wanna Go to Marz" (song), 158

Jagose, Annamarie, 20–21
James, Geraldine, 175
James, Henry, 33
Jane Austen, or the Secret of Style (Miller), 105
Jarre, Jean Michael, 220n9
Jenkins, Barry, 186
Jewett, Sarah Orne, 38
The Jew of Malta (Marlowe), 167
Johnston, Claire, 59–60
Jones, Wendy, 54–55
Journal of Feminist Family Therapy, 130–31

Kant, Immanuel, 163
Kaufman, Charlie, 135
Kelly, George, 65, 74, 206n38
Khamis, Susie, 99
The Kids Are All Right (film), 24–25, 111–13, 124–33, 137, 148–49
Kieslowski, Krzysztof, 221n15
kinship patterns: Australian aboriginal systems, 10–11; gay marriage and, 2–4; same-sex marriages and, 197n39, 198n44
Kipnis, Laura, 14, 19, 196n15, 218n27
Kortajarena, Jon, 90
Kraft, Elizabeth, 135
Kristeva, Julia, 196n14
Kruger, Alma, 62, 82

Lacan, Jacques, 33
The Lady Eve (film), 1, 112
Laine, Denny, 164
Lambert, Mary, 207n5
Lasky, Jesse L., 56
Laurel Canyon (film), 24–25, 111–12, 118–24, 126–27, 131
Lautner, John, 95–97
Lawrence, Julie Fain, 140
Lean, David, 156–57
Ledger, Heath, 107
Lee, Ang, 106–7, 137
legal consciousness model, same-sex marriage and, 5–6
Lemonade (Beyoncé album), 186
Lenton Flats demolition, 149–51, 158, 218n30
Lesage, Julia, 79
lesbian bed death, 217n18
lesbianism: apartment plot in films involving, 136–37; in Arzner's films, 58, 74–81; in Cholodenko's trilogy, 113–15, 124–33; in Hollywood, 82–83; kinship patterns and, 197n39, 198n44; marriage and, 1, 55–56
Lesbian Studies, 131
lesbian superimposition, 206n40
Letter from an Unknown Woman (film), 46
Liberation (Isherwood), 84

Lim, Dennis, 151
literature: cinematic perspectives and, 87–91, 94–99, 101–3; cultural evolution of marriage in, 29–30; marriage plot in, 23, 26, 30–43, 55–56
Locke, John, 32, 163
logic of the couple, same-sex marriage and, 19–21
Lombard, Carole, 64
Love, Heather, 105–6
Loving (film), 10
Loving v. Virginia, 8–10
Luciano, Dana, 211n58
Lurie Alison, 16

Mad Men (television series), 96
The Making of Americans (Stein), 178–79
Mapplethorpe, Robert, 104
Mara, Rooney, 109
Marcus, Sharon, 38–41, 54–55, 197n39, 198n44
Marlowe, Christopher, 167
marriage: black marriage, 184–87; in melodrama, 217n15; remarriage and, 183–89
marriage equality movement: historical roots of, 28, 39–40; *Loving* analogy and, 8–10; in Miller's discourse, 106–8; popularization of, 2, 191n1; queer critiques of, 1–3, 27–28
marriage plot: adultery and, 31–43; in early silent films, 56–57; gay and lesbian innovations in, 53, 55–56, 139–49; in remarriage films, 23, 25–26, 44–52; secondary scholarship on, 53–54
Marry Me: A Romance (Updike), 34
Mascara, Tina, 85
Mating in Captivity: Unlocking Erotic Intelligence (Perel), 184
Maupin, Armistead, 208n22
Mayer, Louis B., 58
Mayne, Judith, 60–61, 72, 80, 205n33
McCall, Mary, 74
McCarey, Leo, 121, 133, 176–77
McCrea, Barry, 51–52
McDormand, Frances, 118–21

McElhone, Natascha, 119
McHugh, Kathleen, 61, 205n36
Meadows, Shane, 150
melodrama, 47, 96, 192n21, 217n15
Melville, Herman, 38
Mercury Rev (band), 119–20
Meredith, James, 109
Meyers, Michael J., 136
middle class: cultural evolution of, 29–30; twentieth-century marriage crisis and, 27–28
A Midsummer Night's Dream (Shakespeare), 43
Miller, D. A., 35–37, 105–8, 196n25, 197n30
Mill, John Stuart, 163
Milton, John, 43, 200n58
Mitchell, Radha, 115–16
Mitchell, Thomas, 69
Mizejewski, Linda, 217n19
A Modern Instance (Howell), 34
modernism: in film, 56–57; marriage and, 55
Modleski, Tania, 132–33, 215n38, 217n16
mood piece, film as, 83–84
Moody Blues, 164
Moonlight (film), 186
Moore, Julianne, 83, 91, 95, 99, 124, 132
Morgan, Julia, 203n21
Morrison, Adele, 9–10
Motion Picture Production Code of 1936, 70, 81–83, 128
Mulhall, Stephen, 199n54
Muñoz, José, 193n28, 201n78
Munt, Alex, 99
My Guru and His Disciple (Isherwood), 100

Narrative and Its Discontents (Miller), 106
narrative closure, marriage plot in fiction and, 31
Nelson, Maggie, 161
neoliberalism, same-sex marriage and, 2
New, Chris, 151
Nichols, Jeff, 10, 123–24
Nichols, Mike, 121
Nietzsche, Friedrich, 163

Nivola, Alessandra, 118, 213n15
Nixon, Nicola, 209n26
normativity: emotional attachment and, 6–7; logic of the couple and, 20–21; neoliberalism and, 2; same-sex marriage and, 2–5
North by Northwest (film), 46
novel: adultery in, 31–32, 196n15; cultural evolution of marriage in, 29–30; post-structuralist perspectives on, 34–35; queer critical analysis of marriage and, 51–52
Now, Voyager (film), 46, 49–50, 215n38
Nugent, Frank, 74

Obama, Barack, 184–85
Obama, Michelle, 184–85
Old Wives for New (film), 56–57
orgasm, interpersonal intimacy and, 21–22
Orwell, George, 86

A Passage to India (Forster), 199n57
Passon, Stacie, 25
Penley, Constance, 59
Perel, Esther, 184
The Philadelphia Story (film), 1, 112, 126; Bronfen's discussion of, 163; Cavell's discussion of, 43–44, 48, 51–52, 141, 187–88, 201n71, 218n20; *45 Years* and, 171, 175
Phillips, David Graham, 57
Place for Us: Essay on the Broadway Musical (Miller), 106
Plato, 163
Platters, 164
popular culture: homosexuality and marriage in, 23; remarriage plot and, 51–52
"Portrait of a Lady" (Eliot), 167
Powell, William, 64
power, female-centered discourse and systems of, 29
Pramaggiore, Maria, 215n30
prenuptial agreements, same-sex marriage and, 13
The Price of Salt (Highsmith), 109
privacy, social publicity and, 44

Proposition 8 (California), 131, 161
Proulx, Annie, 106–7
Puar, Jasbir, 131
Pursuits of Happiness (Cavell), 41–42, 46, 48, 133, 162, 187–88, 198n48, 198n50, 199n57, 200n58, 201n70

The Queen of America Goes to Washington: Essays on Sex and Citizenship (Berlant), 48
queer theory: attachment in, 24–25; Cavell's remarriage discourse and, 47–52; couplehood in, 160–61; criticism of marriage equality in, 27–28; family and, 129–33; marriage in, 1–5, 12–19, 186–89
Quinn, Colin, 160–61
Quinnford + Scout collaborative archive, 160–61

Raban, Jonathan, 87
race: black intimacy and, 184–87; homosexuality and, 211n58; same-sex marriage and, 7–8
Rampling, Charlotte, 164–82, 220nn8–9
Rawls, John, 163
Reading for the Plot (Brooks), 34–35, 55
reattachment: in remarriage comedy, 1, 23, 25–26, 163–82; theory of, 134–61; Winnicott's theory of, 116, 119, 126. *See also* attachment
Rechy, John, 95
Reddy, Chandan, 8
Reiner, Rob, 132
Reisz, Karel, 149, 218n29
remarriage: Cavell's theory of, 23, 25–26, 112, 124–33, 199n57; crisis in, 162–82; divorce and, 41–52, 138–39; in film, 23, 25–26, 41–52, 112, 184–89, 199n57; *45 Years* as comedy of, 177–82; gay marriage as, 171; in popular culture, 51–52; Restoration drama and, 135
reproductive futurism, 4–5
Restoration drama, 135
"Rethinking Infidelity: A Talk for Anyone Who Has Ever Loved" (Perel, TEDX talk), 184

reverse shot, 204n24
Rich, Adrienne, 17, 197n39
Richardson, Samuel, 29–30
Richardson-Self, Louise, 3–4
Rich, B. Ruby, 113–14
Richman, Kimberly, 5–6
Rich Men's Wives (film), 56
#RingYourRellos initiative, 2
Ring Your Granny campaign, 2
Risdon, Elizabeth, 67
Rogal, Kate, 142
Rohmer, Éric, 163, 169–70, 221n11
romance discourse, same-sex marriage and, 14–16
Romney, Jonathan, 165
Ronell, Avital, 213n12
Rothman, William, 46
Rousseau, Jean-Jacques, 32
Ruffalo, Mark, 124, 132
Russell, Rosalind, 23–24, 42, 58–81, 128

"Same Love" (Macklemore), 207n5
same-sex communities, separatist alternatives to marriage and, 37–38
same-sex marriage: adultery and, 33; divorce and, 11–13; domestic experimentation and, 150; kinship patterns and, 197n39; neoliberalism and, 2; overview of, 1; race and, 7–8; remarriage and, 132–33; *A Single Man* and, 101–2
Santi, Guido, 85
Saturday Night and Sunday Morning (film), 149, 218n29
The Scarlet Letter (Hawthorne), 47
Scearce, David, 88
Schaffer, Talia, 53–55
Schwartz, Alexander, 184–86
Schwartz, Pepper, 217n18
Schygulla, Hanna, 114
Scott, A. O., 130
Scott, Donald Ogden, 43
"The Secret to Desire in a Long-Term Relationship" (Perel, TEDx talk), 184
Sedgwick, Eve Kosofsky, 47
Sex, or the Unbearable (Berlant & Edelman), 47–48, 201n78

sexuality: in Cholodenko's trilogy, 121; class conflict and, 29–30; marriage viability and, 27–28
Shakespeare, William, 42, 45–46, 163–68, 199n53
Share, Oisín, 160–61
Sheedy, Ally, 114
Shields, Jimmie, 58, 62, 64
Shumway, David, 14–18, 134–35, 198n48
Sibley, David, 175
Siff, Maggie, 144
Silbey, Susan, 5, 192n13
Silver, Kenneth E., 104
A Single Man (film), 24, 83–84, 86–110, 137, 207n5
A Single Man (Isherwood), 83–84, 87–91, 94–99, 101–3
Sirk, Douglas, 211n58
Sischy, Ingrid, 114
Sleepless in Seattle (film), 132
Smiles of a Summer Night (film), 183, 221n19
"Smoke Gets in Your Eyes" (song), 164
social performance, marriage as, 192n20
social publicity and privacy, 44
Sollers, Philippe, 196n14
Soloway, Jill, 86
Souza, Pete, 184–85
Spector, Phil, 119
Stanwyck, Barbara, 42
state power, marriage as emblem of, 27–28
The State of Affairs: Rethinking Infidelity (Perel), 184
Stein, Gertrude, 55, 178–79
Stella Dallas (film), 46
Stewart, James, 42, 44, 126
Stoker, Bram, 51–52
Stolen Generations (Australia), 10–11
Stoler, Ann Laura, 11
Stone, Lawrence, 30
Sturges, Preston, 1, 199n57
Supreme Court (U.S.), marriage equality cases and, 8
Suter, Jacqueline, 59, 204n24

Tales of the Four Seasons (film quartet), 171–72
Tanner, Tony, 31–36
"TC and Honeybear" (song), 154
Tchaikovsky, Johnathan, 142
theatricality of marriage, 192n20
This Is England (film), 150
Thomas, Kendall, 186–87
Thompson, Kirsten Moana, 109
Thomson, David, 165–66, 177–78, 220n8
Toklas, Alice B., 55
Tongson, Karen, 131
Too Much Wife (film), 56
Tracy, Spencer, 135
transgender experience, 161
Transparent (Amazon series), 86
Trois couleurs: Bleu (film), 221n15
The Trouble with Normal: Sex, Politics, and the Ethics of Queer Life (Warner), 2
Trump, Melania, 184
Trust Your Wife (film), 56

Updike, John, 16, 34

Vers le sud (film), 220n9
Véry, Charlotte, 170, 221n15
Victorian novel, marriage in, 38–40, 53–55, 197n30
Vidal, Gore, 210n39

Villarejo, Amy, 9
Vogler, Candace, 16–17, 194n61

Walburn, Raymond, 70
Warner, Ann, 62
Warner, Jack, 62
Warner, Michael, 2, 19, 108
Wasikowska, Mia, 129
Watt, Ian, 29–31
Weekend (film), 25, 137, 149–61, 169–70
Weigert, Robin, 140, 217n19
Well of Loneliness (Hall), 55–56
Westman, Nydia, 75
Weston, Kath, 197n39
When Harry Met Sally (film), 132
whiteness, rights discourse and, 8
White, Patricia, 82–83, 109–10
Why Change Your Wife? (film), 56
Wiegman, Robyn, 201n78
Wilde, Oscar, 52
The Wild Party (film), 60
Will and Grace (television series), 86
Wilson, Dorothy, 71
Winnicott, D. W., 116, 119, 121, 126, 134
The Winter's Tale (Shakespeare), 42–43, 126, 166–67, 169–70, 180, 183
Women in the Shadows (Bannon), 56
Working Girls (film), 60

Zacharek, Stephanie, 83